THE ISRAELI–PALESTINIAN PEACE NEGOTIATIONS, 1999–2001

The Israeli–Palestinian Peace Negotiations, 1999–2001 is an engaging, compre-hensive and remarkably insightful account and analysis of the Middle East peace process.

The book discusses and supplies:

- an overview of the Israeli–Palestinian conflict;
- the core issues of contention;
- the various "players" involved in the process;
- the extensive covert and official negotiation rounds;
- the possible solutions formulated during the peace process effort.

Gilead Sher provides concise contextual background, thought-provoking analysis and insightful personal impressions. He also outlines the painful compromises that both sides would need to make in order to bring an end to this violent conflict. Sher makes a convincing case that any future settlement to the Middle East conflict will be based on the Barak–Clinton–Arafat formula negotiated at Camp David. This book dissects the political, economic, social and cultural reasons that led to the breakdown of the process and the consequent eruption of violence that has engulfed the region.

The Israeli–Palestinian Peace Negotiations, 1999–2001 provides a new under-standing of the Israeli–Palestinian conflict and will be essential reading for those with interests in Middle East politics.

Gilead Sher, former Bureau Chief and Policy Coordinator of Prime Minister Barak, acted as chief negotiator in the historic talks of 1999–2001 at the Camp David summit and the Taba talks with the Palestinians. Sher is one of Israel's most reputable attorneys.

ISRAELI HISTORY, POLITICS AND SOCIETY
Series Editor: Efraim Karsh
King's College London

This series provides a multidisciplinary examination of all aspects of Israeli history, politics and society, and serves as a means of communication between the various communities interested in Israel: academics, policy makers; practitioners; journalists and the informed public.

Israel: The First Hundred Years (Mini Series)
Edited by Ephraim Karsh

THE ISRAELI–PALESTINIAN PEACE NEGOTIATIONS, 1999–2001

Within reach

Gilead Sher

Routledge
Taylor & Francis Group

LONDON AND NEW YORK

First published 2006
by Routledge
2 Park Square, Milton Park, Abingdon, Oxon OX14 4RN

Simultaneously published in the USA and Canada
by Routledge
270 Madison Ave, New York, NY 10016

Routledge is an imprint of the Taylor & Francis Group

© 2006 Gilead Sher

Typeset in Baskerville by
Florence Production Ltd, Stoodleigh, Devon
Printed and bound in Great Britain by
Antony Rowe, Chippenham, Wiltshire

British Library Cataloguing in Publication Data
A catalogue record for this book is available from the British Library

Library of Congress Cataloging in Publication Data
A catalog record for this book has been requested

ISBN10: 0–7146–5653–4 (hbk)
ISBN10: 0–7146–8542–9 (pbk)

ISBN13: 9–78–0–7146–5653–3 (hbk)
ISBN13: 9–78–0–7146–8542–7 (pbk)

TO RUTI WITH LOVE

To my beloved children
Guy, Neta, Carmel and Maya:
You were in my heart and mind during
the entire negotiations –
These efforts are for you and your generation

CONTENTS

ILLUSTRATIONS

FOREWORD

On the day this manuscript was completed, Al-Quaeda terrorists launched the largest terrorist attack in history: a sophisticated, well-planned, chilling attack on the Pentagon – the nerve center of the United States military – and on the World Trade Center – the heart of the Western economy. This horrifying, apocalyptic act transcended the wildest imaginary scenarios, changing the world for ever.

Israelis are all too familiar with terrorism. Anxiously sending our children to school in the morning and holding our breath until they return home safely is part of our daily reality. But terrorism has not defeated us and it will certainly not defeat the United States and the rest of the free world. While some argue that the attack against the United States is further proof that the pursuit of peace in the Middle East is hopeless, I fervently believe that a political resolution to the Arab–Israeli conflict is within reach and, as importantly, is strategically crucial to Israel's future.

Even before the eruption of violence in late September 2000, no one involved in the peace process had any illusions that a signed agreement would bring an overnight end to a hundred years of violent cultural, religious and national conflict. Conflicts can be settled through political compromise, but people cannot be prevented from dreaming and longing. Hearts and minds cannot be readied all at once. The violence, distress and suffering that have plagued the region since the fall of 2000 make it difficult not to lose hope that a peaceful future can be forged. Are we for ever doomed to be at war with our neighbors? Is the Arab–Israeli conflict truly unsolvable? Are Zionism and the State of Israel but a passing episode in history?

I find these notions unacceptable. No conflict – complex and bloody as it may be – is permanent. Although the scars of the past may last for many generations, hate between people, societies, nations will pass. Undeterred, we must strive tirelessly to find a political solution despite, and because of, the violent events that have besieged our people. There is nothing more dangerous and destructive than the loss of hope.

From the Israeli point of view, the struggle we are currently engaged in involves the realization of the Zionist vision of the establishment of

Israel as a democratic, Jewish state that lives in peace, economic prosperity and good neighborly relations. The goal of the political process over
the past decade, and more intensively during the Barak administration,
was to end the conflict with the Palestinians and free Israel of the abnormal
situation that was created following the Six Day War. One cannot seriously
argue that Israel's existence will be predicated for ever on the occupation
of another people. Occupation cannot last. No matter how justified it may
have been in the outset, at the end of the day, occupation will eat away
at the occupier itself.

The intense negotiations conducted between June 1999 and February
2001 have given both Israelis and Palestinians new insight to the core
issues of our conflict – and to their possible resolution. Thousands of hours
of negotiations that culminated with the Camp David summit led us closer
than ever before to a permanent peace. Long as it may take and elusive
as it may seem, peace is possible.

Many people work for peace. I share a sense of partnership with them.
Based on an open account, my personal notes, official and non-official
documents, this book is my testimony, an attempt to shed light on the
tangible resolution to the seemingly unattainable peace between Israel and
the Palestinians. I have tried to preserve an objective-factual description
of the negotiations, even from my personal perspective as a member of
the Israeli negotiating teams of the elected governments of the late Prime
Minister Yitzhak Rabin and later Prime Minister Ehud Barak.

The obstacles on the way to peace have been disheartening and have
led to heartbreak and despair, but a viable solution exists, a practical
model has been consolidated, and the parameters of an agreement have
been drawn. This book outlines a possible path to a comprehensive
peace agreement that fulfills the Palestinians' national aspirations without
compromising the existence of the State of Israel as an independent, democratic, Jewish state within internationally recognized borders. The issues
under dispute have not changed, and neither have their solutions. The
two peoples will continue living here. When the time arrives for the sides
to agree on an outline for a Permanent Status agreement, I believe it will
look very much like the framework that was developed between 1999 and
2001.

Thus wrote the Arab-Israeli poet Muhammad Ali Taha:

> After our death
> When the weary heart draws the curtain
> Of its last eyelids
> On all our deeds
> On all our wishes
> And on all that was in our dreams,
> Our desires,

Our feelings –
Hate will be
The first thing to rot
Inside us.

The Israeli–Palestinian Peace Negotiations, 1999–2001: Within Reach is about leadership, the lack of leadership, and the human frailties that dictate the course of history.

ACKNOWLEDGMENTS TO
THE ENGLISH EDITION

Since this book was first published in Hebrew, the Middle East has significantly changed, yet the core issues of the Palestinian–Israeli conflict remain, as do the possible solutions. I have made only minor modifications in the original text in order to leave it as authentic an account as it initially was.

I would like to thank Michal Shwarzman for her insightful translation and Jonathan Gillis for his contribution in reviewing parts of the book. My screenwriter-director brother, Eyal Sher, edited skillfully and I took great pleasure in working with him. Last but not least, my gratitude goes to the editors at Routledge.

Gilead Sher
February 2005, Caesarea

ABBREVIATIONS

AGAT	IDF Planning Division
AMAN	IDF Intelligence Corps
AUC	Areas Under Consideration
CAPS	Comprehensive Agreement on Permanent Status
DOP	Declaration of Principles
FAPS	Framework Agreement on Permanent Status
IDF	Israeli Defense Force
NRP	National Religious Party
PA	Palestinian Authority
PLO	Palestinian Liberation Organization
TOP	Treaty of Peace
UDI	Unilateral Declaration of Independence
UNGAR	United Nations General Assembly Resolution
UNSCR	United Nations Security Council Resolution

1

A SENSE OF HOPE

In June 1999 I took a leave of absence from my law firm to work as chief negotiator to the peace talks under the newly elected Israeli Prime Minister Ehud Barak. The Israeli public had high hopes for Barak to carry on the legacy of the late Yitzhak Rabin and Barak seemed determined to fulfill these expectations. Building a broad secular–liberal coalition that would promote a civic agenda while focusing on foreign policy and resolving the Arab–Israeli conflict, Barak did not disqualify any party from member-ship in his government, as long as they agreed on the guidelines that reflected his policies and goals.

The Palestinian–Israeli peace process started immediately after the first Gulf War, in 1991, with agreement on a framework for Israeli–Arab bilateral and multilateral negotiations. The Oslo Accords between Israel and the Palestinians were concluded in September 1993. A result of secret backtrack negotiations, the Oslo Accords marked the unprecedented mutual recogni-tion between Israel and the Palestinian Liberation Organization (PLO). This historic agreement, however, left the most sensitive issues – "the core issues" – to be discussed at a later stage in the negotiations on Permanent Status. The architects of these agreements sought constructive ambiguity; however, it resulted in too broad a space for interpretation. These issues included Jerusalem, the refugees, territory – namely settlements and borders – and security arrangements – interrelated and multidisciplinary issues.

Prime Minister Rabin, who symbolized in his leadership the historic change, was assassinated by a right-wing Israeli in November 1995. A month and a half prior to his tragic assassination, Rabin signed with Arafat the Interim Agreement that has set a detailed regime for the Palestinian–Israeli co-existence until completion of the Permanent Status negotiations. Three and a half years later, in summer 1999, Ehud Barak was elected prime minister. He immediately vowed to make every effort to end the conflict, by negotiating a final agreement and, as a result, ending the occu-pation and bringing into being a Palestinian state.

Benjamin Netanyahu, the exiting prime minister, left his successor challenges on three fronts: Syria, Lebanon and the Occupied Territories.

Netanyahu had engaged in secret talks with the Syrians, with the aim of reaching a peace agreement based on full Israeli withdrawal from the Golan Heights in return for the normalization of relations and suitable security arrangements. But as far as the Palestinians were concerned, the Netanyahu government opted for a political process marked by stagnation, most notably in the implementation of the US-sponsored Wye River Memorandum that called for another Israeli territorial withdrawal. With Israel largely isolated in the international arena, were the Palestinians to unilaterally decide on the establishment of a Palestinian state, they would have most probably been awarded immediate international recognition.

Barak was convinced that Israel's final withdrawal from the Occupied Territories should be tied to far-reaching agreements on the core issues of the conflict, namely territorial boundaries, refugees, Jerusalem, water rights and security arrangements. But the magnitude of the gaps between Israeli and Palestinian positions on these issues led Barak to believe that it was wrong to move forward with implementing the Israeli further redeployment before the disputed issues were further explored and the gaps between the polarized positions narrowed. Conceding additional territories without reaching an agreement on these core issues would leave Israel without any assets to negotiate.

The only incentive for the Palestinians to relinquish their claim for the Right of Return of Palestinian refugees to Israel, would involve transferring a substantial amount of territory as part of a comprehensive peace agreement. Barak assessed that discussing the Right of Return when most of the territory had already been transferred to the Palestinians would leave us empty-handed in the negotiation process. It was only at this point, he believed, that Arafat would reveal his true intentions. This was one of the cornerstones of Barak's approach to the peace process with the Palestinians.

The Barak government thus formulated its position that Israel would not transfer any additional territories to the Palestinians before understandings were reached regarding the core issues. Israel would be ready to discuss ideas on all Permanent Status issues, said Barak, provided that the principle that "nothing is agreed until everything is agreed" is upheld.

Barak often expressed his belief that potential Israeli accomplishments in the negotiations were continually being eroded by global and regional trends such as international terrorism (e.g. Osama Bin Laden), the growing strength and scope of Islamic fundamentalism, and the growing armament of a "second circle" of countries with unconventional arms, including nuclear (e.g. Iran). Time was working against us. Ending the conflict and reaching a finality of claims – on every issue – therefore became a major goal in Israel's negotiations:

- End of conflict was a political demand by Israel that implied that the agreement would mark the formal end of conflict between the two peoples, and the beginning of a new era of reconciliation, peace and good neighborly relations.
- Finality of claims was a political-legal demand by Israel, according to which the claims of both sides would be defined in a framework agreement. This would constitute an agreed interpretation of United Nations Security Council Resolutions (UNSCRs) 242 (November 1967) and 338 (October 1973). It would also bring an end to the "Salami" method, through which Israel's assets, and in particular its territorial ones, were being gradually eroded.

The realization that time was not working in our favor, as well as our main goals of end of conflict and finality of claims, became the two main anchors of our political strategy.

The first meeting between Israel's newly elected prime minister and the chairman of the Palestinian Authority (PA) took place on July 11, 1999. As it had in the past, it was clear that the personal relationship between Arafat and the new prime minister would have a crucial role in the process. The relationship between Arafat and Rabin was characterized by deep mistrust and mutual contempt. Rabin – who had ordered the Israel Defense Forces (IDF) to "break the bones" of the Palestinians who were involved in the first Intifada and ordered the expulsion of 415 members of Hamas – perceived Arafat as a leader of murderers, conniving and ruthless. Even after the Oslo Accords breakthrough, Rabin found it difficult to accept Arafat as a partner in the process. His distant body language during the signing of the Declaration of Principles (DOP) on the White House lawn in September of 1993, revealed his apprehension. With time, however, the two leaders were able to move beyond their mutual suspicion and develop agreed upon rules of engagement. Rabin made a point of updating Arafat before he announced a closure on the Territories or before retaliating following particularly horrific terrorist attacks in Israel, and Arafat was relatively willing to accept these measures. Despite their differences, the two leaders were committed to the political process, their relationship reflecting the strength of the "Peace Covenant."

With the end of Netanyahu's administration, Palestinians expected Ehud Barak, who was elected as "Rabin's successor," to forge a relationship based on the same mutual trust and partnership. Arafat restated these sentiments when, during the first meeting with Barak, he said: "You are my partner and friend."

Emerging from the meeting, the prime minister made the following statement:

3

... We must foster our mutual respect, and seriously aim to jointly bring peace to the Middle East ... Israel is committed to the agreements it has signed; we will implement the Wye Agreement and, together with Chairman Arafat and the Palestinian Authority, we will finalize a mechanism for promoting Permanent Status negotiations together with the implementation of Wye ...

But while the Israelis welcomed Barak's commitment to a permanent peace solution, his statement delivered a severe shock on the Palestinian side that interpreted the introduction of the Permanent Status negotiations as a tactical move to avoid implementing the Wye Memorandum – which set a timetable for the implementation of numerous other Israeli obligations. Worn and wounded by three years of confrontations with the Netanyahu government, the Palestinians expected the new prime minister to announce the immediate implementation of the Wye Memorandum. "He can forget about fifteen months of Permanent Status negotiation," fumed Arafat in Cairo. The Palestinian media raged with angry analyses of Barak's intentions. During the Netanyahu administration, the opponents to the peace process among the Palestinians and in the Arab world at large often blamed Arafat for surrendering to Israeli edicts. Palestinian sensitivities on every nuance were particularly high, and their willingness to convey flexibility and compromise was minimal. An agreement to alter the Wye Memorandum and to postpone the implementation of Israeli commitments was perceived as further surrender. The Palestinian Cabinet demanded the implementation of the Wye Memorandum within three weeks.

Had Barak discussed his vision for the peace process with Chairman Arafat, without media attention, Arafat might have responded favorably. In numerous communications, the Palestinians clarified that Arafat would be willing to assist Barak in a getting a "better deal" from Israel's perspective than the one reached with Netanyahu. However, getting the Palestinians' cooperation could not be achieved with an edict from the conqueror to the conquered, but rather on a basis of mutual respect and direct dialogue between the leaders. Unfortunately, this pattern of brash behavior by Barak would repeat itself numerous times in the upcoming months, severely hampering efforts to restore the trust between the two sides.

However, at the end of July, after completing the task of coalition building, a highly publicized meeting with President Clinton at the White House, an encouragingly positive meeting with President Mubarak of Egypt, and two meetings with Arafat, Barak had succeeded in energizing the political process with the Palestinians. A feeling of hope that the new government would find the illusive road to peace began to reawaken within the Israeli populace.

4

2

DIRECT AND BLUNT
DIALOGUE

The negotiations began in earnest on Thursday July 29, 1999, in Jerusalem. The Palestinians were represented by Saeb Erekat, head of the negotiations and Mohammed Dahlan, Gaza security head. The Israeli team included Brigadier-General Michael (Mike) Herzog, head of the Israel Defense Forces Strategic Planning Division; Colonel Daniel Reisner, head of the IDF's International Law Branch; and myself. A sense of excitement filled the room as both sides, friends and old rivals, felt they were embarking on a new path that could potentially lead to an historic agreement.

"Advocate Sher, are you optimistic?" I was asked by a television cameraman, who followed me to the hotel's parking garage before the meeting. "I am always optimistic," I replied, "I do not know of another way to deal with life in our region."

In discussions with Prime Minister Barak prior to the negotiations, we defined Israel's core interests:

- Jerusalem shall remain under Israeli sovereignty; retaining Jewish and Israeli linkages to the holy sites;
- territorial compromise will leave contiguous settlement blocs under Israeli sovereignty for the majority of settlers;
- the Jewish and democratic nature of the State of Israel will be preserved;
- the future Palestinian state will be demilitarized and there should be appropriate long-term responses to Israel's security concerns; and
- Israel will not assume responsibility for the refugee problem and there will be no Right of Return of refugees to Israel. The refugees must be duly compensated however and Israel will partake in the international effort to rehabilitate the refugees.

Adhering to these vital interests empowered our negotiating team throughout the difficult negotiating process.

At the onset of the negotiations, Erekat, who participated in the previous meetings between Arafat and Barak, conveyed his impression of Barak as an honest and direct person. He described a very bleak picture of Palestinian society, having lost any hope of peace, largely as a result of the past few years during which it was suffocated and humiliated. Erekat stated the Palestinians were thus ready and willing to engage in Permanent Status negotiations, but not as an alternative to the implementation of the Wye Memorandum.

I knew Saeb Erekat well from many previous encounters. Born in 1955 in Abu Dis, near Jerusalem, he spent most of his childhood in Jericho, although he had American citizenship. He holds a Ph.D. in Political Science from Bradford University in England, and was a lecturer at A-Najah University in Nablus. Saeb is a warm family man and good company. At his childhood home in Jericho – his young son Mohammad jumps into his welcoming arms and his charming twin daughters tease their father lovingly, while their mother, Naame, looks on, smiling. One of his daughters is a member of "Seeds of Peace," which brings together Jews, Christians and Arabs – Israelis, Palestinians, Jordanians and Americans. Pictures of Erekat with Arafat and other Palestinian leaders fill the living room. In earlier pictures Erekat can be seen with a dark mane of hair and thick beard. Over the years both have turned gray and have been shortened slightly.

Unlike other Palestinian leaders, Erekat is not characterized by any of the common symbols of status. He did not belong to the old guard of the PLO, for example, nor did he participate in armed struggle, a clear disadvantage when vying for a position of leadership among the Palestinians. But his eloquence, fluent English, and love affair with the world's media, have put him on the international center stage, where Erekat is identified as much if not more than others with the Palestinian national struggle. In 1986, what Israel considered inflammatory material was discovered in Erekat's office at A-Najah University. He was subsequently arrested a number of times for his activities in Fatah.

Erekat is a man of peace, a democrat and a liberal who believes peace has to be made between people, rather than between governments. He is an experienced, tough and shrewd negotiator, with a phenomenal memory. He does not hesitate to raise his voice and stomp his feet when necessary. In an effort to stall, he can be the most meticulous, petty and even irritating person; while, in an effort to advance, he will bypass all the mines he himself had laid out. Of all the members of the Palestinian leadership, Erekat experienced the most substantial transformation of thought – from defiantly donning the famous Kaffiah during the 1991 Madrid Conference; through promoting the democratic process in Palestinian elections and fighting corruption; to investing all his time and effort in the peace process. His dedication and commitment to the peace process throughout the years translated into hours of tedious negotiations and drafting sessions.

When it was Dahlan's turn to speak, he too expressed his personal appreciation of Barak as well as his own commitment to peace. Dahlan identified the PA's commitment to fighting terrorism as the root of its confrontation with Hamas during the Netanyahu administration. "We were surprised and disappointed," he continued, "by Barak's request to re-open an agreement, which was signed by Netanyahu, and his rejection of Israel's commitment to implementation. No Palestinian would accept such an offer," he emphasized. "It would be a disgrace on our part, if Arafat were to accept it. In such a case, I personally would resign from the Palestinian Authority."

Born in 1961, Dahlan is one of the most fascinating people on the Palestinian side – clever, eloquent, impulsive, calculating and completely dedicated to the Palestinian cause. He is fluent in Hebrew and very knowledgeable about Israeli history and politics as a result of his detention, between 1983–4, in Israeli prisons. Despite having many friends in Israel, the Israeli public's perception of him is divided due to his alleged involvement in acts of murder and terror against Israelis and for promoting anti-Israeli riots among Palestinian prisoners. His many critics view him as a hooligan who has settled down, and accuse him of involvement in political corruption in the PA. From 1993 onwards, he lived in Khan Yunes, first serving as head of internal security and later as head of the Preventative Security Service. Cooperation and coordination of security and intelligence activities, in which Dahlan had a central role, was one of the tenets of the relationship between Israel and the Palestinians following the signing of the Interim Agreement in Taba in September 1995. A close confidant of Arafat, Dahlan became a major player in promoting the peace process. Although he understands and speaks English very well, in bilateral discussions he ensures that Saeb Erekat – who masters the English language better than anyone else in the Palestinian delegation – translates what is said into Arabic. Dahlan then puts down every word in his notepad.

Until the rioting and violence erupted in September 2000, Dahlan never hesitated to show the scope of Palestinian flexibility, where it existed. Yet, he was never afraid to raise his voice, be blunt, curse or even turn the table over, if he felt that the Palestinian cause was being compromised.

Despite the intensity of dialogue during our discussions on July 29, the meeting ended in good spirits. It was agreed that the joint steering and monitoring committee would reconvene. The issues on the agenda had far-reaching consequences for both sides.

The plans for the construction and operation of a seaport in Gaza, for example, required a deep assessment of its security implications in light of Israel's quest for the demilitarization of the future Palestinian entity. Issues relating to the safe passage between the Gaza Strip and the West Bank also had ramifications on Permanent Status since Israel would not compromise its sovereignty over the passage, including the right to stop suspects in transit. The most sensitive issue, however, was that of security prisoners. At the time, Israel held 1,894 prisoners, of which 1,714 were residents of the West Bank and Gaza Strip. The remaining prisoners

7

were residents of East Jerusalem, thus holding Israeli ID cards. The issue of prisoners was, and continued to be, a central theme in the Palestinian political struggle. Almost every clan (in Arabic "Hamula") had a son in Israeli prisons. The Palestinian public honored the prisoners and their families, considering them heroes who were paying the day-to-day price of the Palestinian struggle for independence. The issue was equally charged on the Israeli side where many citizens were victims of these prisoners' terrorist acts that resulted in death, handicaps and deep emotional grief, underscoring the Israeli public's resistance to releasing many of the prisoners. Israel had set criteria for the release of prisoners. First, Israel would not release security prisoners who were Israeli citizens or residents of East Jerusalem. Second, it would not release prisoners with "blood on their hands" – i.e. who had murdered or injured Israelis or Palestinian collaborators with Israel. Third, Israel would release prisoners who committed their crimes prior to September 13, 1993, the date of signing the DOP in Oslo. Interestingly, most of the prisoners who met these criteria had already been released. The Palestinians now demanded to break through these criteria proposing a principle by which prisoners who had served two-thirds of their term would be released. This would imply the immediate release of nearly 300 security prisoners.

On September 18, 1978, serving as a reserve company commander in the IDF Armored Corps, Haim, one of the commanders under my command, woke me up at 5 a.m. "Gilli, wake up, there is an agreement! Begin and Sadat signed a peace treaty."

I was twenty years old when the 1973 Yom Kippur War broke out. Three of my classmates were killed, among them Amos Tene, one of my best friends. We lost many of our friends in the battles of the 401 Armored Brigade. Several hours after the engagement near the banks of the Suez Canal, our brigade was left with a third of its troops. The painful loss of dear friends in the Yom Kippur War, along with the feeling that we Israelis could have done more to prevent the war, shaped my outlook on life.

The good news from Camp David arrived five years after the war. It seemed that thirty-year-old Israel was finally heading toward normalization of its existence in the Middle East. But was that really the case? Prime Minister Begin had sacrificed the Sinai Peninsula in order to keep the West Bank and the Gaza Strip. The Palestinians for their part missed once more an opportunity to establish an independent entity, and eventually a state, in those territories.

It was with the deep understanding that the negotiated two-state solution would be the only realistic way out of the bloody Israeli–Palestinian conflict, that I joined the peace talks; first as head of the Palestinian Negotiation Project at the Planning Division of the IDF and as delegate under Prime Minister Rabin in 1994–5, and later under Prime Minister Barak, in 1999, as chief negotiator.

In the upcoming weeks, the Palestinians continued to press for their demands. On August 18, the Israeli Security Cabinet met to discuss the issue. At the end of a long meeting, it was decided that the criteria would not be modified. The Cabinet decided not to release those who had murdered Israelis, members of the Hamas and Islamic Jihad, prisoners who committed their crimes after September 1993, or residents of East Jerusalem.

On that day, the meeting of the teams lasted for only half an hour. It was dedicated entirely to the issue of prisoners. At the beginning of the meeting we reported the Cabinet's decision to the Palestinians. Dahlan and Erekat were irate. "Without 650 released prisoners – there will be no agreement," Erekat warned. Dahlan's position was more conciliatory: "400 prisoners will be released in the agreement, and we will continue to discuss the rest." "We will not release a single prisoner who does not meet the criteria set by the Cabinet," I responded, "and we will not be party to fabricating numbers in order to satisfy your public." Erekat refused to discuss any other issue, insisting that the two teams would meet again only when our side had a ready answer to their demand. We knew a crisis was brewing.

3

THE FRIENDS OF PEACE
MUST BE STRONG

The Egyptians decided to increase their involvement in the hope of facilitating a compromise and advance the parties toward an agreement. Four people led the process in Egypt: Foreign Minister Amre Moussa (now head of the Arab League) who was known for his tough stance against Israel, and insisted that there was no real difference between Barak and Netanyahu; political adviser to the president of Egypt, Osama El-Baz; head of Egypt's Intelligence Services, Omar Suleiman, whose position with Mubarak was very strong (Suleiman had been effective and positive in transferring information, messages and ideas to and from Mubarak); and the Ambassador of Egypt in Israel, Muhammad Bassiouni. The latter's knowledge of the political players and Israel's social and economic background made him a confidant of both Israelis and Palestinians, and a reliable analyst of the Israeli reality.

From August 24 onwards, Bassiouni played host to a series of meetings at his residence. Bassiouni was the perfect host. At every meeting he insisted that we "eat something." When we sat at the table, we were served a feast with the best the Egyptian kitchen had to offer. Dahlan and Erekat were offered "Shisha," a private nargila (water pipe) reserved for them at his home. Bassiouni knew when to leave us to our negotiation work and joined occasionally to make sure that everything was going well. When negotiations would continue into the small hours of the morning, he would – in pajamas and robe – excuse himself, leaving his droopy-eyed guests to be tended by servants. I carried out telephone consultations with the prime minister from the ambassador's lawn, far from wandering eyes and ears. These conversations would sometimes last over an hour.

During one of these meetings, on August 31, I had to leave Bassiouni's home at 5 p.m. at the latest in order to get to a lecture that had been scheduled months before at the Chamber of Commerce in Be'er Sheva. The discussions dragged on, and I was able to leave only at 8 p.m. The lecture had been scheduled for 7 p.m. When I finally arrived at 10 p.m., I was surprised to find dozens of people still patiently waiting. I lectured and answered questions for approximately an hour and a half, returning to the Bassiouni residence at 2 a.m. to continue negotiating. In the meantime, however, a new bone of contention had been discovered. Erekat, on behalf of Arafat, rejected the Israeli proposal to name the first agreement between the two sides "Framework Agreement on Permanent Status." He proposed other alternatives, including: "Conceptual Framework Agreement," "General Framework Understandings," "Understandings on Principles for Permanent Status," "Framework for Conceptual Understandings." I, nevertheless, sensing that this seemingly phrasing divergence was rather significant, insisted on the term "Framework Agreement on Permanent Status."

We passed on a clear message to Arafat through Erekat, reiterating our demand to explicitly mention the "Framework Agreement on Permanent Status" as the first necessary step in a process aiming to conclude a Permanent Status agreement, and February 2000 as the envisaged time-table for implementation of the second stage of the Third Further Redeployment of Israel in the Territories agreed upon at Wye. I clarified that we could not hold a summit between the three leaders, President Clinton, Chairman Arafat and Prime Minister Barak, unless these issues were agreed upon beforehand at the level of the negotiators. Further agreement or flexibility with regard to the other remaining issues – release of prisoners, safe passage between Gaza and the West Bank, Gaza seaport, and the city of Hebron – were contingent on Palestinian agreement to these two demands. Erekat responded angrily: "Meetings during the last few days went well. There has been progress in the positions of both sides. The ultimatum is definitely unnecessary at this point of the negotiations."

The Palestinians emphasized the importance of creating a reliable and secret channel of dialogue between Barak and Arafat. This channel was to be discrete and accessible to both leaders. During the Rabin administration, Yossi Ginossar created and was responsible for this dialogue. The Palestinians now offered to renew this mechanism. It appeared that on the Palestinian side Mohammed Dahlan was the person most fit for this assignment. Yossi Ginossar remained the most qualified person for this role on the Israeli side. I often compared Ginossar to either an expert plumber who effectively unclogs obstructions in the channels of communication, or to a gifted surgeon who could bypass thickened arteries.

The impending crisis on the issue of the prisoners was looming heavily over the negotiations. At around midnight one day, a pale-faced Osama El-Baz returned from the Office of the Prime Minister, accompanied by Yossi Ginossar. They had come directly from Ramallah. It was a dead end. Two days later, in the midst of Mubarak's Herculean efforts to bridge the gaps between the sides, Ariel Sharon was interviewed on the religious radio station Radio Kol Hai. "Egypt is Israel's greatest enemy," he claimed ". . . could anyone consider Mubarak or his adviser El-Baz friends? They are enemies who are at our throats daily . . ."

More surprises were yet to come. Without warning the Palestinians announced, on behalf of Arafat, that he wished to delete a paragraph from the agreement, which ensured that both sides would refrain from unilateral actions that could affect Permanent Status negotiations, including building new settlements and declaring a Palestinian state. This request, although typical of Arafat's negotiating method, surprised all those involved – the Americans, Egyptians and Israelis – and raised new suspicions that Arafat was preparing a Unilateral Declaration of Independence (UDI) in case the negotiations failed. I informed Erekat that without full agreement on these issues, there would be no meeting between the leaders. "We are to leave Barak and Arafat," I said, "with a limited number of issues to negotiate, among these, the number of prisoners, dates, or the pace of the Israeli Third Further Redeployment."

On Thursday September 2, the US Secretary of State Albright and the Middle East Peace Team arrived in the region. A meeting with the prime minister, Foreign Minister David Levy, Chief of the Political-Security Staff Danny Yatom and myself, took place at 1 p.m. on Friday. During the meeting, Albright lavished praise on the Egyptians and their important role in persuading Arafat to accept the prime minister's proposals. The general feeling was that this was a last necessary push before an agreement.

On Friday September 3, right before the planned signing of the agreement, Dennis Ross arrived in Ramallah, to meet with Arafat. Ross was responsible for packaging the understandings and agreements in a manner that would appease Arafat and would prevent the latter's well-known last-minute attempts to press for concessions. Media from around the world descended on Alexandria for live broadcasts of what appeared to be the first sign of hope since the new Israeli government came to power. Albright and Mubarak tried to convince Barak, on the one hand, to come down to Egypt to "close the deal" there on the outstanding issues, and Arafat, on the other hand, to refrain from his traditional and tiring insistence on racking up achievements by exploiting the last stage of negotiations.

Barak did not heed their appeals. "If it is not clearly stated in the document that we intend to exhaust every opportunity to reach a framework agreement – and a full agreement on Permanent Status, thereafter – we have achieved nothing." Barak further told the Americans and Egyptians that, "in addition, all that has been agreed upon between the negotiators will not be re-opened for negotiation at the last minute. This includes both the issue of prisoners, and the possibility of a UDI. Until I receive a clear and final answer from Arafat on all these issues – I will not go." Barak's insistence on getting clear responses from Arafat, rather than postponing a momentary crisis by yielding to the chairman's dodging, remained since then – and throughout the negotiation process – a typical characteristic of his policy.

Despite the feeling of urgency and crisis, as well as the label of tactician in his refusal to sign, Barak was unequivocal. "This is the heart and core of the agreement," he emphasized. After a series of nerve-racking back-and-forth exchanges between Arafat and Barak, which Albright carried out for a period of two days, Arafat finally agreed to Barak's three demands. On Friday September 3, at 8.30 pm, Arafat called the prime minister to express his agreement with the all the conditions agreed upon in the negotiations.

Small teams from the Ministry of Foreign Affairs, the IDF's Attorney-General, and the Office of the Prime Minister worked feverishly to prepare the ceremony that would be held during Saturday evening. The ceremony was to be held in Sharm El-Sheikh, rather than Alexandria, despite the objections of the hundreds of reporters and the media. The leather binders were unearthed from storage and dusted off, the last logistical and ceremonial details were finalized, and a forward guard from the Prime Minister's Office along with security officers made their way to the signing location.

In a number of phone conversations, Daniel Reisner and I finalized the wording of the agreement, the signatories to the agreement, and the procedures. Haim Mendel Shaked, Barak's chief of staff, marked the date "4 September 1999" and the location "Sharm A-Sheikh" on a set of pens from the Prime Minister's Office set aside for signing the agreement.

On Saturday evening, my father drove me to the airport. I believed that in doing so he felt he was taking part in this historic event; or maybe it was yet another chapter in his forty years of work in the Israeli Foreign Service. The symbolic importance of this moment – the intergenerational continuity – was clear as we passed the Castel, the site of a key battle in the 1948 Independence War en route to Jerusalem, where my grandfather had fallen.

In the halls of the Hotel Jolie Ville, where the ceremony was to take place, Saeb Erekat was seen, breathless. "Where's Gilead?" he asked. When he finally found me, we sat in a side room to go over the final draft of the agreement. He had one request for a correction, with which I had no difficulty complying. "I would like to request that the term 'PLO' be replaced by 'Palestinian Liberation Organization.'" With the printer running, and fine quality paper in hand, the first agreement of the Barak government was ready to be signed.

The ceremony hall was in a flurry of excitement. The top echelon of the Palestinian leadership, the American Middle East Peace Team headed by Albright, President Mubarak and his senior government officials, His Royal Highness King Abdullah of Jordan and his ministers, Prime Minister Barak, Foreign Minister Levy, and the Israeli delegation were all present. Mubarak, Albright and King Abdullah signed the agreement as witnesses. For many, this ceremony symbolized a new, successful and promising beginning, having overcome the first hurdle. "Through this agreement the parties have cleared the way for the beginning of serious Permanent Status negotiations," remarked Madeline Albright in her speech.

The main accomplishment of the Sharm Memorandum was the anchoring of Barak's thinking, in terms of the transition from Interim Agreements to a Framework Agreement on Permanent Status (FAPS), and creating the necessary conditions as a foundation for discussing the core issues. The Sharm Memorandum stated that the "Permanent Status agreement" would include both a FAPS and a Comprehensive Agreement on Permanent Status (CAPS) that would be signed on the basis of principles, guidelines and timetables defined in accordance with the framework agreement.

It was agreed to release 350 security prisoners in a two-phase process. Concurrently, a joint committee would be created to consider the potential release of additional prisoners. The committee would present its recommendations to the relevant authorities in Israel, especially around the time of Ramadan. The Palestinian side committed itself to abide by its obligations to security cooperation, collection of arms, arrest of suspects, and the transferring of a list of the Palestinian policemen to Israel for review. The two sides pledged to refrain from unilaterally changing the status of the West Bank and Gaza Strip. Finally, Israel had rehabilitated its standing in the international arena and in the region. The Sharm Memorandum set the mechanism for the continuation of the process, ensured stability for another year, and removed some substantial disputed issues from the negotiating table.

Secretary Albright was excited but cautious:

> I especially want to congratulate Prime Minister Barak and Chairman Arafat and their respective negotiating teams headed by Gilead Sher and Saeb Erakat. They have toiled long hours under great pressure in a noble cause and they have succeeded . . .
>
> The accord Israeli and Palestinian leaders have just signed provides a long awaited boost both to the substance and to the spirit of the search for Middle East peace . . . The two sides have begun to rebuild their partnership . . .
>
> Through this agreement the parties have cleared the way for the beginning of serious Permanent Status negotiation . . . The obstacles that Permanent Status negotiators will face are daunting. They are tough, laden with emotion and deeply rooted in the region's troubled past. They involve life and death issues for both sides. But the road to reconciliation has always been strewn with obstacles . . .
>
> If a permanent settlement is to be achieved, the friends of peace must be strong. Those who seek peace must be persistent, and the advocates of peace must make the case over and over again that negotiations are not just one option among many. They are the only way.

We were now ready to begin the journey toward negotiating Permanent Status.

The following day, September 5, the Israeli government approved the agreement. Twenty-one members voted in favor of the agreement but Ministers Yitzhak Levy and Natan Sharansky opposed, causing the first crisis within the coalition. "Yahadut Hatorah," the ultra orthodox religious party, announced that it was leaving the coalition following a decision by the Israeli Electric Company to transfer a superheater to the new power plant in Ashdod during the Sabbath. Almost as an aside, the party also noted its dismay that the preparations for the signing agreement were carried out during the Sabbath.

On September 8, the prime minister delivered a statement of policy in the Israeli Knesset, indicating that:

> The Sharm Memorandum . . . creates the initial conditions that are best suited for Permanent Status negotiations . . . we have achieved the following: first, in terms of security, we have postponed the third phase of the Second Further Redeployment by nearly three months. Implementation of the further redeployment on the basis of the timetable detailed in the Wye Memorandum would have compromised the political and security interests of the State of Israel. This postponement provides us with five months for intensive discussions regarding the Framework Agreement for Permanent Status, as a jointly agreed upon goal with the Palestinians. This discussion will be carried out under more conducive conditions at the onset in terms of our political and security concerns. . . . Another achievement of the Sharm Memorandum involves rebuilding trust between the sides, while strictly upholding Israeli interests, in general, and our security concerns, in particular. We maintained the principle of direct, open, and sometimes blunt dialogue with the Palestinians.

Unfortunately, my colleagues and I felt Barak failed to mention the most important issue – the vision of a fair compromise, two states side-by-side, and joint development. In general, curiously, Barak's speeches failed to convey his agenda, vision and steadfast energy, falling short of engaging and motivating his audience. Nevertheless, with a majority of fifty-four to twenty-three the Sharm A-Sheikh Memorandum was approved. Permanent Status negotiations began ceremoniously almost immediately, on September 13. In a show of solidarity with those of the prisoners that were not to be released, Mohammed Dahlan was conspicuously absent.

One month later, capitalizing on the political success, Prime Minister Barak called on the president of Syria, Hafez El-Assad from the Knesset podium to engage in negotiations toward a peace agreement of "courage and honor."

4

POLITICALLY,
I'M STRANGLED

In the following months, substantial professional work, especially in mapping positions, was invested. The people involved in the official channel – Oded Eran, ex-Mossad official Meidan-Shani, Peace Administration Chief Colonel Arieli, Negotiation Coordinator Grinstein and Arieli's Deputy Cristal – produced a lot of in-depth work that outlined the principles and possible guidelines for a framework agreement. A summarized document was used by the "peace administration" to assign tasks and to discuss possible scenarios that might arise during the negotiations.

Barak and Arafat intensified their meetings. On December 21, Abu Mazen hosted the two leaders in his Ramallah residence. Three consecutive monthly meetings took place in various locations.

Even during the roughest, most violent and most hostile times, Arafat remained the perfect oriental host, heaping food on his guests while settling for a pinch himself. Arafat was always the only one speaking during any dialogue meeting with the Palestinian leadership; there was no doubt about who the boss was. He was concentrated and alert, however, one would always feel that during large parts of the conversation he did not grasp either the information transmitted by his interlocutor or the nuances. Suddenly, a somewhat detached Arafat would cut back into the conversation, making strange statements, unrelated to the issues discussed and accompanied by complaints on marginal matters.

Dressed in his military outfit, he is very theatrical, using his arms extensively, insisting on reminding his guests of the myriad titles he holds: army commander, engineer, president, "Rais," deputy chairman of the Arab Conference on Jerusalem, and his positions in various Arab, Muslim and international bodies. Arafat's associative world is rather enigmatic. Jumpy and confused, and in stammering anger, he sometimes shares – out of any context – details of biographical events. Examples of this are his early 1960s training in the Syrian army, his exile in Tunis or his childhood in his uncle's house in the Old City of Jerusalem. The periods mentioned would not always correspond to the real ones, but that never seemed to bother Arafat, a master in elastically adapting his words to any audience: extremist, repetitive and inflammatory in Arabic, diplomatic and moderate in English.

On April 1, several possible action items were analyzed in a document that was presented to Barak. The working assumptions of the analysis were that the framework agreement would be signed by the beginning of summer; that the Palestinian state would be declared at the end of 2000/beginning of 2001 and that discussions on the core issues would take place after the summer of 2001. The internal document reviewed changes in existing agreements that would be necessary as a result of signing new agreements and stated specific issues that needed to be addressed in order to obtain the Palestinians' agreement to the new timeline. Those included the establishment of a Palestinian state, the formulation of a CAPS, and/or Treaty of Peace (TOP) with the Palestinian state, agreeing on refugees, implementing the Third Further Redeployment, releasing prisoners and agreeing on the finality of claims.

For the first time the Americans began talking explicitly about accelerating the negotiations toward a planned summit between the leaders in September. In Washington, Clinton met with Barak, and then with Arafat. Barak declared to Clinton that he had no intention of retaining Israeli sovereignty over populated Palestinian areas around Jerusalem. He also noted that Israel would not assume moral responsibility over the Palestinian refugee problem but would be willing to participate in the effort to solve it. Most of the conversation, which lasted for a few hours, focused on the withdrawal from Lebanon. Clinton promised to enlist the support of the international community in recognizing the implementation of UNSCR 425 as a full and necessary step for Israel to proceed.

The American plan was developing as follows: an accelerated round of talks on the framework agreement in Eilat aiming to formulate a draft framework agreement by July 2000. And, concurrently, continuing secret talks at a ministerial level, with the active participation of US Middle East envoys Dennis Ross and Aaron Miller. Barak and Arafat would become involved in the process whenever major decisions were necessary. Finally – a trilateral summit, to conclude the details of a comprehensive agreement.

Among the most difficult issues to settle was that of the Palestinian refugees. A solution to the refugee problem affected issues of demographics, security, national identity and economics, as well as legal and moral aspects such as assuming responsibility, the Right of Return, and the finality of claims. Equally important for the purpose of resolving the issue were practical aspects such as defining "who is a refugee," allocating resources between different countries, and the way in which claims for property or compensation would be addressed. Until then, Israel focused mainly on moral questions and points of principle. Its position was that the refugees were an unfortunate result of Arab aggression against Israel and that Israel would therefore not assume moral, legal or political responsibility for the creation of the refugees problem. Moreover, refugees would not return to Israel under the "Right of Return" but arrangements would be made for their return to the Palestinian state. Legally, collective claims would be blocked and additional personal claims against Israel would be limited.

Formal discussions in Eilat proceeded, albeit in a very tense atmosphere, partially due to the publication of an Israeli tender for constructing apartments in Ma'ale Adumim. It is a large city east of Jerusalem, considered by many Israelis as an integral part of the Zone of Jerusalem despite its location in the Occupied Territories. "The government of Israel is negotiating with the National Religious Party, not with us," Erekat complained. Much later, on Holocaust Remembrance Day, Dennis Ross arrived at the sight of the formal negotiations. The Palestinians stood silently to attention when the public siren of remembrance was sounded.

Managing the negotiations team and operating the supporting systems were complex assignments that required coordination and strict control. The core team included Shlomo Ben-Ami and me; permanent members Israel Hasson and Pini Meidan-Shani from the Prime Minister's Office; Shaul Arieli, the head of the "peace administration," and his deputy Moti Cristal; Ephraim from the IDF Intelligence Corps (AMAN); Eli Haram and Miri Lapid from the Prime Minister's Bureau; and Gidi Grinstein, the team secretary.

Within the close and immediate circle, the core team coordinated and cooperated with attorneys Colonel Daniel Reisner from the IDF prosecutor's office and Ehud Keinan from the Ministry of Foreign Affairs. There was close coordination with the national security adviser Uzi Dayan, the head of the IDF Planning Division (AGAT) Major-General Shlomo Yanai, and the military secretary to the prime minister and minister of defense, Brigadier-General Gadi Eizencot.

This core team would meet on a regular basis for updates, assessments, planning and monitoring sessions, allocation of tasks and assignments, brainstorming processes with external organizations, and implementation of the work plan vis-à-vis all the government apparatus.

Danny Yatom, the head of the security-political staff, Yossi Kucik, the director general of the Prime Minister's Office, and Yitzhak Herzog, the Cabinet secretary, were part of the circle we reported to and updated. Minister Amnon Lipkin Shahak and the late Yossi Ginossar were also included in the discussions. And so was Deputy Minister of Defense Ephraim Sneh, albeit less frequently.

At the staff level, things were carried out with full transparency; problems and dilemmas were discussed freely; information was examined; and recommendations were contradicted and criticized. The work products were raised to the political level – which included the "peace cabinet,"[1] the security-political Cabinet, and when necessary the prime minister.

Slowly, the components of the Permanent Status core issues were outlined – Jerusalem, refugees, borders, settlements, security. Division of tasks developed over time and underwent some changes with the onset of the Al Aqsa Intifada and my appointment in October 2000 to the position of the prime minister's chief of staff.

It was tedious work, carried out by many dozens of people, over a long period of time. This complex network of professionals provided a strong, indispensable foundation for the upcoming negotiation effort.

In hindsight, a thorough analysis of the Oslo Accords may well bring up certain deficiencies. The process did not take into account the need to establish effective mechanisms of implementation. Such mechanisms could have provided a rigid framework that would impose the requirement to continue negotiating the Permanent Status agreement despite changes in circumstances and tumultuous politics. The instigators of the Oslo Accords could not have foreseen the difficulties arising from the daily friction, frustration and loss of confidence during the interim stages. On the one hand, under these Accords, Israel continued to sow settlements in the Territories, while, on the other hand, the Palestinians consistently pursued their venomous incitement against Israel, the Jews and Zionism.

Nevertheless, the Oslo process was right in principle. In any historic breakthrough there is no other option but neglecting certain details on behalf of sustaining the core principles. It might have been the only option for Prime Minister Rabin's government for starting the ploughing in the hard soil toward reconciliation.

In the subsequent negotiation process an integrative dynamic developed. We had to maintain parallel, extensive dialogues with the prime minister, with our Palestinian counterparts, and with the Americans. We also communicated extensively with the various political factions – some hostile to the government's agenda – as well as with direct staff and supporting systems.

I used to first listen attentively in order to be able to analyze the positions of the other side, its interests and intentions. The ability to connect with the people sitting across from me did not dilute my mission, which was to achieve the best possible results as defined in the strategic objectives of the leadership. I found out that empathy for the arguments of my interlocutors often helped overcome real and imaginary obstacles.

---

1 Ministers Peres, Beilin and Shahak, Member of Knesset Sarid, national security adviser Dayan, Yatom and myself.

Shlomo Ben-Ami and I made an effort to be fair and accurate in presenting the positions of the other side, as we understood them. By so doing, we attempted to increase the chances that they would trust the veracity of the positions we presented.

The integrity and morals of a person are an inseparable part of the personality. Professor Richard Shell of the University of Pennsylvania posed high standards for a negotiator, saying that personal integrity is a central component in the success of the negotiations. The lower your credibility, the more damage to your reputation. This ultimately has negative implications on the negotiations. The same goes for your counterpart. The lower his credibility, the more you have to be careful, alert and determined to protect your positions and interests.

Beside the trust that had emerged in countless hours of negotiations, one of our main tools was doubt. Never were we too sure of our counterpart leader's reliability, and seldom did we mix substance with friendship. In order to produce the desired result in the laden, complex negotiations, I had to be very direct, ask a lot of questions, and focus the entire time on what we – as well as the Palestinians – were trying to achieve around the negotiations table. Time and time again we had to identify when the discussion had ended, and when we, the negotiators, got stuck on marginal rather than main issues. Like a truck driver with a heavy load, the negotiator must return slowly but safely from the low road to the high road. Finally, dealing with the most sensitive issues, we had to maintain a delicate balance between secrecy of the content and the need to consolidate public opinion that would support the results of the negotiations and foster a supportive press.

The decision-making process on the Palestinian side was of major concern as we prepared to engage the Palestinians in a comprehensive effort to resolve our century-long conflict. With Arafat as the sole decision-maker and the quality of reporting to him infamously unreliable, we feared that he could get a distorted picture of the progression of the negotiations and miss the historic opportunity for reconciliation between our people. On his part, progress in negotiations meant either moving toward his positions or compromising on the Palestinians' maximum demands.

At most, under the best of cases, we negotiators believed we could bring the sides to the point at which the concessions of one side corresponded to the interests of the other and vice versa – the point at which agreement can be reached. In order to conclude the agreement, however, decisions were necessary by those responsible, the leaders. It was imperative that both leaders made the central decisions.

5

THE SWEDISH GOVERNMENT
AT YOUR SERVICE

On April 1, 2000, Pär Nuder, a special emissary of the prime minister of Sweden, Göran Persson, arrived secretly in Israel. The prime minister, a strong friend of Israel, was involved in a political struggle with his pro-Palestinian foreign minister, Anna Lindh. Pär Nuder, who served as the state secretary, and was in practice the chief of staff in the Prime Minister's Office in Stockholm, carried a personal message for Ehud Barak:

> The chances of what we all dream of – a just and lasting peace in the region – look better than ever, largely thanks to your personal and dynamic contribution to the process . . . the Palestinians are very worried that the current process is not working fast enough to produce results on time. They see a need for better options for secret talks, for more informal contacts between the sides, and for ways and means that will allow free and completely secret discussions on the core issues, together with you. To this end, Abu Mazen has asked us to help promote the creation of such contacts. He specifically asked that I contact you personally on this issue. After careful consideration, I have decided to convey this request from the Palestinian side. I have asked my state secretary, Pär Nuder . . . to convey this message to you personally. He can explain in more detail what the Palestinians propose.

It was around this time, that Barak felt that Ben-Ami and Shahak's discussions at the ministerial level with Abu Mazen and Abu Ala had exhausted themselves, and that there was a need to move forward toward a more practical level via a secret channel. This is how the Swedish channel known as the "Stockholm talks" was created. Shlomo Ben-Ami, a dedicated, quick-thinking scholar turned politician, empathetic to the plight of the Palestinians, was appointed the head of the Israeli delegation to the "Swedish channel." Our first meeting with the two senior Palestinians, Abu Ala and Hassan Asfour, was held under the stringent security conditions assuring us that the existence of the meeting would not be leaked to the press.

Abu Ala was born in 1937 in Abu-Dis, just outside Jerusalem. In 1989 he became a member of the Fatah Central Committee. A successful banker, he was perceived as having had an instrumental role in setting the economic foundation for the operation of the PLO. He was Uri Savir's counterpart during the Oslo Accord negotiations (1993–5). The two remain good friends to this day. He is independently wealthy, industrious and thorough. He has a rolling laugh, is a consummate storyteller, and a notorious chain smoker.

Born in Gaza in 1950, Asfour studied Agronomy in Baghdad and started his political career in the Communist Party. He joined the PLO in 1979 and participated alongside Abu Ala and Maher Al-Kurd in the exploratory talks that led in 1993 to the Oslo Accords. Asfour, married and father to two daughters, is proud of living in the village Abassan in the Gaza Strip. He served as minister for non-governmental organizations and as head of the PLO Negotiations Department.

Most of the discussion focused on borders and settlements. From the beginning, Abu Ala reiterated the Palestinian position that "settlements do not set borders." "Settlers can become Palestinian citizens, if they so wish, under one – Palestinian – legal system," he added. "We must differentiate between the status of the 'settlement area' and the status of the 'settlers in the area,'" Ben-Ami replied. "We could try a method of 'leasing' the territory to the Israeli government, or even to the settlements themselves. Settlers who prefer to remain in Palestinian sovereign territory will retain their Israeli citizenship but will become citizens of the Palestinian state," Ben-Ami added. "Most settlers will probably prefer to move into Israel proper. In which case, the settlements could be used, for example, for the rehabilitation of refugees. In the settlement areas that will be annexed to Israel, it will be necessary to provide the Arab inhabitants with a status similar to that of the settlements that remain in the sovereign territory of the Palestinian state," he explained. Abu Ala objected: "This is extremely artificial, forced and too complicated to work in reality. We understand that you want some changes to the 1967 border, but we cannot do so to the extent the Israeli public would like. We have people collecting a million signatures today in support of the Right of Return. As for Jerusalem, the same territorial rules must hold. If a special regime is created, it must be implemented both on the western and eastern parts of the city. If not, the East will be ours, and the West will be yours." Ben-Ami and I replied: "We propose extending the boundaries of Jerusalem to include all 200,000 Arab inhabitants. In the Old City and Temple Mount, a special regime with international elements must be implemented," emphasizing that as the capital of the State of Israel, Jerusalem, has been and will always be the capital of the Jewish people, alone.

After the meeting, Ben-Ami and I met with the prime minister at the Ministry of Defense. "We have eight to ten weeks of work ahead of us, in order to provide time for the US Congress to budget and allocate the billions dollars of aid necessary to help resolve the refugee issue, to advance projects in Jerusalem, to promote desalination plants and means of physical separation," Barak began. "The message that should be conveyed to Arafat is that this is a unique, singular, and historic opportunity." He emphasized that the Palestinians should agree, in principle, that as part of the negotiations process we would jointly prepare a document that outlines all the agreements and disagreements in advance of Permanent Status. The essence of Barak's approach was to "unmask" the Palestinians' intentions in case their involvement in the process was not to negotiate in good faith but to ultimately lead to confrontation.

As our secret channel discussions with Abu Ala and Asfour continued, we were joined by Dennis Ross, head of the American peace team, and Rob Malley – Director for Near East and South Asian Affairs at the National Security Council and Special Assistant to President Clinton for Arab–Israeli Affairs. Ambassador Martin Indyk joined us shortly thereafter. Ross, Indyk and Malley, together with Aaron Miller and Jamil Hillal, felt personally committed to the peace process and had accumulated extensive "frequent flyer" miles while flying back and forth to the region, working tirelessly to promote it. They knew the details of the process and the various people who were involved in it over the past decade. Indyk, a diplomat with an amazing career by any standard, began a second term as Ambassador to Israel several months before. And until the end of this term, he was intensively involved in the development of the peace process.

Disagreement about borders resurfaced. Abu Ala argued, "We are concerned about the nation, the people, and the land. You – with security. Ma'ale Adumim and Ariel will never become part of Israel. Border modifications will not be made on the basis of settlements, but primarily on the basis of security considerations." "We never said that we would agree to the '67 borders," we quickly replied. "Barak will not agree to an arrangement whereby most Israeli settlers will not be under Israeli sovereign rule." Abu Ala reiterated his position that "the settlements are illegal, and cannot constitute grounds for changing borders. However, we will assume a 'soft' approach to these borders. We must develop a new approach to address security concerns in the context of a Permanent Status agreement, possibly including joint patrols, American presence, or early-warning posts. We can go further into details regarding the eastern border of a Palestinian state. As for the western border – tell us what your needs and demands are – and we will discuss which border modifications will be necessary. First we will try to get something down on paper that will narrow the gap between our positions. Issues that cannot be resolved through negotiations will be handed off to the political leaders to decide. If the gap between the positions is not large, President Clinton will invite the sides to a summit, in the spirit of Camp David," predicted Abu Ala.

But Barak still had reservations regarding Palestinian negotiations tactics. "Gilli," he asked when we met later that evening, "what do you think are the chances of successful negotiations?" "I believe, less than fifty percent," I answered. Barak feared that an internal Palestinian coalition might be created, between Dahlan, Mohammad Rashid and Abu Ala, that would strengthen Arafat's belief that he had already relinquished too much, and it was now time for Barak to compromise. We discussed several ideas regarding territory, including for example, defining three types of areas – those that would remain under Israeli control, those under Palestinian control, and Areas Under Consideration (AUC). The status of latter territories would be postponed for at least five years. We discussed the possibility that at this stage of the negotiations, the emerging text would be presented to a reputable international jurist and attorney, perhaps Sir Professor Elihu Lauterpacht. Sir Lauterpacht, an international law expert with a world-renowned reputation, teaches at Cambridge University, and serves as a barrister, arbitrator and expert-witness in international disputes. In the past he, together with his assistant Daniel Bethlehem who is a legal expert in his own right, consulted the Israeli government on different issues relating to the peace process. Lauterpacht, who was born in 1928, is a second generation to a family of international jurists. His father assisted the team that both drafted Israel's Declaration of Independence, and handled all related international legal aspects. Israel has always striven to gain international legitimacy for its borders and its capital, Jerusalem. The legitimacy of its Declaration of Independence was rooted in the Lord Balfour Declaration and UNSCR 181. This was the mirror image of what happened on the Palestinian side. For them, international legitimacy was like a religion. Negotiations took place in conference rooms, but their battle was taking place around the world.

The following day, May 9, was Memorial Day. We held a meeting in Barak's office at the Ministry of Defense in Tel Aviv. Major-General Amos Malka, head of AMAN, anticipated that the Palestinians might agree to Israel annexing five to six percent of the territory. On the other hand, Minister Amnon Lipkin Shahak estimated that the area under consideration was more like four to twelve percent. I suspected that the Palestinians were preparing their own draft of a framework agreement and suggested that we would be in a better position if we were to present our conceptual document first, and subsequently use that draft as a basis for discussion. On the issue of territory, we needed to present a concept without specifying numbers or completing the missing parts on the map. In any case, it was necessary to prepare a fully fleshed out document that would leave us with substantial maneuverability in negotiations further on in the process. The head of AGAT, Major-General Yanai proposed exploring characteristics of military activity in special security areas, such as the Jordan Valley, in terms of presence and time; we discussed longer

Israeli presence in the Jordan Valley, but with fewer forces or a less "visible" presence – in order to accommodate Palestinian sensitivities. The head of the Shin Bet, Avi Dichter, emphasized that we must anchor the developing document with Palestinian commitments to combat terrorism. He also called for physical separation in the city limits of Jerusalem, between the Palestinian state and the territory of the city of Jerusalem. The prime minister concluded:

> We are on the brink of some of the most difficult decisions of this decade, if not of the history of this country. We do not really know how far we can go in terms of reaching a reasonable balance between the needs of one side and the needs of the other. It is important to be aware of the need to change our own perceptions – a change from a system of supervision to a system of defense from within. We must therefore concern ourselves with creating simple outlines for separation.

Barak directed us to proceed with the "package" and consolidate it before our next meeting:

> The Palestinian state must, of course, be demilitarized, and we should recognize the state as soon as it is established. As for the territory, in return for Palestinian understandings regarding the need for settlement blocs and security areas, we can propose thirteen to fifteen percent of the territory for Israel, seventy-seven percent for the Palestinians, and eight to ten percent areas subject to future negotiations.

It is worth mentioning that during the same period, senior politicians from the Israeli left, including Minister Haim Ramon, were discussing a formula of seventy percent (Palestinian)/twenty percent (AUC under Israeli control)/ten percent (annexed to Israel). Peres had said that an agreement could be concluded on the basis of twenty/eighty. Barak was convinced that these formulas were unacceptable to the Palestinians, but he could not allow himself at this stage to sidestep his party colleagues from the left.

With regard to Jerusalem, Barak felt that presenting any substantive public position too early could blow up the negotiations in terms of the internal Israeli public debate. He suggested hinting at possible solutions, including expanding the area of Jerusalem, or establishing a supra-municipality, but directed us to defer negotiations on Jerusalem until the very end.

On the same day, May 9, Arafat met with Egyptian President Mubarak and informed him that the talks were in "deep crisis."

In secret and with subdued excitement, Abu Ala, Hassan Asfour, Shlomo Ben-Ami, Ilan (chief of staff for the head of the Shin Bet) and I took off at 10 p.m. the next day from a concealed airfield at Ben Gurion airport in the private airplane of the Swedish prime minister. The pleasant atmosphere on the flight was underlined by palpable apprehension. Our mission was to effectively prepare the upcoming summit between Barak and Arafat, which would be an important stepping-stone toward concluding a FAPS. Ben-Ami and I looked over documents, Abu Ala had written notes, while Asfour was busy reading the newspaper sports pages, particularly those from Egypt.

At around 2 a.m. we landed in Stockholm, where we were met by John Hagard, the former Swedish ambassador to Israel and current deputy director general of the Swedish Ministry of Foreign Affairs. The fatigued teams were then discreetly led to Harpsund – the official countryside residence of the prime minister of Sweden, a beautiful, pastoral estate from which we could see the breathtaking view of a lake, small boats and a wooden pier. Security forces dressed in shorts and carrying backpacks were everywhere but were hardly felt. When I went for a run the next morning in the adjacent hills, they rode after me on their bicycles ensuring that I was never out of sight.

Pär Nuder opened the discussion: "We, the government of Sweden, and its representatives here, are committed to the future of the Middle East and to efforts aimed at resolving its conflicts. It is you who will decide if Sweden has a role – as a friend to both sides – and if so, what such a role would be. We have a lot of admiration and respect for the courage of the Israelis and Palestinians in going forward with the step that has brought you here. From this point on, we will be here, around, at your service."

Abu Ala summarized our mission: "I am glad that this group has gathered here. This is our ninth meeting and the most important thus far in the peace process. We should begin trying to draft something on paper – borders, refugees, Jerusalem, security. We must also prepare public opinion for difficult decisions on both sides." I proceeded to present the draft I had prepared following my meeting with Barak, skimming over its contents – introduction, territory, borders and settlements. Ben-Ami continued, detailing the Israeli position on refugees. "It is not correct to discuss Jerusalem at this point, but it is clear that to complete the framework agreement, we will have to discuss it in detail and reach agreement." Abu Ala was upset. "On all the substantive issues, we have returned to 'square one.' Israel has no need for our land. What Israel needs is security," he said. "Our approach to security requires control on the ground," I emphasized. "Even if it is for a limited period of time." Abu Ala, for the first time, understood the concept of "territory" in contrast to the concept of "posts." "If you need deployment of forces or equipment in the Jordan Valley, we can discuss this. In terms of the western side [of the Palestinian state], the '67 ceasefire lines will be the border. We will be willing to discuss small changes along these lines, as long as such measures are reciprocal, and completely equal in quality and size," he replied. Ben-Ami and I presented the approach to security, and the need to demilitarize the Palestinian state. "I am interested in building and developing a state," Abu Ala responded, "not in security investments. I accept your right to use our airspace. The details will be finalized in the framework agreement that will be signed in September." About an hour after the meeting began, Raviv Druker, the political correspondent for Galei Tzahal (Israel's military radio station), called my mobile phone. "Gilli, can you confirm that meetings are taking place in a European capital between Abu Ala, Shlomo Ben-Ami, Hassan Asfour and yourself?" "I'll get back to you later," I replied, hoping my voice did not give away my surprise. The radio station went ahead with the news item that afternoon. Demoralized by the leak, we decided nonetheless to continue with the discussions. It was clear, however, that from this point on, the rules of the game had changed. We suspected that the story was leaked by Abu Mazen, who actually initiated the Swedish channel, but was later bypassed as the person to spearhead it. Then again, the leak could have come from an Israeli source privy to the talks. On both sides there were those who clearly had an interest in exposing the talks in order to prevent an imminent agreement.

Having known Abu Ala as head of the Palestinian delegation to the negotiations on the Interim Agreements in 1995 ("Oslo B"), I knew that such exposure would limit his willingness to negotiate and compromise on the difficult issues. It was hard for him to work in the limelight. The potential criticism within the PLO and the PA could completely paralyze him.

Hoping to overcome this hurdle, I prepared a first draft of an agreement and gave everyone a copy, stressing: "this paper does not represent the Israeli position, it's neither an official nor an unofficial document. Rather, it is my own private attempt to present the issues that we are discussing. We will have to continue working, editing and correcting it together." After reviewing it, Abu Ala was clear. "The effort is admirable, but we completely disagree with the substance," he said. We went over the document, paragraph by paragraph, and noted the Palestinian positions as articulated by Abu Ala. Hassan Asfour pleaded with us to put a map on the table for discussions. The map we laid out outlined 76.6 percent for the Palestinians, 10.1 percent AUC, and 13.3 percent annexed to Israel. "This isn't a proposal," we emphasized "it is a snapshot, illustrative." "This kills any desire to continue," Abu Ala responded. "We have such strong pressure on us to leave . . ." "Look, Abu Ala, we know you cannot accept our plan, but would you at all consider '100 percent minus?'" Ben-Ami asked in an attempt to instill calm. "There is no justification for this," Abu Ala replied. "What about our needs? What did you mean when you signed the Declaration of Principles in 1993? Borders, as one of the issues to be discussed during Permanent Status negotiations, meant the

1967 borders." "It is clear to both of you, that this map is the kiss of political death to Ehud Barak and Shlomo Ben-Ami if it were to become public," I answered. "We are ready to make changes, but no annexation. Most of the annexation you have requested is not related to the settlements," Asfour said, expressing a widespread Palestinian argument that the total area of settlements was 1.8 percent of the total land in the West Bank and Gaza. The annexation that Israel was requesting was much larger, and it was therefore occupation under the guise of "needs."

Focusing on the division of territories in percentages of the total territories held by Israel since 1967 was one of the most damaging results of the Interim Agreements. Everything was calculated in numbers, not in quality of land, its importance, or other significance. The Palestinians believed that the settlements were clear proof that Israel was working toward infinitely perpetuating the occupation and maintaining control of the land. The Palestinians, together with the rest of the Arab world were not the only ones who held this position. The policy of the Barak government was quite clear however. The only construction carried out in the settlement during his administration had been authorized by the previous government; new private construction was officially frozen.

Any hope for further progress in our negotiations dissipated with news from Israel regarding Palestinian prison riots, a hunger strike, and trouble in the Territories. The climax came two days later, on the day of the Nakba ("the Disaster"), on which the Palestinians commemorate the establishment of the State of Israel. A dozen soldiers were injured, five Palestinians were killed, and more than 180 were wounded. These were the most serious events since the Temple Mount Tunnel incident in September 1996. "Stop this," Ben-Ami begged, this time in his capacity as minister of internal security, who is responsible for the jails. "Take control of what is going on. The prison riot is out of control." "We are ashamed to look the families of the prisoners in the eyes," Abu Ala replied.

Nevertheless, on May 13, 2000, I prepared an additional draft and passed it on to the negotiating teams. Hassan Asfour's response suggested willingness to allow Gush Etzion, Ramot and others to be annexed. "It is clear that you have to find a solution to these problems, and at the end, maybe we could accept that you annex these problematic areas." He qualified this with a declaration, "I will not repeat this, and I will deny I ever said this in the future." But the meaning was clear. We had finally breached the stiff paradigm of the "1967 borders." This was the first time in a formal negotiations channel, that an Israeli demand for border modifications to include settlement blocs in the West Bank would not be unequivocally rejected by the Palestinians.

On the afternoon of May 14, Dennis Ross, Aaron Miller and Jamil Hillal arrived. The latter was an American of Egyptian descent who began his work in the peace team as an Arabic translator, and with time gained the respect of the team and a standing of his own. The Americans first met with the Palestinians, and immediately after received a complete and detailed report from Ben-Ami and me. "My impression is better than I would have anticipated," Ross concluded.

That night, the Palestinians announced that Yasser Abed Rabbo had resigned as head of the official negotiating team because of the reports of a secret channel and in solidarity with the striking prisoners. Abed Rabbo was able to gauge popular Palestinian sentiment very well. Modest and inconspicuous in his demeanor, he nevertheless zealously protected his position in the Palestinian leadership. The following day the riots continued. Fifteen Palestinians were wounded.

We returned home on May 17. In a meeting with Barak, Shlomo Ben-Ami defined the main problem. The Palestinians wanted to advance on the marginal issues, and we wanted to discuss a substantive framework agreement. We wanted to move from agreed arrangements to principles that would lead the negotiations on the disputed issues. The Palestinians wanted to move in the opposite direction.

Two days later, we were again on a night flight on the Swedish prime minister's jet back to Harpsund. This time my assistant Gidi Grinstein joined us. The Palestinians added attorney Hiba Husseini. I tried to organize my thoughts before we began with the next round of the negotiations. Both sides needed to overcome the limits of conventional, one-dimensional thinking but both the central government in Israel and the PA feared being de-legitimized. Lobby and pressure groups that draw on slogans and demagoguery were encouraging factionalism, intensifying disparities and deepening social and political divisions that impeded far-reaching compromises.

Back at Harpsund, Abu Ala opened the morning session. "We reported home," he said coolly. "We received an okay to move ahead. I suggest addressing a different topic each day, in an attempt to reduce the number of Israeli and Palestinian differences." "The events of the last few days are not a constructive contribution to the creation of a conducive environment for both peoples, and do not contribute to the preparation of the huge step we are about to make," Ben-Ami said. "Prime Minister Barak's commitment to the process and its goals remains intact." I proposed moving forward by identifying the issues for the summit and trying to minimize the gaps between our positions on paper, even if not necessarily bridging them. I raised a series of questions that needed to be addressed. What would happen if the committee on refugees could not complete its work by September 2000? What would happen if all the territorial questions were not resolved in the framework agreement, and then what would happen with the third redeployment? When would "Permanent Status" begin, and what would happen until the establishment of a Palestinian state? When would end of conflict be achieved? When would the PLO change? Since Palestine would be liberated, Israel would no longer be a target of annihilation. The rationale for the existence of the organization should change accordingly, both substantively and in terms of the main mantra of the organization.

Abu Ala took note of my questions. "If the framework agreement will give clear answers and solutions to all the major issues, both in detail and in principle – this would essentially be the end of conflict. One thing should be clear: the framework agreement must include a timetable for implementation of Israeli withdrawal and the transfer of territory to the Palestinians. As for the PLO, we have no intention of discussing changes to the organization or its charter," he said.

At around midnight we received reports from Israel of riots in the Territories. In Netzarim, there were casualties on both sides. The Palestinian team received translations of articles and reports with alleged details of the developing agreement we were working on. A deflated Abu Ala conducted intense ongoing phone calls with people in the West Bank and Gaza. It appeared as if the Swedish channel, like its predecessors, fell victim to Palestinian infighting, thus undermining once again any attempt to move toward an agreement. The violence in the region cast a dark shadow on the negotiations. The feeling on our side was that our Palestinian counterparts had received orders not to go ahead too fast in drafting and putting things on paper. It was clear to both sides that the main issues under dispute were still a long way off.

6

FIRST MOVEMENTS

The two Days of Rage that the Palestinians announced on May 19–20 resulted in numerous injuries and harsh images, including a soldier injured at a junction near the Gaza Strip settlement of Netzarim, settlers from Netzarim airlifted to their homes by air force helicopters, and an Israeli baby wounded by a Molotov cocktail in Jericho. These events finally ended with five injured Israeli soldiers and over 100 wounded Palestinians. Barak reversed his previously announced proposal to transfer control of three Arab villages near Jerusalem over to the Palestinians and ordered us, the Israeli negotiators, to return from Sweden.

Upon our return to Israel on May 21, Ben-Ami and I met with the prime minister to discuss whether to proceed with the next stage of discussions, and if so, under what conditions. Ben-Ami wanted to have a comprehensive and secret discussion with Barak on the issue of Jerusalem. In the meantime, it was agreed that I would prepare a document, in advance of a possible summit, which would detail the issues that would be raised and the flexibilities we had with each issue. Another document would also be prepared that would outline the more "generic" issues which included water, economics, regional cooperation, law enforcement, and bilateral relationships in other areas that were not part of the four contentious core issues.

Early on the morning of the following day, I met with Ehud Olmert, the mayor of Jerusalem. We were old friends and our relationship was based on trust and mutual appreciation. We discussed the "yes" issues (administrative, community) and "no" issues (no Palestinian power over planning and construction). In private conversations Olmert is a very practical person, significantly less extreme than "Olmert the Likud politician." Olmert knew the practical problems of Jerusalem better than most experts.

At a little after midnight on Wednesday, May 24, Barak and I met privately at his Jerusalem residence. Ehud Barak's working hours had a tendency to completely disrupt the biological clocks of those working close to him. During the coalition negotiations, we believed that the regular meetings we held in the early hours of the morning – at 1, 2, 4 a.m. – were a negotiation tactic aimed at wearing down potential coalition partners but as it turned out, the insane working hours were a way of life for Barak. He simply could not sleep during what we would consider "normal" hours. The Prime Minister's Office employees and Barak himself rarely left the building before the early hours of the morning. This was Barak's modus operandi throughout his administration. Consequently, we all became accustomed to receiving phone calls at our homes at 2 a.m., as if it was midday. I was particularly relieved on the Saturdays, when Barak chose to remain in his Jerusalem residence. It meant that I would not have to travel out of Jerusalem for meetings at his private residence in Kochav Yair.

Barak feared that if we deferred the summit beyond June 23, the Palestinians would claim that we had not implemented the scheduled Third Further Deployment and accuse us of failing to implement agreements, derailing the negotiations on the framework agreement and precipitating an out-of-control crisis. Hoping to accelerate the pace of the negotiations, he urged his ministers to find ways to soften Palestinian public opinion by taking unilateral steps, such as the release of prisoners who met certain criteria. Toward that goal, we also generated a document entitled "Toward the Summit: Toward a Framework Agreement on Permanent Status," that summarized the present positions of both sides on each issue, along with a proposal of a possible accord that could serve as a basis for continued negotiations. The central theme of the document was that FAPS would constitute an historic end of conflict and a finality of claims. This differed from the Palestinians' demand that the comprehensive agreement (CAPS) would constitute an end of conflict and a diluted statement regarding the finality of claims. The final agreement on Jerusalem, it was reiterated, would remain pending, requiring additional negotiations, and ultimately left for the leaders to resolve as part of the Permanent Status agreement. The issue of land swaps at any ratio was considered a key territorial issue. Israeli agreement to land swap would allow the Palestinians to accept most of Israel's territorial demands, including settlement blocs, circumventing Jerusalem, military sites in the Jordan Valley, etc. Without agreeing to a land swap, a difficult Palestinian struggle was expected on every paragraph, and it was altogether doubtful that an agreement could be reached. It was agreed that this issue as well would be left for a summit between the leaders.

On May 31, 2000, I met with Minister of Foreign Affairs David Levy and updated him on the latest developments. "Don't rush to a summit," Levy warned. "We still have nothing, and we are tearing the coalition apart. A little break won't hurt anyone. The Palestinians have to get used to thinking in terms of profit and loss. I want to protect Barak, to prevent everything from falling on him at once. We cannot allow people from the Jordan Valley and kibbutzim, as well as Barak's other hard-core supporters to join Yesha[1].

---

1 The Settlers' Council.

Palestinian presence along the Jordan River will compromise our relations with Jordan. This king, Abdullah, is not as stable as his father. He may turn to the East."

Barak was convinced that the substantive political process would take off once the Palestinians understood that Israel was genuinely willing to sign a real framework agreement. By the end of May, it appeared that June would be a critical month for the process. The meeting of the Syrian Baath party was scheduled for June 17. At such conferences, decisions are made that help anchor Arab or Muslim positions. Every Arab summit, on any issue, could bind Arab leaders in radical, hostile resolutions and impede political activity and compromise. Barak urged us to explain to the Palestinians the full significance of not having President Clinton involved in the process should we not move forward fast enough. Indeed, the Clinton administration was more involved than any of its predecessors in the Middle East conflict. No American president has been more knowledgeable, committed and empathic than Bill Clinton, whose familiarity with the disputed issues, down to the smallest details was impressive. Clinton remembered the names of the neighborhoods in Jerusalem and the difficulties involved in physically connecting between them. He was in command of the statistics and demographics of the area, as well as the history and tenets of the different religions with respect to the Temple Mount. He sometimes embarrassed the negotiators themselves with this proficiency. And when he did not know something, he was never ashamed to ask.

At that time, only a few people knew about the planned withdrawal from Lebanon, which was scheduled for that week. In hindsight, we underestimated the potential impact of the withdrawal from Lebanon on the process with the Palestinians. The withdrawal would ultimately have a difficult, even critical, effect on that process as the interpretation given to it in Arab capitals suggested that with force and determination you could apparently expel Israel from Arab soil. Barak's decision to withdraw was actually rooted in complex and deep political considerations that were consolidated before he took office.

The Palestinians failed to understand that southern Lebanon and the West Bank and Gaza Strip were not comparable. Southern Lebanon is not part of the historic land of Israel, the internationally recognizable border with Lebanon dates back to the British mandate period, southern Lebanon had no settlements and the security issues in the two areas were completely different. Still, a few days after the withdrawal, Arafat told Minister Dalia Itzik in a meeting in Ramallah that Palestinian public opinion was putting a lot of pressure on him to act like a "Hezbollah hero." And when we next met with the Palestinian delegation in the "Swedish channel," Abu Ala complained about the withdrawal from Lebanon, describing the difficult week the Palestinians experienced as a result. "We have been attacked and slandered from every possible direction following your withdrawal from southern Lebanon. The Israeli press fuels these flames by claiming that the Palestinians have allegedly compromised on every-thing – refugees, Jerusalem, and borders. How do you expect us to function in this type of environment, within our own circles, and in the Arab world? In Sweden it was clear that you were avoiding discussions on certain issues like Jerusalem and prisoners. But this time we will not let you get away with it. We are also willing to talk about security," he added unwillingly.

Despite our consistent attempts, our Palestinian counterparts had until then staunchly refused to discuss security matters. But as one of the core Permanent Status issues, security could not be ignored at such an advanced stage of the negotiations. In preparation, we met with Major-General Shlomo Yanai from AGAT for a short pre-brief. Yanai described Israel's strategic approach to the issue of security. He explained that expanding the narrow waist of the country was more important than the Jordan Valley. "The Jordan Valley," Yanai said, "does not have to be under Israeli sovereignty, as long as it remains a border that separates Israel from Jordan, the crossing of which constitutes *casus belli* [a legal term describing an event used to justify war]." He also noted that we needed to take into consideration the 3,000 Israeli inhabitants of the Valley and ensure the demilitarization of the envisaged Palestinian state. "Control over security in the Jordan Valley can be carried out jointly with the Palestinians, by a third party [i.e. with Jordanian participation], or by leasing. Sovereignty is of course preferable over key areas, but we could be satisfied by just having an Israeli presence." By the end of the briefing, Ben-Ami and I believed that the IDF had both internalized our need to provide Palestinians with sovereignty over most of the Jordan Valley, and understood that its role was to focus only on security-related issues. What is not necessary for security therefore would not be necessary for Israeli sovereignty. But we could not shake the feeling that the army was presenting an outdated perception that was detached from political reality. This included, for example, the demand to designate territories for IDF use within the Palestinian state during a time of emergency.

Yanai laid out a white map marking the distance from the Green Line to Israel's main centers of population. "There are 120 kilometers between Gaza and Haifa," he began. "It is a narrow strip which contains eighty-five percent of the Israeli population." "Get to the point. What you need from us is our territory. You just want to annex. That's all," Asfour interrupted impatiently. "With all due respect, General Yanai," Abu Ala continued, "there will be no territorial complications under our sovereignty. If we agree to it, there may be foreign forces, but not you. What will we agree to? Warning posts, American forces, UN forces – something of that kind. And one more thing, we will not be willing to lease the strip of land along the Jordan River. What are we, crazy? We are very sensitive to the presence of Israeli military forces. Do not surround us with military forces from every direction. When will you understand that before the peace process we were enemies, and now we are partners. Make use of our help." "We are willing to fight to defend you. No one will do this as well as we will. You also know what we have done to preserve the peace," Asfour added. "Tell me," Yanai replied, "how do you want to convince me that you will be able to defend my vital interests when I am not able to convince you that these interests exist?" "As a theoretical exercise, let us follow through with your logic," I turned to Asfour. "Let us say that we withdraw in a few years and are replaced by 'other' forces, which will not be named today. Where exactly do you think our forces will deploy in a state of emergency? A decision regarding a state of emergency is a sovereign Israeli decision and therefore your demand that we decide on this together is really absurd." "You will not really wait for authorization from us and you will deploy when you feel like it," Asfour replied. "We will not let you. And in any case, who said that we would be a demilitarized state?"

Security has a central place in the Israeli psyche. For many Israelis an agreement is acceptable as long as it is endorsed by the security establishment. Israel has always been a unique society in that respect. Ordinarily, in order to placate the concerns of the average Israeli, it is sufficient for a "security personality" of some military rank to assure the public – in a confident voice – that all of Israel's security needs are addressed in the agreement. This was the case during the first Gulf War, and the "no choice" wars in 1956, 1967 and 1982. Our working assumption, therefore, in the negotiations team, was that if we had reasonably solid and satisfactory security arrangements and saw that they reached the public through reliable information channels, it would be easier for the Israeli constituency to swallow the bitter pill on other issues.

Israel's conservative concept of security has for years linked holding onto the Jordan Valley and Mountain Ridge with the level of national security. This outdated approach was never really examined in a systemic, serious and thorough debate. The map of Israel's vital interests does not necessarily coincide with the map of military needs. National security means much more than the number of troops or the size of the territory. It is the synergy between the resilience of society, a strong economy, national identity, solidarity and recognition of the right to exist. To this one must add military strength, size and composition, fighting ability, national leadership and public support of it, and military leadership of the commanders. Thus, for example, it is much easier to protect places on which there is a national consensus, such as the larger settlement blocs, as opposed to the more remote points of settlement. Not only is the level of daily friction between the military and the Palestinian population very high, but it is also subject to sharp public debate within Israeli society. If however a decision is not made on evacuating settlers, they should be entitled to protection and the civil rights of every Israeli citizen.

Shlomo Yanai appeared open-minded. He was willing to examine all arguments – for and against – regarding security. He was also conceptually flexible in terms of the different components that made up the overall approach to security, such as early warning, demilitarization and emergency deployment. It was easy for me to get along with Yanai who, like me, had served in the armored corps of the military. The Palestinians, however, were not as impressed with our relative openness, and basically refused to listen to what Yanai had to say. "Let's create a joint group of experts that will listen to these remarks, discuss them, and present us with understandings they would reach," Yanai proposed. "We have no need for sovereignty over the roads to the deployment areas. The same goes for the airspace above the Palestinian state. We need control, not sovereignty." "Of course," Abu Ala mocked, "we will go to our people with this and say, 'we have sovereignty' . . . You do not understand, we are under occupation! Once we have an independent state, we will be willing to discuss all this. With the exception of the early-warning stations, we reject your concept. All of it."

When this difficult and derisive discussion finally ended at 1 a.m., Ben-Ami and Abu Ala met privately. "Arafat wants an agreement," Abu Ala began. "The Hezbollah in Lebanon has embarrassed Arafat in the eyes of the entire Arab world and humiliated him. But, if we are able to reach an agreement on Al-Quds [Jerusalem], the Arab world will rejoin us. Al-Quds needs to be an open city on the basis of the 1967 borders; not some 'capital' in Abu Dis. On the issue of refugees we must have the Right of Return. The key will be in implementation. Do not go too far on territory. The thirteen percent you wish to annex is too much. Prepare a more modest proposal. The settlements territory currently totals only two percent. Present a realistic request with regard to the settlement blocs. Offer us options for land swaps." "I suggest that we do not re-open the document we concluded in Sweden on the refugees. You have not presented any proposal either on the issue of borders or on Jerusalem. What if we postpone the discussion on Jerusalem for three years?" Ben-Ami asked. "No way!" jumped Abu Ala.

In the meantime, I phoned Barak and suggested that he speak to Yanai about the map. I also reported to the prime minister that the Palestinians rejected our security approach, but that it appeared to be a tactical move. They were hoping to rack up gains on other issues and then concede on security. It was clear to them that unless we were satisfied with the security arrangements, there would be no agreement. We had to discuss the security and settlements in the Jordan Valley. "So Albright should not rush to the region on Wednesday?" Barak asked. "That's not really important now," I replied. "Let us see how this round proceeds in the next couple of days, and then decide. In the meantime it is imperative that we conduct a low-key dialogue with the settlers, using one contact person." I urged Barak to meet with their leadership personally to help keep the dialogue discrete, to clarify our positions, and to make them part of the process before actual decisions that directly impacted on their future were carried out. Barak agreed and authorized me to continue a discreet dialogue with the settlers, including Ze'ev "Zambish" Hever, Pinchas Wallerstein and Uri Ariel.

My contacts with the settlers were based on complete mutual trust. Of the many meetings and tours we had, only one – in the Jordan Valley – was leaked to the press. Our meetings were characterized by open-mindedness and a joint search for long-term solutions within our policy constraints. I never concealed the fact that I knew that the advent of Permanent Status and the end of conflict would necessitate a massive evacuation of settlements.

Under a cloud of heavy Palestinian suspicion, we continued our discussions on the issue of security but we realized quickly that we were walking on the spot and wasting precious time. We felt that our interlocutors were holding the issue of security hostage in return for concessions in other areas. It was particularly frustrating because security involved less emotional weight and cultural ethos than almost any other Permanent Status issue and could have been resolved rather easily. Instead it turned out to be a difficult nut to crack. We did not doubt that we were right to raise and defend our security interests. The concessions we made were not a result of Palestinian pressure, but rather an outcome of our own desire to reach an agreement. We focused on the most vital and important security interests of the State of Israel. And we knew very well that at least part of the military would be severely shocked if the ideas we discussed were to become public prematurely.

Abu Ala and I left to speak alone in the other room. "Give us sovereignty over East Jerusalem," he said, "and all the rest will fall into place. There is no way we can discuss Israeli sovereignty in the eastern part of the city. We could maybe think of a special status or standing for the newly built Jewish neighborhoods east of the 1967 lines. They are like settlements. If we can agree about special arrangements for the holy sites, with the rest of the Old City under Palestinian rule – respecting the rights of Israelis who live there – we will have an agreement. Do you know what Arafat calls Jerusalem? 'Al-Quds Al Sharif' – the revered Al-Quds. And Abdullah, the Crown Prince of Saudi Arabia, warned us a number of times not to give up Jerusalem. Jerusalem and refugees – these are lethal to the agreement. Arafat will not yield, not in front of his people, not with a view to his legacy, and not toward the Arab world." I presented Abu Ala with our proposal of expanding the definition of the Jerusalem area to include Ma'ale Adumim to the east, Gush Etzion to the south, and Givat Ze'ev to the north, as well as that of the two capitals: Jerusalem and Al-Quds. In a parallel private meeting between Asfour and Ben-Ami,

Asfour did not dismiss the possibility of an interim solution for Jerusalem. When we reconvened, there was some minimal feeling of initial movement on the issue of Jerusalem.

The following day, June 3, Ben-Ami opened the meeting by explaining to the Palestinians that the Israeli government was nearing the moment of truth. "We cannot fail the leaders and we cannot fail Clinton. Shall we work on the maps or on the drafts?" he asked. "There is no difference between what you presented to us on the territorial issue now and what you proposed at Eilat [the formal negotiations track] in November 1999," Abu Ala replied dryly. "On security – everything is in your hands. On refugees – you agreed to the mechanism but not to the principle of the Right of Return. On Jerusalem – we cannot even begin to draft. If you cannot make progress on these major issues, there is no chance that we can reach a full agreement. Let us begin discussing the eastern border and then move to security arrangements. After that we can address the western border and settlements. Unless there is an agreement on borders, we will be unwilling to move forward with drafts or any other issue." "Our approach to the Jordan Valley is different from our approach to the western border," Ben-Ami replied. "For the first time I am pessimistic," Hassan Asfour said, discouraged. "It is possible that we – all of us – are not correctly foreseeing what will happen in the next three months. You – the Israelis – are destroying our honor. But no one will prevent us from dying with honor. Put yourselves in our place. Don't kill our hope and our future." "You realize by now that if we would reach a comprehensive agreement – at the end of the process, after a period of a number of years we will agree upon – most of the Jordan Valley will be yours. It is therefore clear that you are tactically postponing progress on the negotiations. Our role is to prepare our political leaders for the summit, and only we – the negotiators – can honestly value the real situation with regard to every issue. You and us. Put the Americans and Egyptians aside for a second," I replied. "What are you talking about?" Abu Ala erupted. "Our signature constitutes the signature of the entire Arab world. Eight million people are waiting for this and are keeping an eye on our movements. You are worried about borders and settlements leading to calm. We are concerned about the people, the nation, and the land."

I laid a map out on the table. Asfour extended his hand toward the map, to look at it more closely. Abu Ala got up from his chair and stopped him. The two had a very vocal exchange and were actually fighting. Finally, Asfour submitted to Abu Ala's authority. The map stayed on the table. Everyone calmed down, or so it seemed. I decided to suggest a new idea. "How about it if you, the Palestinians, update Barak; and we the Israelis will in our turn update Arafat?" "Actually, why don't all four us update them together?" Ben-Ami added. Our Palestinian counterparts were not impressed by these ideas.

In the evening I met with Barak to describe the results of the discussion. I presented a schematic representation of the proposed arrangement in Jerusalem, which involved maintaining the status quo on the Temple Mount, a special regime in the Old City, and separation of the remaining areas on the basis of interest and demographic considerations.

The Swedish channel had ended.

7

DO YOU WANT
AN AGREEMENT?

In a meeting between Barak and President Clinton in Lisbon it was agreed that Madeleine Albright would come to the region to assess the progress and the potential for a successful summit between the leaders. The president was optimistic, stating in one of his reports that he believed there were few issues remaining to be finalized.

On Sunday June 4, Secretary Albright arrived in the region. "The moment of truth is approaching. If each side realizes that it cannot achieve a hundred percent of its demands, there is a chance for an agreement," Albright announced. Barak accused Arafat and his people of dragging their feet and of deliberately delaying negotiations. He labeled the events surrounding the day of the Nakba "scandalous" – Palestinian policemen were firing at Israeli soldiers!

It appeared that the Palestinians, headed by Abu Mazen, were preparing – albeit unwillingly – for a possible summit on June 21. It was very difficult for the Palestinians to deal with the nearing, and quite unavoidable, historic decision to which the process was leading. They could no longer hide behind the veil of international legitimacy, Interim Agreements, and UN resolutions. We would now be confronting both the core issues at the heart of the deepest disagreements between the two peoples, and the painful compromises that each side would be required to take in order to resolve these differences, without which there would be no agreement.

The Palestinian leadership, and primarily Abu Ala, tried to postpone the inevitable by arguing that the issues were not discussed thoroughly enough. There was, of course, no substance to this argument since the latest round of negotiations had not advanced the convergence and understandings beyond those reached in the preparatory discussions in Sweden. It was time for the leaders to take center stage. The summit was ready, the decisions that needed to be made respectively by Barak and Arafat were identified and defined, and no one besides them could make the necessary decisions on the issues.

Gidi Grinstein and I flew to The Hague to meet with International Law Professor Lauterpacht, whose advice and expertize we solicited some weeks before and who had generously agreed to "do whatever I can to help Israel." I sent him the topics I wanted to discuss in advance, as well as the written conclusions from the Swedish channel.

On the plane, I was approached by an orthodox businessman who wished me luck and offered his political insight. He thought that if most Israeli citizens would remain under Israeli sovereignty in settlement blocs, there would be no problem with the remaining settlers. It was a very heartfelt meeting. Our negotiating team was always concerned about how our negotiations outcome would be perceived by the religious community. This accidental dialogue, and others like it, were very encouraging. "Do what you need to do. For peace, we are willing to make compromises, even hard ones" was the overwhelming message.

We met Lauterpacht and his assistant Daniel Bethlehem at his hotel room, which was filled with law books, boxes, huge red binders brimming with documents, maps and papers scattered on the floor. The questions that were sent to Lauterpacht were drafted from the perspective of international public law, focusing specifically on relations between countries (or state-like entities such as the PA): What are the implications of the structure of Permanent Status agreement? What should be the hierarchy and relationship between a framework agreement and a comprehensive agreement? Legal questions regarding the end of conflict and finality of claims in relations to the Palestinians' claims such as the Right of Return; legal implications of the different categories of the Territories and agreed arrangements as far as military sites, settlements, roads for joint use, safe passage and holy sites; legal-constitutional issues relating to the establishment of a Palestinian state; Jerusalem; and refugees.

Professor Lauterpacht was incredibly quick and sharp in articulating the issues. He would read aloud while drafting, as he focused on a certain word and waited for a better one of his own or from us, checking and rechecking every formula, attacking it from every possible direction, always remaining open to versions different from his own, as long as they were "on the mark." He wrote his proposals with a thick Mont Blanc pen with a handwriting we later spent hours deciphering. It was worth it. There was no substitute for Lauterpacht's clear, focused and comprehensive thinking, which resulted both in a unique perspective in terms of the text, and a fresh view of the issues we were dealing with.

Upon my return to Israel, Barak instructed us to urge the Palestinians to speed up the negotiations but also warned against mediation efforts that could potentially erode our positions. "Everything that was raised as an idea," Barak emphasized, "might be very close to our final positions and our red lines." The prime minister was concerned that the Palestinians would document the Israeli positions as they were being presented in the negotiations, identify differences within our team and between the individuals who negotiated, and would use these differences to achieve a tactical advantage in the negotiations. "The State of Israel is prepared to negotiate in good faith, not as an entity that intermittently releases something in return for nothing," he said.

The political crisis within the coalition had reached an important crossroads. On June 7 the coalition suffered a setback with a preliminary vote of sixty-one to forty-eight on a bill that called for disbanding the Knesset, thus calling for new elections. Representatives from Shas, the National Religious Party (NRP), and Israel B'Aliya, all members of the coalition, were among those who voted for the bill. This marked new heights of outrageous behavior by Israeli politicians as the ministers sitting in the government on behalf of these parties did not resign from their positions in advance, the most basic protocol in any democracy.

On Saturday June 10, 2000, Syrian president, Hafez El Assad passed away.

Clinton was instinctively ready to convene a summit, but requested that he be provided with "ammunition" to ensure its success. "We do not have much time," the prime minister emphasized, "given the death of Assad, the withdrawal from Lebanon, the presence of Clinton, and even of Mubarak at the summit. All these undermine the enemies of peace. In just two months' time, however, we will not be able to convene such a summit, given possible developments in our region. The US administration will focus on the elections. And we will not know what will happen with the coalition and with the government. Be careful with the issue of Jerusalem. Do not document positions. We cannot have drafted or written documents; only notes and discussions," Barak warned.

The timeframe the Americans set for a possible summit at Camp David was after Independence Day on July 4, and before the national Democratic and Republican conventions in mid-August. This was neither the first nor the last time they would set such arbitrary deadlines that would ultimately be postponed time and again. In private discussions some mentioned that Arafat wanted the summit, but had to appear as if he was being dragged to it, kicking and screaming, unwillingly.

I was asked to update the national security adviser Sandy Berger at the White House. Berger, an attorney by profession, was considered the "strong man," in terms of foreign policy, in the Clinton administration and a close personal friend of the president. In the past, he had been identified with the positions of Israel's "Peace Now" movement, and had very clear views about solutions to the conflict. He was experienced, smart, focused and short-fused when it came to nonsense. When he identified someone who could endanger the president, he became a pit-bull. Both his assistants, Bruce Reidel and Rob Malley, were extensively involved in the peace process.

En route to the US on June 11, I was highly aware of the magnitude of the national responsibility with which the prime minister had entrusted me. I was Barak's confidant and an emissary for the State of Israel. Focusing on this thought throughout the day, I had been trying not to lose my concentration and not to give in to fatigue. The emotional – and sometimes even physical – toll was heavy. Months of work could be ruined by a word that was spoken out of place at the negotiations table, in the press or anywhere in between.

I prepared for the meeting with Berger much like I prepare for court. I never doubted the validity of the policy I represented. The concept of "larger Israel" – the one which perpetuates occupation – may not be a monster, as philosopher Yesha'yahu Leibowitz has said, but it certainly corrupts every good part in our nation and society. He who cares for the Jewish people, the Israeli society, the future of the country, understands that we are at an historic crossroads. A brave choice needs to be made regarding the norms of a moral, healthy society confident in itself and reconciled with its conscience. To me, that meant a society that values the sanctity of life over the sanctity of land; it is the national home of the Jewish people, in practice, not as a slogan lacking all substance.

It was in this spirit that I approached Berger. "The reality created on-the-ground over the past thirty years does not allow all parties to implement their aspirations. I refer primarily to the inability, in practical terms, to agree with the demands regarding the Right of Return of Palestinian refugees, and a return to the borders of June 4, 1967." "Israel," I continued, "does not demand more than accommodating its most basic needs. On territory, we will be satisfied with what is strategically vital to us. We can find arrangements for the main settlement blocs as well as border modifications. In all, we are talking about a low percentage, between ten and twenty percent of the land. As for our security needs, these are not 'for ever' and could be addressed through special arrangements, especially in the Jordan Valley."

Berger was very attentive. I described the proposal that was developed in Sweden which involved creating an international mechanism for addressing the issue of refugees, with a commission and fund, and the initial thinking on Jerusalem. I said that on these two core issues, a gradual multi-phased process would be necessary, which incorporated stabilizing and supportive elements. I emphasized that during the negotiations we came very close to the red lines of Barak's position. We negotiators could not have compromised more than we had, given our domestic political constraints. The situation was getting worse; the Tanzim – a militant arm of Arafat's Fatah movement – was involved in numerous violent shootings, the last on May 15. "Despite all this," I said, "Barak is determined to make the final push toward concluding a substantive package for a framework agreement. This is an historic opportunity that cannot be missed."

"The failure to reach agreement with the Syrians in Geneva proved that we must be hard on ourselves before such critical high-level meetings, and that we must neutralize the significant risks in case of failure," Berger said. "In order to ensure success, therefore, the implication is that we must be very careful about the prior conditions to the summit and lay all the necessary groundwork in advance. We, the Americans, also feel a sense of urgency, importance and opportunity. We do not doubt that Barak is committed to achieving a Permanent Status agreement, but it is the prestige of our president that is on the line." Berger criticized Israel's decision in the aftermath of the May 15 riots, for the freezing of funds that were supposed to be transferred to the PA. "By not transferring tax revenues to the Palestinian Authority you caused the president, for the first time, to break a promise he made to Arafat. You have to provide the president with something he can give Arafat, something really tangible," he urged me. "The second hurdle," Berger continued, "is the Third Further Redeployment that must be postponed for about a month and a half. If these two things are doable, I will be able to tell the president, 'this is possible.' We intend to make the same clarifications with Arafat on June 15. Only after these clarifications are made will we be able to determine the guidelines for a possible summit. In the next few weeks, you have to make an effort to build as much trust as possible in your channel. If there are things you cannot tell *them*, but that could help *us* make a decision regarding the summit – please tell us, and we will keep it locked away. The most difficult issue is Jerusalem. I do not believe Arafat will be able to accept any postponement of this issue. This would not be good for you either, since any postponement would encourage violence."

We knew that within the Palestinian leadership Abu Ala was the strongest opponent to the summit. He had been de-legitimized by his political rivals and subsequently marginalized. The Palestinian leadership was without a leader, impractical, fractured, conflicted and weak. It would disappoint us, time and again, later in the process. In any case, recalling that the Americans had said that the summit would not take place before the weekend of July 4, Abu Ala wanted two to three more weeks of preparations. In the interim, Ben-Ami had arrived in Washington, joined by Yanai and Ephraim from the intelligence branch of the IDF (AMAN). The Palestinian delegation, headed by Abu Ala, also arrived in Washington with the explicit goal of setting a date for the summit.

We met with the Palestinian team on June 12 at the Willard Hotel in Washington DC. "We recommended to Arafat that he examines the possibility of attending the summit, contingent on the success of the current round," Abu Ala emphasized, then added: "On Jerusalem, we will not be satisfied with general declarations without talking about details." "We were able to present and clarify several issues in Sweden," replied Ben-Ami. "No other Israeli government has offered you what we are offering you today, particularly on territory, thus considering the dismantling of settlements. This is something in the order of a domestic political earthquake in Israel. What are you afraid of? We will negotiate now for a week, maybe two, and then attend the summit. You are here – so close to an agreement – thanks in large part to your own political struggle rather than international law, which was supposedly on your side for the past fifty-two years. Do you want another UN resolution or rather an agreement?" "Shlomo, Shlomo," Abu Ala cut him off. "All you have to do is just talk to us like you did with the Syrians, the Egyptians and the Jordanians. No more and no less. Otherwise this summit will be a disaster, a catastrophe." I stressed that "the final map will be very close to what you saw in the most updated draft of the Israeli proposal relating to territory." "If so," Abu Ala replied, "we cannot accept the offer, and we completely reject your proposal for territorial arrangements. The deal should be 'what is yours is yours, and what is ours is ours,' and no other."

Convening the summit was necessary to exhaust all possibilities of bringing Arafat to a decision-making stage; otherwise, years could pass, once again, without any real progress toward a permanent solution.

The last phase of preparations for the summit began on June 13 at Andrews Air Force Base, just outside Washington DC, home to Air Force One, and the official portal where foreign dignitaries land upon arrival in the capital. It was an intensive round of negotiations, however it was clear that it served the parties as a tactical stage in the process. In our joint discussions, the Palestinians used their usual ammunition – "perpetuating the occupation," "Israeli dictate," "stealing territory under the pretext of security." They were trying to get the maximum Israeli concessions before the summit.

The members of the American peace team arrived and met with both teams. There was a feeling that we were standing in place, and basically treading water. Without definite decision-making by our respective leaders there was inability and unwillingness to move forward. Ben-Ami and I believed that our Palestinian counterparts were at the "end of their tether." No progress would be made unless Israel demonstrated flexibility in its positions, which clearly did not correspond with our plans at that point. We perceived Permanent Status as a package deal in which mutual concessions are made by both sides toward an historic compromise on all issues. "Interests" come in place of "positions," and disagreements are settled on the basis of common interest. Unless we sensed readiness to "give and take" on the Palestinian side, we would continue to pursue measured progress on all issues concurrently.

This, in fact, is how Abu Ala presented the situation to the American team. "The positions the Israelis presented on Jerusalem, borders and security, cannot serve as a basis for negotiations," he argued. "If the Israeli team would not be authorized to make progress, we will announce that this channel has exhausted itself. We do want a summit, but one that will result in an agreement." He further stressed that "the visibility of the agreement in the eyes of our people is imperative. If the people see the occupation continuing with settlements and Israeli soldiers – it will not work. The agreement will not be realized."

Dennis Ross tried to calm the atmosphere. "We told you, in the early stages, that no better group exists to carry out these negotiations between Israel and the Palestinians. We cannot rush toward a summit. The higher the expectations, the greater the disappointment." As usual, Dennis Ross tried to promote continuity. "Let us meet separately with each of the sides and hear how it understands and interprets the positions of the other."

I responded that we were authorized to move forward on nine miles out of ten. The mandate of our counterparts, however, which was supposedly very wide, was in fact very limited. "How is it possible," I asked Dennis, "that from that day in Sweden in which you claimed that the most important move in the peace process was taking place, we have arrived at this dead end? We had it right in Sweden, and we lost momentum. We can achieve it again, as long as we do not confuse tactics and substance." I concluded by saying that it is only together with the Palestinians that we could create the "critical mass" of convergence necessary for both the success of the summit and the completion of the framework agreement.

"Peace is indeed important to the Israelis," Abu Ala replied, "but for the Palestinians it will determine the future. We must therefore be careful to complete everything necessary to ensure the success of the summit."

Ben-Ami and I were aware that the strongest "cards" our counterparts held were the security arrangements and the end of conflict. Among ourselves we predicted that the Palestinians would be willing to let Israel retain two to three percent of the territory, without land swaps. It was actually the Americans, in a meeting with the Israeli team, who requested that we get rid of "gray areas," and reduce the size of the required territory.

It was clear that the Americans were looking for a safety net for the president. But the Israeli team was adamant about seeing some kind of movement on the Palestinian side. Albright decided to call Barak, with us in the room. "I don't know how to operate one button on this phone, with the exception of this one, which connects me with my secretary," she apologized. Dennis Ross made the call. Albright told Barak what she had already told us. "We are very disappointed from the release of only three prisoners. This is really an insulting number. It was difficult, but we convinced Arafat not to make a crisis. You need to say that discussions on the issue of the Third Further Redeployment will continue." We heard similar things, later that same day, from Sandy Berger: "The Clinton–Arafat meeting was one of the worst they had in the past seven years, including during the Netanyahu administration. The president will not go to a summit without momentum or without a foundation. Be creative about what Israel can do to give the US a safety net, without throwing Israel into an internal crisis.

You have to be entrepreneurial and innovative, and you must be sensitive to the Palestinian situation." "We have more to lose, in this story, than anyone else," Ben-Ami replied. "If we do not succeed, our situation will be very difficult. We are all in the same boat. But unless our partners have the authority to move forward to narrow the gaps – we will never succeed."

That night, Ben-Ami, Minister Vilnai and I met with Arafat, before his flight back to the region, at the VIP lounge of Andrews Air Force Base. He was joined by Abu Ala, Abu Mazen and Hassan Asfour. The latter two had not exchanged a word since 1998. "We must jointly create the basis and conditions for the summit," Ben-Ami began. Arafat interrupted before Ben-Ami could finish his sentence, and began a tirade: "The issue of the prisoners was intended to hurt Clinton and me. We can create a reality on the ground that is similar to what you had with the Hezbollah in Lebanon."

We tried to focus the conversation back on the substance of the negotiations: "Authorize Abu Ala to discuss security," we pleaded with Arafat. "I am convinced that we can reach an agreement if there's good will and each side is authorized to move forward," Ben-Ami added.

The short meeting ended. The importance of the meeting, we thought, was in that it actually took place, it helped ease the repercussions from Arafat's explosive visit to Washington, and it coordinated expectations.

The next morning, in a meeting with the American team, we proposed some working assumptions that we felt were necessary to complete the agreement. We again felt that the Americans were not focused enough on content and did not create a coherent and clear image of the situation, the interests and the positions. For a decade, these talented individuals dedicated their time to resolving the Middle East conflict, by looking together with both sides for possible solutions to incredibly complex issues. As they grew closer to adopting the positions of one side there was natural erosion in their impartiality as mediators. With six months to go before Clinton left office, and under the almost certain knowledge that the succeeding president would not be nearly as involved or as knowledgeable in the details of the process, the team did not want to make mistakes, fearing that it would not have time to correct them. To complicate things, Permanent Status issues posed huge conceptual, seemingly insoluble challenges. As far as Arafat was concerned, Secretary Albright's prestige and authority were at an all-time low while Dennis Ross was being unfairly de-legitimized by the Palestinians as Barak's voice.

The American team realized that the current round of talks was not likely to produce any significant outcome. Ross suggested that they present each side's position to the other in hope that "it may be easier for each side to concede a difficult position to a third party, rather than to the opposing side." He continued to request that we share our "flexibility" with the Americans: "We promise you that we will not turn the real positions you present into the opening positions for the next stage." He did not get what he wanted but thanked us nevertheless for our honesty, creativity and effort.

Ben-Ami, Yanai and I were convinced that the direct stage of negotiations had been fully exhausted. With or without American mediation, it was time for our leaders to discuss the disagreements and bridge the gaps. Knowing Arafat's patterns of manipulative, edgy and evasive behavior we recommended to Barak that confidence-building measures be prepared for the days of the summit. Ben-Ami suggested releasing prisoners and turning the village of Abu Dis over to Palestinian control.

Barak feared that the political noose would tighten further around his neck the closer he came to reaching an agreement. He asked me to convey that concern to the Americans. As much as Barak was willing to stake his political survival on this historic agreement with the Palestinians, it was clear that the Knesset would try to stop it. He would therefore have to go to elections and present the agreement to the judgment of the public. Shas ministers resigned from the government on June 20, but returned to it the next day. Consequently, Meretz ministers submitted their resignations, but promised that they would continue to support the political process from "the outside." "If it will pacify the NRP and Israel B'Aliya, I will not transfer Abu Dis at this stage," Barak said.

Much of our effort at this time was invested in updating and consulting with various parties whose support of the process could have a positive effect on the negotiations.

Assessing that Mubarak had a substantial influence on Arafat, I met with Egyptian Ambassador Bassiouni and briefed him on the status of the negotiations. Bassiouni, who began his career not as a diplomat but as an intelligence officer for the Egyptian military in Syria, was very optimistic. He was confident that in a referendum, seventy percent of Israelis would vote for an agreement, and that the Knesset could do nothing to prevent it. The Egyptian ambassador anticipated that the summit would begin in the first week of July, and would end three weeks later, immune to failure. But he also warned that Jerusalem and sovereignty were not Palestinian issues. "These are issues," he said, "to which the eyes of the entire Arab world are turned." He added that we could not allow Arab Muslim extremists a foothold in developing a solution for Jerusalem. His warning did not fall on deaf ears. We knew that within the Arab and Muslim world there were those who did not look favorably upon the Palestinians monopolizing the issue of Jerusalem. Of the four Permanent Status core issues, Jerusalem was the only one that was not strictly a Palestinian issue. It was more of a pan-Arab issue. The Al Aqsa Mosque was the third most important place among Muslim believers.

I then flew to Paris to meet with the advisers of the French President Chirac and with senior French Foreign Ministry officials. Although I thought

I had won them over somewhat, it was surely not enough to bring about any movement in the traditionally pro-Arab French position. Old France did not want to risk French interests.

The American peace team informed us that the president had asked that the outline of a possible agreement be clarified before a summit was convened. Clinton assessed that in light of the limited time horizon as well as the complexity of the issues, the agreement should not include the issues of water, economics, law enforcement, and other "generic" issues. Ben-Ami and I believed that this type of agreement would lack the vision and the details necessary for carrying out day-to-day life. It would be seen as just another "contract" rather than an historic peace agreement. Other members of the peace team, namely Rob Malley, were more optimistic about the possibility of attaining far-reaching understandings but wanted to gather as much information as available on possible compromises, in order to protect the president from failure.

At the residence of the US ambassador to Israel, Martin Indyk, on June 22, Ross geared the discussion toward the issue of Jerusalem. "We have an indication," he said, "that the Palestinians may be willing to allow the Old City to be designated as Area B[1], under the assumption that the rest of the Arab neighborhoods will be under full Palestinian sovereignty." I suggested that the discussion on the issue of Jerusalem be carried out – in principle and in practice – with the prime minister in attendance.

The prime minister was considering whether the entire area of Jerusalem should be enclosed within a "bubble" on the map, or whether a fence separating Israel and Palestine should cut through the city. "Jerusalem is a city that requires special, unique municipal arrangements. The most important thing is to ensure access – a bridge or tunnel – to whoever wishes to worship at Al Aqsa. But Jerusalem will stay united," Barak had emphasized to us. "You can hint to the Palestinians that we understand that they have certain aspirations regarding the Temple Mount and Arab neighborhoods but don't set any precedents on sovereignty or on a Permanent Status solution. Our struggle is on the 'American mindset,'" he added. "We cannot give up quite yet. The Palestinians are standing in place, waiting for us to make the concessions. Whatever you say, always qualify it, to avoid being bound by a certain position." Barak knew that in the case of failure, he would be the only one held responsible, and he would have to pay a very dear political price. But he was nevertheless not afraid to do so, and was determined to exhaust all possibilities of achieving Permanent Status.

1 Palestinian civil responsibility, Israeli security responsibility.

8

TRAPPED IN A
NATIONAL MYTH

On Sunday June 25, we continued to prepare for a meeting with Arafat. On the very same day, Arafat told thousands of cheering Fatah faction supporters in Nablus "Palestine is ours, ours, ours! . . . We don't get threatened by tanks and planes – no one can threaten us."

Jamil Hillal, who probably knew Arafat better than any other American, noted that "Arafat's mindset must be changed. He has to acknowledge the achievements and progress in the Swedish channel. His current view that nothing is moving forward has to shift."

While I met with the American team again later, Minister of Justice Yossi Beilin came to meet privately with Dennis Ross. In a government session earlier that morning, Barak criticized the unofficial and unauthorized meetings that government members were having with Palestinians. Although he did not "name names," it was clear that his message was directed toward Haim Ramon. "This really sabotages the negotiations," he reprimanded the ministers, "because the Palestinians use this to press for concessions. They grab on to these discrepancies."

Ben-Ami and I drove to the meeting with Arafat in Nablus from Yossi Ginossar's house in Kohav Yair. The Palestinians picked us up with drivers and bodyguards from Avnei Hefetz checkpoint in the dead of night.

Yossi Ginossar, like many other former senior officials in the Shin Bet, including Carmi Gillon, Ami Ayalon, Israel Hasson and Shimon Romach, realized the limits of power. The Shin Bet had shouldered most of the responsibility for preventing terrorist attacks for the past thirty-four years. It did so effectively and with great dedication. It was this experience that led these senior officials to conclude that operational success and supremacy in the field would not result in a long-term solution to the Israeli–Palestinian conflict. They ultimately became the strongest proponents of a radical and deep solution to the conflict as a means of protecting Israel's vital interests.

We met the Palestinians at the house of the mayor of Nablus, Ghassan Shakaa. They were seated in a huge room, and as usual, at a great distance from one another. Abu Mazen and Abu Ala sat on one sofa, with Ginossar seated in between, a cigar in hand. I sat to their right with Erekat and

Shakaa. Arafat and Ben-Ami were seated on yet another sofa. We started with the usual small talk that always precedes the real meeting.

"I want to update you on progress in the back channel," Ben-Ami began, leaning toward Arafat on the sofa, "or as some of your people joke 'the bad channel.'" Arafat stopped him after two sentences. "I am told," he raised his voice, pointing a trembling finger at Ben-Ami, "that the Hezbollah are better than us and that Barak mocks us. He wastes time until Clinton is no longer relevant. Then another year and half will pass until Bush or Gore is in the White House." Ben-Ami replied that "Barak cannot allow himself to waste time, and he's not alone. The summit is where all of us will have to make a concerted effort to succeed, for the sake of history." "We have to prepare well for the summit. That is your mission, together with our people," Arafat replied. "Because of Geneva [the failed summit with Assad], the US will not allow us to fail. We will not allow the process to be derailed," Ben-Ami continued. Arafat then returned to his usual lamentation. "June 23 passed, and everyone – Mubarak, Moratinos, and Albright – pressured me to accept Barak's promise to withdraw. He promised again and again and did not fulfill. What about the forty-three settlements [meaning the illegal strongholds] that he promised to evacuate and did not? Why not bring the villages [three villages near Jerusalem] to the Knesset?" Yossi Ginossar interrupted. "It is only with you that Barak can reach an historic agreement," he said in an attempt to persuade and soothe. Ben-Ami continued to update as Erekat translated from English to Arabic, leaning toward Arafat on the other side. "We began with fifty percent of the territory. Now we reached eighty-seven percent of it – seventy-six percent immediately, and the remaining ten percent through a gradual withdrawal," Ben-Ami explained. "And don't forget – the additional thirteen percent will be negotiated in the US. This is in no way the final situation." "Why did you withdraw from all of southern Lebanon?" Arafat asked. "Territory is only one of the many issues involved in the Israeli–Palestinian conflict; in Lebanon it was the only issue," Ben-Ami replied. With the experience of a gifted lecturer, he captured the attention and focus of his audience. "The Palestinian people have suffered too much. But an agreement is the only way to enlist the support of the entire world, including Israel, toward the great effort necessary to rehabilitate refugees. If there is no agreement, it will be very difficult to build up public support. Let us create an international fund, a commission. We are split only on one issue, the Right of Return. Please understand, Mr Chairman, our society is vulnerable and fragile. Twenty percent of our population is Arab. I may not disagree with the morality of your claims, but we have to find a formula, on the basis of which, the Right of Return will be strictly symbolic. We are all prisoners of our national myths and are at the same time part of it." "Do you really think those who live in Chile will return to Ramallah?" Arafat wondered aloud. "In Jordan, ninety-nine percent of the economy is dependent on Palestinians, on refugees. In Syria, Palestinians have senior positions in the military. They may not have citizenship, but they have all the rights of a Syrian citizen." Ben-Ami now turned to the issue of Jerusalem. "You are aware," he turned to Arafat, "of the extent to which you, as Muslims, have autonomy on the Temple Mount. This has been the situation since Moshe Dayan's decision to do so in 1967. No agreement can harm the status quo. You will have full and secure autonomy for all worshipers." "Al-Quds," Arafat responded, "is an issue for Arabs, the Vatican, Christians and Muslims. I remind you of the letter Peres sent to Holst [former foreign minister of Norway] and the 'Covenant of Omar.'[1] Is there an Arab, a Muslim, who would accept your offer? The issue of Al-Quds Al Sharif unresolved? Forget it. I will be kicked out. I cannot have nothing in Jerusalem." "But Mr Chairman," interrupted Ben-Ami, "this is an issue we need to discuss at the summit. We can at least agree on the holy sites, and return to discuss the rest in two years. In the meantime, in the Old City, you will have some elements of sovereignty. The municipality of Al-Quds will have special municipal governance over the Arab neighborhoods in Jerusalem. Even today, inhabitants of East Jerusalem have almost complete autonomy in health, education and welfare." "It's like – how do you say, Saeb – it is like a guillotine to our necks," Arafat replied.

It was clear throughout the meeting that this was the first time Arafat was hearing of Israel's updated positions. The Palestinian negotiators had not relayed the actual positions, progress on the negotiations, or our openness on many issues, back to Arafat. Despite his disgruntled demeanor, Arafat understood that substantial – though conditional – progress had been made toward achieving his major goals of sovereign control over most of the territory, a reasonable international solution to the refugee issue, accompanied with a genuine willingness to compromise in Jerusalem.

"We did not have a real negotiation on Jerusalem," I turned to Arafat. "The principles should include: mutual recognition of the capitals of both sides, preserving the status quo for a period that will be determined, and maintaining the claims of sovereignty of each side. We will have to resolve this issue in a way that would be acceptable to both peoples, without completely closing off future options. We do not expect Barak and you to negotiate this at the summit. That will be up to us, while you will make the decision."

"Do you know who was the first to suggest a Palestinian state? It was Begin. But I could not accept because there was enormous pressure from

1 This was referring to an agreement from 638 BC in which Caliph Omar Ibn al-Khattab granted the people of Jerusalem and the Patriarch Safronius a covenant of peace and protection, and ensured the care and protection of Christian and Jewish Holy places. He also forbade Jews living in the city.

the Syrians," Arafat said. "Do your utmost this time – whatever is necessary – for your people," Ben-Ami hurried to tie both issues together. Arafat nodded thoughtfully, saying "We have a lot of hard work to do before the summit. We should think about this together with Albright and Mubarak."

We met with Barak a few hours later, on the morning of June 26, to provide him with a full report of our meeting in Nablus. Barak made the following points on the issues going forward. The Right of Return for refugees will be implemented in Palestinian territory only. Israel will accept few refugees, only on the basis of humanitarian considerations. On Jerusalem we may not able to achieve end of conflict. If we do not conclude all related issues, and all the aspects of the arrangement and its details, we will face an explosive situation. There is a need to make an effort to hold on to the Jordan Valley for thirty years. Every ten years we will examine whether sections can be transferred to the Palestinians. The Americans will guarantee implementation of the arrangement and will strengthen Israel in terms of security and military. This will provide justification – maybe the only justification – for concessions on the eastern front. "The Palestinians are not moving forward," Barak said. He expected that they would want to postpone the summit, and in the absence of an agreement, they would blame us for a crisis involving the Third Further Redeployment. We felt that time was working against us. Arafat was using this to his advantage, hoping to arrive at the summit under the pretext of someone who was being dragged to it unwillingly, in order to assuage Arab criticism.

The next day, on the morning of June 27, I met again with Jerusalem Mayor Ehud Olmert. "A Palestinian flag over the holy places – no way," started the mayor. "On planning and construction – Israel should always have the authority to decide, even if a joint Israeli–Palestinian committee is established. Finally, there has to be symmetry between arrangements in the Tomb of the Patriarchs and arrangements governing places holy to the Arabs," Olmert affirmed. As expected, he did not reveal all his cards and articulated himself very carefully. At the same time, I noticed that he was willing to make certain compromises in the city – which largely amounted to the term "separation." He knew the city well, and he understood the internal logic that guided Barak's position on Jerusalem. But ever the politician, he sat on the sidelines and waited. He knew that I would not relay our conversations to anyone but Barak. This was largely true until January 2001, when six months after our meeting, deep into the election campaign, Barak and Olmert violated the code that had formerly defined their relationship. Olmert attacked Barak publicly on his supposed position on Jerusalem. Barak returned the favor revealing that Olmet had presented him with far-reaching maps and possible arrangements.

On the morning of Thursday June 29, a meeting was convened in the Prime Minister's Office in Tel Aviv to discuss the possibility of a Palestinian

UDI and our potential reactions to such a development. The participants included the chief of staff, the heads of AGAT and AMAN, the head of Central Command, legal advisers and others. The prime minister explained that if we did not respond immediately to a unilateral declaration, our political position would be compromised in the international arena, and we could ultimately be drawn into conflict. Under this scenario, a Palestinian state, which the UN would recognize, would declare its sovereignty over the Jordan Valley and East Jerusalem. Barak feared that a UDI would result in an all-out conflict.

Later that day, I met with the American peace team to discuss possible models for documents, timetables and frameworks. Aaron Miller's impression was that the Palestinians did not believe Barak's intentions. "If so," I said, "maybe we should have a two-phase summit. In the first phase we will negotiate, and see where this leads. Only thereafter will the political leaders meet." Dennis Ross was concerned that "the president knows more about the Israeli positions than of the Palestinians positions, and we have more clarity on the issues of territory and refugees than on the issue of Jerusalem. The president will make a decision next week." In a meeting in Ramallah, Albright suggested mid-July to Arafat as a target date for the summit.

Camp David was two weeks away.

Before departing, we prepared the major talking points for our discussions with the representatives of the settlers. Our attempt to sweeten the bitter pill of evacuating settlements was the assurance that under Permanent Status, approximately eighty percent of the settlers would be accommodated under Israeli sovereignty in settlement blocs adjacent to the 1967 line, which would be incorporated as an integral part of Israel. We finalized the format and timetable for the summit over the next few days. First, the Palestinian team headed by Abu Ala and Asfour, and the Israeli team headed by Ben-Ami and myself, would fly out for two days of preliminary discussions. The summit itself would begin on the morning of Monday July 11.

In announcing the summit, Clinton said that his decision to convene the summit was taken "after lengthy discussion with the two leaders." He explained that "while Israeli and Palestinian negotiators have made real progress . . . the truth is they can take the talks no further at their level . . . Movement now depends on historic decisions that only the two leaders can make." Clinton added that "to delay this gathering, to remain stalled, is simply no longer an option. For the Israeli–Palestinian conflict, as all of us have seen, knows no status quo . . . The decisions will not come easier with time . . . I think that if we work hard we can get it done in several days."

Ambassador Indyk provided us with further details regarding the summit. Secretary of State Albright would meet with the negotiating teams on Sunday evening, before the full delegations arrived in Camp David. The summit would include discussions focusing on the core issues. The delegations would each be comprised of twelve people, including the respective political leader. Discussions on the other "generic" issues would take place with teams comprising twenty people per side in nearby Emmetsburg. "Get yourselves ready for a two-week period," Indyk hinted, "the dress code will be casual, with the exception of the opening ceremony, and perhaps the closing ceremony . . ." he added, grinning.

The PLO's Central Council called on Arafat to move toward a declaration of statehood "within a year." Off the record, Arafat said that if progress was made in the negotiations, the declaration would be postponed.

On July 7, 2000 the prime minister convened another meeting with Eran, Yatom, Rubinstein, Major-General Orr, the military secretary Brigadier-General Gadi Eizencot and me. We discussed the issue of the holy sites, focusing in particular on questions of sovereignty, management, ensuring free access and status of worshipers. Barak then met with a smaller forum, which included Ben-Ami, Yatom and me. In the course of the discussion a possible "give and take" position emerged with regard to the core issues – territory versus components of sovereignty, Jerusalem versus refugees. Lack of compromise, on the one hand, would require flexibility on the other. The prime minister then left for Europe to meet with British Prime Minister Tony Blair and his French counterpart Lionel Jospin, to update them and enlist their support for the process.

The Shas ministers, together with Yitzhak Levy (NRP) and Natan Sharanski (Israel B'Alia), resigned from the government. David Levy, the minister of foreign affairs, announced that he would not be joining the prime minister at Camp David. The personal and political damage to Barak was irreversible. He was heading toward the most difficult and dramatic political campaign in the history of the State of Israel, supported by a shaky parliamentary minority. "I will continue with the negotiations even if I remain with nine ministers and a quarter of the Knesset members." This declaration – which was meant to express Barak's determination in pursuing an agreement – was interpreted as inappropriate arrogance, and further exacerbated Barak's political de-legitimization in the eyes of the Israeli public.

At the final briefing before our departure to Camp David, Barak asked that I bring the following books: *A World Restored: Metternich, Castlereagh and the Problems of Peace, 1812–22* by Henry Kissinger, *A Savage War of Peace: Algeria 1954–1962* by Alistair Horne, and finally *The Battle for Peace* by Ezer Weizman, which describes the author's perspective on the first Camp David summit in 1978. He asked Major-General Yanai to bring along maps and aerial photos of Gaza and of the settlement blocs that were to be annexed to Israel, corrected according to his instructions. He then suggested names of people who would be responsible for explaining in the media the developments in the US to the Israeli public. These included Yossi Beilin, Haim Ramon, Yossi Sarid, Uri Sagui, Matan Vilnai, "Fuad" Ben Eliezer, Menahem Einan, Amram Mitzna, Ilan Biran and Amiram Levin.

It was clear to Barak that failure at the summit meant deterioration into violence. This was backed by the assessments of our security establishment that Arafat had instructed his people to prepare for armed conflict in case the negotiations failed.

Before leaving for Camp David, I went to my law office to clear my desk in advance of what would be a long absence. Two orthodox businessmen came to my office for a brief meeting. One of them took out a bill worth NIS50 (approximately US$10), and handed it to me. "This I give you, so that you will return with an agreement," he said to me. When I now see this businessman from time to time he reminds of that bill which I still have folded up in my wallet.

The first preparatory meeting took place amid a feeling of great uncertainty at the Madison Hotel in Washington DC on July 9. "Management of the summit will determine its success or failure," Abu Ala began. "Do not forget that the deadline for a declaration of a Palestinian state is September 19. Then, the interim period will actually be over. It is a decision of the authorized Palestinian institutions. A Palestinian state is our right, and preparations toward its establishment will begin immediately." Abu Ala refused to discuss security before the permanent borders were determined through negotiations. "The prime minister wants a summit that will yield results," Ben-Ami replied. "We must, therefore, discuss security arrangements, which is something we have not done before. We must make an effort to find areas of agreement between us." Abu Ala was concerned about the prospects of an American proposal. It appeared that he feared we knew something he did not. "We are in the same boat," we tried soothing his fears. "Are you optimistic?" Abu Ala asked Ben-Ami. "I am impressed by Barak's determination," Ben-Ami replied. This exchange, however, was not followed by a substantive discussion. I called Rob Malley at the White House and asked him to make Arafat understand that "it's now or never."

"President Clinton would like to move ahead quickly. He thinks that all the people Arafat brought to the summit are there to help him make political decisions," Malley said. "I think this summit will result in an agreement," Ben-Ami added.

It was 9 p.m. The preparatory teams – Israeli, Palestinian and American – gathered around a large table at the State Department. "Those seated here have worked harder than anyone else in the world for peace between Israel and the Palestinians," Albright began. "We are at a difficult historic moment. We intend to stay at Camp David – a comfortable, isolated and protected location – until we reach a conclusion. The president will do all he can. The US will do all it can." Albright then went on to outline the code of conduct for the summit. This reminded me a little of summer camp. First, there would be a complete media blackout. There could be no press leaks. This was meant to help us create a relationship based on trust, which would allow deliberations on the most critical issues to take place without the press. Only the political leaders would have an outside phone line – only one – in their room. "We, the Americans, will set the agenda. And starting from tonight," she smiled, "no ties. Dress casually."

Abu Ala thanked the secretary of state for preparing the summit: "We agreed that the agreement would be based on UNSCR 242 and 338, would be clear, and would include all the issues. We still have gaps, but we will work hard to bridge them."

Ben-Ami followed. "The political situation in Israel does not detract us from the goal of putting an end to conflict. Even with majority support in the Knesset, we would do a referendum. Barak arrives here on a mission, and he does not plan to avoid negotiating any issue. Our problem," Ben-Ami continued, "is how to settle our national myths with the need to compromise. We will have to work together in order to achieve our goals."

"It is completely clear to us how difficult the discussions and decisions will be," said Dennis Ross. "The concerted effort everybody has invested in this summit is unlike anything any of us has experienced thus far. We have been granted with an opportunity to make an historic change. We will really work with you, in the process – bilaterally, trilaterally – and the president himself with the political leaders." Ross then asked what paper would serve as the basis for our discussions. "We need to prepare a document of 'I' and 'P' positions, of Israeli and Palestinian positions, respectively," Ben-Ami replied. "The president will leave in eight days for the G8 summit in Okinawa, Japan. It is very important that we finish our work by then, so that the president can raise funds. This, therefore, is the timeframe. We don't have the entire summer for this," Albright explained. "We must reach a breakthrough on the core issues of Jerusalem, refugees and borders. There are very difficult problems in these areas. Indeed, we will need to discuss several issues concurrently. But I must emphasize again – think in terms of a week, not longer," Albright replied. "What is this, an ultimatum?" Asfour roared. Then Erekat: "I am very concerned. Failure will immediately create unwanted tension in the street. Most importantly, we did not prepare properly for rebuilding trust between Barak and Arafat, which at this point is below zero." "The president knows this," Albright interrupted. "It is clear to him that the relationship between Barak and Arafat is not what we had hoped for. But we also have a calendar of our own, and this cannot wait until September 13. Give us a chance."

We later met with Ross to get a better idea of American perceptions going into the summit. "The president must support Arafat and get him out of the mood he is in – change his emotional concept of reality," Ross explained. "Arafat may understand the negative implications of failure, but he has yet to internalize the benefits inherent in this achievement. Camp David is an extension of the White House – it is small and intimate, and it allows the president to have his hand on the pulse. Our intention is for the work to be carried out in small groups – which will negotiate territory, borders, security – and will bring the results of the discussions to the president. After two days of discussions we will assess the situation and see how we move forward."

"You," I told Dennis, "master the issues better than anyone else. You know the Non-Paper from Sweden, the current agreements, the possible future points of agreement. Detailing Israeli and Palestinian positions in a document will therefore not move us forward."

"Had the president not seen potential for an agreement," Ross replied, "he would not have convened the summit, despite the fact that even within the Palestinian leadership there are disagreements regarding refugees and Jerusalem, especially between Abu Mazen and Abu Ala. Jerusalem is definitely the most difficult issue. In the Jordan Valley the formula should be 'security for sovereignty.'" With this formula, the Americans had effectively "erased" our sovereignty in the Jordan Valley in return for satisfactory agreed-upon security arrangements and guarantees. We reported to Barak that the Americans would indeed address the political, municipal and religious dimensions of the Jerusalem issue.

In a meeting we had with the American team the next day, July 10, I emphasized that we expected to find that all issues would be addressed simultaneously in every document the Americans would submit, if they in fact did so. "Our willingness to present you with all the possible understandings, fairly and thoroughly, should not ultimately hurt us." With this, our final meeting before Camp David ended.

The prime minister and his entourage were already on board the Israeli Air Force plane bound for the US and the Israeli advance team had finished its preparations. On the Palestinian side, the reasonable possibility of ending this violent conflict between Israelis and Palestinians was undermined by Arafat's manipulative indecisiveness, deceitfulness and potentially explosive political maneuvers. On the Israeli side, Barak's ability to undo the Gordian knot between the Territories and Israel's future stood in stark contrast to his inability to maintain domestic political support in Israel.

We were asking ourselves whether we had really reached that unattainable point of an historic compromise. Did we have additional flexibility on the issues in dispute in order to produce an agreement? Was it possible that we still had not begun scratching the surface for solutions?

As always, Arafat remained the largest unknown. Arafat's image, as a leader and person, has occupied more than a few writers and researchers. Opinions – of course – are split. There are those who view him as a great leader, with a deep sense of history, who actually created and consolidated the Palestinians as a national entity. Still others view him as a fraud and as someone who purposefully misleads, using premeditated terrorism as a political tool. A few months after the summit, I received a book entitled *The Mystery of Arafat* by the renowned *Haaretz* daily columnist Dani Rubinstein. I finished the book in one sitting. It was riveting. Arafat, however, remained a mystery.

On his way to Camp David on the morning of July 10, Barak met with President Mubarak in Egypt. When he returned to Israel, he responded to two no-confidence votes.

The prime minister was quoted as saying that:

> ... We will not return to the 1967 lines. Jerusalem [will remain] united under our sovereignty. No foreign army will be west of the Jordan Valley. The majority of the settlers of Judea and Samaria will be in settlement blocs under Israeli sovereignty. Israel will not recognize moral or legal responsibility for the creation of the refugee problem ... there are governments in our history that have maintained the situation, and there are governments that have changed reality from the core ... I am departing ... in order to come back with an agreement that will strengthen Israel ... To the citizens of Israel I say, that peace is not only giving up beloved parts of the land. Peace is the key to deep change in our way of life.

Barak ultimately lost the vote with fifty-four Knesset members voting no confidence and fifty-two opposed. Having received his mandate as prime minister directly from the people in the elections, this vote had no implication on Barak continuing to hold the prime minister position, however it still was a very painful personal blow. He left for Camp David knowing he lacked parliamentary support. If an agreement were to be reached, he would have to return to the people through a referendum in order to approve the agreement. "I am not going alone. Together with me are two million voters," he said as he boarded the plane.

We were at the threshold of a decisive stage, the climax for which we had extensively prepared during the past year. There was a sense of subdued excitement, a fear of the unknown, a feeling of sharing an historic event. Just like before a competition, exam or long voyage to an unusual, distant and unknown location. Behind us were dozens of meetings, efforts and tensions, consultations and hundreds of hours of negotiations. In front of us was a long and unknown road. At stake were the well-being of succeeding generations and the future of our region.

9

AN HISTORIC
OPPORTUNITY

On Monday July 10, the members of the Israeli advance team left Washington for Camp David. We drove ninety kilometers northwest in the Israeli embassy's cars, into the heavily wooded Catoctin Mountains of Maryland, to a green, hilly and magnificent retreat. We arrived at Camp David having passed through some tightly controlled barriers manned by police with police dogs, FBI personnel and Marines.

Shlomo Yanai, a veteran of Shepherdstown, warned the others, "We will be searched, from head to toe, no matter who we are or what our position is – all our bags and clothes will be checked." It turned out to be a false alarm. In two well-organized and refurbished trailers, the American administrative team simply issued badges that we were asked to wear during our entire stay.

At Camp David itself, a few minutes drive away, we were received formally by an officer on duty. Camp David was guarded by the uniformed Marines – polo shirts with a terracotta emblem of Camp David and khaki pants. We had clear instructions, accurate descriptions of who stayed where, and directions about transportation by electric golf carts, on bicycles and on foot. We were told the timetable for meals, laundry and the cafeteria. Leaving the site was prohibited without special permission. Only the prime minister's cabin had an outside phone line. The American well-oiled machine worked perfectly. The very welcoming and efficient American staff made themselves available to any need, request or problem. Nothing, down to the smallest and most marginal detail, was left to chance.

Ben-Ami and I lodged together in Walnut cabin. In the first 1978 Camp David, our cabin had housed the personal physicians and consultants of President Anwar Sadat. Amnon Shahak, Shlomo Yanai, Yossi Ginossar, and Attorney-General Rubinstein stayed in the adjacent Sycamore cabin. Israel Hasson, Oded Eran and Gidi Grinstein were housed in the Redwood cabin. During dinner we heard about the results of the no-confidence vote in Israel. Barak would arrive at Camp David at the lowest point of his political career since creating the coalition.

Upon Barak's arrival the next morning, we proceeded to the prime minister's room, in Dogwood cabin, which was just across the way from President Clinton's Aspen cabin. We poked fun at the American cabin-switching exercise – in the first Camp David summit in 1978 Menahem Begin was housed in the Birch cabin and Sadat in Dogwood, this time it was the other way around. On a more serious note, Shlomo Ben-Ami, reviewing possible American intentions for Camp David, nicknamed the summit the "Jerusalem summit." The two issues that will be discussed, he predicted, would be Jerusalem and the eastern border of the Palestinian state. I noted that the mechanism of negotiations and the American process management in the summit would have a considerable impact on the substance. "I suggest taking into account the possibility that the Americans will surprise us. Only a comprehensive package would stop the erosion process in which we have found ourselves since the Oslo process." I also updated those present regarding our legal work, particularly on Palestinian commitments, ratification of the agreement – when reached – in the UN, and domestically in Israel. Barak remarked that this was one of the most complicated, difficult and delicate moments in recent years; we were dealing with our fate. "We have come a long way to bring about a real dialogue. I will not be able to sign just about anything. The whole process is 'Gestalt' – everything versus everything. Our domestic political situation is no better than Arafat's. On both sides, there are certain conditions with which we cannot go back to our people. Jerusalem, for example, is clearly not a Palestinian issue, but an issue that focuses the entire attention of the Muslim and Arab world. From here on," the prime minister emphasized, "this is an official delegation of the State of Israel. There will be no more non-committal channels or meetings."

Among ourselves we had different assessments and opinions about what the prime minister was referring to in terms of "hard-core" Palestinian positions. Each member of the Palestinian leadership had his own definition of "rock bottom" positions and set his priorities in a different way. Abu Mazen, a 1948 refugee from Safed, considered the refugee problem as the primary issue. Abu Mazen was guided by considerations of territory, sovereignty and equality on all dimensions of the relationship between two sovereign states, living side by side. Dahlan placed security considerations, independence and symbols of sovereignty, and in the short term – full release of all security prisoners – at the top of his priority list. Jerusalem was the highest priority for Erekat. He also demanded that the Palestinian state should not be perceived differently than any other sovereign state.

It was clear that the negotiations should be based on a "give and take" on the core issues. This should be done without compromising the vital interests of Israel while looking for the widest possible common denominator between the members of the Palestinian leadership. An indispensable condition for progress was that Arafat would endorse such a common denominator.

I felt that the basic Palestinian position was comprised of both substance and appearance. On territory and borders, the Palestinians were determined to create an area with reasonable geographic continuity. It was important to them to be able to present to their constituency that they received no less than other Arab countries, Egypt and Jordan, had received in their own peace agreements with Israel. A possible formula for this 100 percent, however, could include most of the territory occupied in 1967, to be vacated in an agreement, plus land swaps, less a small percentage of the land, which Israel would continue to retain. While they found it very difficult to compromise on the principle of returning all the occupied land, they could have presented flexibility on the length of time taken for withdrawal, at the end of which, this Palestinian perception would have been achieved.

On the issue of refugees, again, perceptions overpowered the reality. It evolved as an ethos that was created and developed over dozens of years and fostered as one of the pillars of the national Palestinian struggle. The Palestinian negotiators saw it as their duty to prove that the suffering of the refugees was over, and that the dream would be fulfilled, even if only formally. For many of our Palestinian colleagues who worked on this issue, the formulation of the agreements was much more important than the practical mechanisms that would be created to rehabilitate the refugees and the effort to mobilize the international community in order to end their plight. I was under the impression that in return for Israeli flexibility on formulations that could have satisfied the Palestinian need for appearances, the Palestinians would not have demanded the actual exercise of the Right of Return into Israel, which I thought was not a component of their "core position."

On the issue of security arrangements, the Palestinians wanted to present national pride in the form of power – which, though not necessarily military, would be perceived as such: a military-sounding name for the Palestinian police force; and use of the phrase "a state with limited arms" instead of "demilitarized." All these were supposed to satisfy the need for symbols of sovereignty related to security issues. The border, according to the Palestinians, must be under the sovereign control of the government of the territory, meaning Palestine. There was willingness, however, to agree to foreign – non-Israeli – control over some of the borders and passages, for a limited period of time.

With regard to Jerusalem, there were those who believed that the Palestinians would not accept an agreement that did not give them explicit sovereignty over "Al-Haram al-Sharif," the areas around the mosques, two Quarters in the Old City and over the majority of Arab neighborhoods outside the walls. I wasn't sure.

The complexity, sensitivity and the myriad of connections and relationships between the core issues, made it very difficult to define exactly the "hard-core" Palestinian position. The negotiations at the summit, and the rounds of negotiation that followed, however, have reinforced my opinion that – putting aside propaganda manipulations and tactical considerations – *these* were the real "core" Palestinian positions.

At 2.30 p.m. the delegations gathered for their first and last festive plenary session at Laurel cabin. The president of the United States, the secretary of state, the national security adviser, and the rest of the American team were seated around a large wooden table, approximately fifteen meters long, in the central hall. Barak was seated across from them on the left, and Arafat on the right. The members of the delegations sat beside their respective leaders. At the narrow end of the table, Erekat and I faced each other. We were given white writing pads with the insignia of the "White House" and a simple Parker pen carrying the signature and seal of President Clinton. It was an electrifying and truly festive atmosphere.

"This is an historic opportunity," Clinton began, looking directly at both leaders. "We look to the future we want to build in your region. I am glad to be here. I have gone over the material, night and day, in preparation for this summit – the geography, Jerusalem – and I am sure that at one stage or another you will test my knowledge of the material. However, resolutions and decisions are yours alone. The United States is here to enable the process. We will set the agenda, the events, the set-up and the forums. But the real substantive issues – these need to be examined by you, not on the basis of short-term considerations, but in light of the future you want to build. If I can leave here to the G8 summit, to enlist international support for an agreement – it would mean a lot. Rest assured," the president continued, "we will not let the press know about any substantive details. It is important to maintain contact with the press, although there will be a complete blackout of the actual issues."

Barak spoke next: "We have come here with great responsibility and great hope, to provide a better future for our children. But this will not be easy. A similar opportunity might not repeat itself in the foreseeable future. We will therefore respond to this historic challenge. Every one of us has faith in the United States. And, although we respect the Russians and Europeans, they do not come close to the contribution and help we have from the Americans – from President Clinton – on the Israeli–Palestinian issue."

Arafat concluded: "We believe that what happened in the first Camp David will repeat itself here. With the help of Allah, we will bring a solution to both sides."

In the evening, President Clinton met privately with Arafat to discuss the issues of the refugees and Jerusalem. "We want recognition in principle of the Right of Return," Arafat began, "later we can discuss the practical aspects. As for Jerusalem, it's simple. East Jerusalem – ours, the west – for the Israelis."

On the second day of the summit, July 12, during his second meeting with Clinton, Arafat told Clinton, "You invited us here to blame us for failure? I remind you that Barak voted against the Oslo Agreements, and he intends to bring the Likud into his government." The first signs of what was going to happen were raised later, in a conversation between Albright, Abu Ala and Erekat. "The Israelis have nothing to look for in the Jordan Valley," Erekat responded to the secretary of state's question about a possible land swap. "The entire border with Jordan – is ours," he added. Nevertheless, Sandy Berger and Rob Malley informed us that the next day they would submit the full US paper, which would serve as the basis for further discussions, to both sides. The intention was that negotiations toward the conclusion of an agreement would take place between Friday July 14 and Sunday July 16.

The golf carts that were innocently left outside the meeting areas with the keys in the ignitions – in accordance with the instruction we received – started disappearing. We had to walk and bicycle back to the cabins. Danny Yatom tried to instill some sense of order. He collected all the vehicles and returned to distribute them on the basis of some sense of social fairness. A barber was called from a nearby town, so that we could get a more reasonable haircut than that of the Marines on the base. We discovered the gym, which Yatom, Grinstein, Yanai, Meridor, Eran and I often used, only a few days later. We were developing our own routine in Camp David.

The following day Shahak, Ben-Ami, Rubinstein, Grinstein and I met with Dennis Ross, Aaron Miller, Rob Malley and John Schwartz. The Americans said that the document they would present would address the issue of Jerusalem in a "limited" manner, but would push the rest of the issues, and would indicate a direction for a possible solution. John Schwartz, the attorney, defined the developing document as a "primitive framework agreement." "On settlements," I told the Americans, "we ask you to include the principle of 'blocs,' meaning that settlements, which will become part of these blocs, will remain in place." I indicated that we expected to see the issues of borders and territory, which we presented, fully detailed. We had to ensure that everything was written down and understood.

After midnight, Clinton summoned Arafat, who arrived with Erekat. "The document we are about to present," said the president, "will reflect both positions on the issue of Jerusalem."

"I do not think I can accept this document," Arafat replied. At 2 a.m. Dennis Ross gave the American document to the Palestinians. Erekat translated the paragraphs relating to Jerusalem into Arabic. "Wake everyone up," commanded Arafat. The Palestinians, meeting in Arafat's cabin, were in agreement that the American document was drafted in coordination with Israel, and it was therefore necessary to immediately reject it. "Return this to Clinton!" Arafat told Erekat. "It is 2.30 a.m. Maybe we can return it to Albright?" Erekat replied. Abu Ala and Erekat hurried to the secretary's cabin. It was 3 a.m. "We reject this document. You prepared it with the Israelis," Erekat said to Albright. "That's not true. This document is not meant in any way to anger Arafat, but rather to try and move things forward. The Israelis contributed ideas, you did not," Albright answered.

Upon receiving the American document, Barak convened a meeting with Ben-Ami, Rubinstein, Yatom, Yanai and me, to analyze and discuss our preliminary reactions to the proposal. The general feeling was that the Americans were trying to push us beyond our positions, without requiring similar movement from the Palestinians. "This is a difficult point of departure," Barak concluded. "It serves as a bad basis for dialogue." It was clear that the Americans were feeling their way, hoping to ensure success at a relatively early stage. This came across in terms of the unevenness with which certain issues were addressed, as compared to others. Shahak complained that the Americans tried to surprise us. "They prepared this paper in haste. They improvised it. Now, I have no doubt that there will be a crisis. The question is if there will be movement beyond that crisis." "There is an attempt to sneak in positions through trickery," Barak agreed. Yanai, a veteran of the Wye negotiations carried by the Netanyahu government, described the American action as a litmus-paper test. "Before they present their real paper, they want to check the strength of our response."

On the evening of July 13, Shlomo Ben-Ami met with President Clinton, and emphasized three main points on territory that the American document did not address to our satisfaction. First, the safe passage between the Gaza Strip and the West Bank was an integral part of the comprehensive territorial package. Second, the eastern border and the adjacent security area would remain under our sovereignty for an extended period. Third, land swaps would also be a part of a comprehensive package. Ben-Ami came back and reported that the president was definitely well informed on all the issues, and that he criticized the waste of time and the "game" the Palestinians were playing.

Abu Mazen believed at that stage – as he conveyed to his Israeli counterparts – that the American paper was the only way to bridge the methodological gaps. Israel wanted to move from the agreed to the disagreed, and from arrangements to principles. The Palestinians, however, wanted the opposite. It appeared that they thought at this stage of the negotiations, that the Americans were leaning more toward their positions than toward ours. The Palestinians would therefore try to postpone their decision until the very last minute. In this way, the decision would be in their favor, focusing mainly on "principles." But they understood that the prime minister would not move in their direction, if they did not move toward ours.

Arafat had proposed creating three working groups. Barak instructed that the following groups be created: Ben-Ami and I – borders and settlements; Rubinstein and Grinstein – refugees; Shahak and Yanai – security. "But if our working assumption – that it is difficult to move forward in the working groups – proves correct, we will start working one-on-one on Saturday," Barak noted. "On Saturday night, we are expecting a full American draft. If they do not announce its presentation to the sides, there will be no dynamics for negotiations."

We organized our comments to the American draft. There were many, on almost every paragraph. When we presented our reservations to the Americans, they were very disappointed.

At 10 a.m. on July 14, the prime minister gathered Ben-Ami, Meridor, Shahak, Ginossar, Yatom, Yanai, Rubinstein and me. Barak informed us that the Americans had been e asked to correct points and wording in the document that damaged Israeli positions. The American team apparently preferred to return to an "I" and "P" document, with several alternatives for each possible wording. They also preferred to begin one-on-one discussions, in order to examine initial drafts on the core issues. Clinton told Barak that Arafat refused to receive the American paper. Arafat had asked the president to move to a two-on-two discussion format with a note-taker on each side. Barak responded, "This is a procedure that will substantially slow down the process. Everyone will be careful of what they say." "In any case," Clinton insisted, "we have to give this mechanism a chance, and on Saturday – return to one-on-one discussions." Warm, captivating, perceptive and incredibly eloquent, Bill Clinton demonstrated mastery of compromise through identifying shared interests.

"What builds a state for the Palestinians," Barak emphasized, "is the length of borders combined with the safe passage. These are important bargaining chips. We are not starting the negotiations today," he added, "and I do not intend to move forward without progress from the Palestinian side. If we fail, just the fact that we have gone the distance will speak for itself."

Dan Meridor objected to the American presentation of the territorial issue as a struggle between rights – theirs, and needs – ours. "This is simply an area over which there's a dispute," he said. "According to the paper, we have agreed to most of the central Palestinian demands. That will be the point of departure for the negotiations." "Negotiations are a process of overcoming obstacles, not of documenting reasons for failure ahead of time," Barak responded.

The dynamics of documents and papers is completely different than that of talking. The paper continues to exist. Unlike the spoken word, it becomes a new point of reference. If the paper is good, know how to preserve it, focus the discussion around it, and improve it. If the document is bad for your position, present another paper, which will help balance and provide a basis from which to improve the first paper. It is preferable to abandon the document and build a more comfortable skeleton.

Shahak asked that we have an internal discussion on Jerusalem. "What are we going to discuss in the working group on Jerusalem?" he said. Barak responded that "there is little leeway between the opening and closing positions. We want to allow them free access to the Temple Mount and special status on the Mount. We also need a wider definition of Jerusalem that includes territory that belongs to us and to them. In this enlarged area, the capital of Israel will be established. It will be the biggest and strongest Jerusalem ever, with the largest Jewish majority. The Arab capital will be in Al-Quds. Certain areas will be subject to special arrangement, although still under Israeli sovereignty. We can, for example, turn the Atarot airfield into a Palestinian terminal, and we can examine the possibility of flexibility in other areas. We have to look for solutions, rather than being dogmatic. We have to operate on the principle of simplicity." Barak thought that Arafat had flexibility that would allow him to accept this, and the Muslim world to support it.

On Saturday July 15, right before noon, the secretary of state visited Arafat. "You will have a state," she told him. "I already have a state," he responded dryly. "If Barak does not want to recognize this now, I do not care if it is recognized even in twenty years. Our situation is like the one in South Africa, the whole world supports me."

The president turned to both leaders during their mutual meeting and asked them to enable the teams to move forward. The delegations have done good work, Clinton reported to Barak and Arafat, and it should be continued. Arafat responded favorably, and the general atmosphere reflected a willingness to make supreme efforts to move forward. However, Barak, during a consultation he held with us later on, was skeptical. Was Arafat pretending in order to avoid pressure? "We will not have another president like Clinton, with this level of commitment," Barak emphasized. "Still, the dialogue must remain non-committal, until a final agreement is reached. As of tonight we have three days and a few hours to achieve this." Ben-Ami shared the prime minister's concerns. "Arafat does not want to be perceived, at this stage, like someone who caused the process to fail. So, he appears to allow the process to move forward."

The point at which the conference was to become a summit of leaders was nearing. Without leaders taking the "bull by the horns," the agreement would not come. Shahak was practical: "Half of our time here has passed. I don't know how to predict what is going to happen in the next few days. Even if we hurry now, I don't see how we can finish everything by Tuesday night. Arafat won't move forward on anything, until he gets what he wants on the basic issues." Shahak then moved to the issue of Jerusalem. "In our discussions thus far, they have not given a formula for resolving Jerusalem. Therefore there is no agreement. We have not clarified ourselves what is Jerusalem for us. Qalandiya, Shoafat, the Temple Mount, is it really all the same? Are we fighting for everything until the end? In 1973, if we had made an agreement, we would not have the 'Talmonim No. 29' settlement that was built a year and half ago . . . I'm not willing to fight for that." [Shahak was sarcastic about a ring of small settlements around the first settlement of Talmon, near Ramallah.] Shahak focused his criticism inward. "We are not even close to a discussion amongst ourselves on our red lines. About 300,000 non-Jewish Russians immigrated to Israel. Is that moral, when you consider the people we are not willing to accept?" The moral issue kept me occupied as well. "The substantive internal debate must be carried out," I told Barak, "and much more openly. Otherwise, we cannot go on. On Wednesday we will not have an agreement, and our impact on the final product – the American paper that will 'land' tonight, is decreasing. It is true that we haven't yet touched on the core issues with the Palestinians, but there are a few issues that can be concluded. We are being lulled by the Americans," I warned, "and if we don't wake up to an accelerated process of drafting with them and the Palestinians, I am not sure that the process will result in a legal document that will be binding for us. I agree that at the end we will have to decide that Talmonim No. 29 is not part of sovereign Israel." The prime minister summarized the discussion: "We have internal red lines – real ones – which everyone will be able feel by basically defining the vital interests of the country." He finished but did not explain.

At 10 a.m., the working group on territory met at the Holly cabin. President Clinton, who came to each of the working groups to get updated, was in attendance. Abu Ala presented the traditional Palestinian moral demand for 1967 borders and implementation of UNSCR 242. A furious Clinton lost his self-control. "You are not acting with integrity," he shouted at Abu Ala, "and you are breaking my agreement with Arafat and Barak. You are not acting in good faith. This is no way to manage negotiations!" he barked and slammed the door on his way out. The yelling was heard all over the cabin. Abu Ala, white as a sheet, left the room, very hurt. This was a breaking point of greater significance than was initially thought. Abu Ala lost faith in the fairness of the American mediation, convinced that Americans accepted the Israeli positions without considering the Palestinians'.

The working group on refugees also met, first on its own – with Abu Mazen, Nabil Sha'ath, Elyakim Rubinstein and Gidi Grinstein – then later with the president and his team, and then again in a joint bilateral meeting. It was at this meeting that Nabil Sha'ath first responded favorably to the claim of Jewish property in Arab countries, although he prefaced this with the argument that Arab countries did not transfer this property to the Palestinians.

In the evening Barak convened a small meeting with Dan Meridor, Israel Hasson and me. It was clear that sovereignty was the main dilemma regarding Jerusalem. It was primarily a nationalistic issue. Barak emphasized the uniqueness of the situation in Jerusalem. "The responsibilities and authorities that we should keep in East Jerusalem are security, law enforcement, planning and zoning, and of course, our religious ties with the holy places. The more we detail the practical issues, the better. We need coordination on infrastructure, including transportation, sewage and water. Coordination can be carried out between Al-Quds and Jerusalem." Israel Hasson doubted whether our sovereignty could be maintained if we assigned civilian authority to the Palestinians. He thought sovereignty would be eroded over time. Barak stressed that "sovereignty is of the utmost importance. That is why the independent administrations should be under the authority of the municipality of Jerusalem. In areas such as security and jurisdiction there will be no signs of Palestinian sovereignty. I'm not sure we can solve this problem. In this case, we have two alternatives: division of the city, or an agreed-upon postponement of the issues in dispute."

As the evening progressed, we were joined by the entire delegation. "We are at a crossroads," opened Barak. "If the Palestinians do not initiate a serious dialogue, there is no practical chance of completing an agreement, and certainly not of formulating it. If, within a few hours, the positions of the sides are not clarified, we will not be able to assess if we could eventually reach an agreement at all. In case of failure, the president's assistants will look for someone to blame. It is important that they do not claim that we were an impediment." The prime minister reviewed the disparities in the positions. "The gap on territory remains, but it appears that we can bridge it on the basis of the principle that we do not want to annex Palestinians. On the issue of borders, we disagree about the eastern border – the Jordan River – and the narrow strip on the northern part of Gaza, which we want to leave in our hands." The demand for minor border adjustments in the northern Gaza Strip, instead of completely withdrawing, was superfluous and puzzling at this stage, since we had yet to raise it during the negotiations. "On refugees," Barak continued, "we must draft commitments and come to some agreement on the numbers. As for security, it appears that the issue can be resolved, and that they will agree to a phased withdrawal. The issue of Jerusalem is linked to the end-of-conflict notion. We may have to reach agreements on the remaining issues, and agree on principles for solutions in Jerusalem and on postponing the detailed negotiation on the basis of these principles for a later date. It is unclear whether solving the issue of Jerusalem will take a short period of time, such as a year, or longer." "Right now," Barak noted, "the most difficult gaps are on the issue of Jerusalem, including sovereignty in the Old City, sovereignty and arrangement on the Temple Mount, and a link – under our sovereignty and for their use – between Bethlehem and Ramallah. The Palestinians expect sovereignty in both East Jerusalem and the Old City."

Barak concluded: "We have arrived at the moment of truth. It's history versus politics, on both sides. From our perspective it is a real and substantive question involving the Jewish identity of Israel. The solution in Jerusalem should be based on long-term demographic considerations, and time is working against us. The separation that we can do today, will not be possible tomorrow. In settlement blocs, as well, if we wish to preserve the principles important to us in the long term, we need to ensure that we have the minimum number of Palestinians incorporated within."

Dan Meridor reacted first. "It is very important to reach an agreement, and there is no easy and clean agreement to be made. It will be a difficult and traumatic national event, despite the clear advantage of the end of conflict. On refugees, let's not delude ourselves that the numbers will be less than 100,000. As for Jerusalem, the Americans are likely to postpone the question of sovereignty. Nevertheless, we can transfer responsibilities and different functions in the city to the Palestinians. We are negotiating with the Americans, not with the Palestinians. Clinton's anger toward Abu Ala will eventually be channeled toward us."

"In order to come out with an agreement we need to conclude things quickly. So far, there has been no negotiation on security," Shlomo Yanai added. Barak warned that "the danger is that the Palestinians are trying to expose our positions and to secure indirectly a series of summits, even without Clinton. If we put our final positions on the table, there will be no way back. But if they would move toward us, we would move forward."

In Tel Aviv, on July 15, 2000, there was a demonstration of the Israeli "right" in Rabin Square with about 150,000 participants.

Preliminary positions on the various issues were presented, one after the other, by the working groups from both delegations, to President Clinton in the first few days. The president held meetings, accompanied by the American peace team, on the large porch of his cabin. But this orderly process of presenting positions, mapping interests, and giving the sides "homework" did not have any follow-up, which could have provided the impetus for decision-making. The process dissolved, and the relevance and substance that characterized its beginning faded away. The beginnings of many concrete and assertive processes lingered without being continued.

We were very wary of the danger of an unstructured and unplanned process. In a process in which in addition to the two sides, a third party participates in the role of a mediator, it is expected that the third party, which convenes the summit, would enforce effective management to ensure the summit's success. This requires, among other things, that the mediator insists that both sides present their comments in an orderly manner at each stage. The Americans did in fact invest great efforts in preparing the working papers. If, in addition, there had been thorough and tight supervision of the proceedings, these working papers could have contributed substantially to our moving forwards – on all issues – toward a conclusion. But the supervision, management, control and follow-up were insufficient. The fact that this was not done had a critically negative impact on our progress on different issues at the summit. We alerted several people in the American delegation about this, including Rob Malley and Dennis Ross. Unfortunately, we were not adamant enough. Ultimately, this was a conflict between the Israelis and Palestinians, not the Americans.

Maybe the most serious shortcoming of the American team was that some of its members appeared to be less knowledgeable than the president in the details and implications of the process. From my perspective, this type of dynamic was unwanted. The leader needs to focus on leadership, on setting principles and general policy, not on the mechanism of negotiations. Clinton had to deal with the small details, instead of preserving his precious time for trilateral "cracking-heads" meetings with the two leaders with the aim of softening their positions.

The following morning, Erekat and I were to present President Clinton with our positions on Jerusalem. This would be the first time I would meet the president of the United States face to face. Nothing seemed obvious, and I came to the meeting on Jerusalem with real trepidation. I was going to present our positions on the most sensitive topic discussed, on behalf of the State of Israel, to the leader of the free world.

Clinton, with a Diet Coke in one hand and an extinguished cigar in the other, set a comfortable tone. His questions were focused and to the point. He mastered the details. He had read a great deal of material about the history of the city, its topography, demographics and urban problems. At that short meeting, a personal bond was created, which was not broken, even after he left the White House. I laid out an aerial photograph of the city, to which each of us – Erekat and I – referred in turn. The conversation deteriorated to shouting when Erekat went off with the familiar Palestinian narrative regarding Jerusalem. "We have given up our justified demand for the western part of the city. In all the remaining parts you having nothing to look for, everything should be turned over to us." We responded accordingly.

Clinton calmed the atmosphere. "My entire adult life, during the past twenty-eight years, I have been involved in politics. I have tried to identify interests and resolve them, and bring about a positive result that serves all sides, instead of conflict. Go to work, you have a lot to do. I'll meet with you once more after you have had another round of discussions."

10

GOD BLESS YOU

Thus far in the summit, the Palestinians withdrew from all the under-standings reached in the Swedish channel, re-opening everything up for discussion – including refugees, end of conflict and finality of claims.

Malley came to our cabin at around 11.30 p.m. on July 16. "Arafat will demand land swaps. Not symbolic ones," he told me. "Informally and implicitly he has agreed to leave eight to ten percent in Israeli hands," Malley added carefully. "But we have to get a deal on Jerusalem – putting all the alternatives and possible ideas on the table. . . . As for the eastern border – Palestinians should have all of the Jordan River," Rob continued, convinced that this was the right solution.

The Americans made it clear to us and to the Palestinians that they had no patience left. In a very tough conversation I had with Sandy Berger, he argued that Barak, who had wanted the summit and who had "pressed on all of us," was now retracting from his previous positions, and was not showing enough flexibility. "As of tomorrow," he added, "I end my commitments to the peace process and start protecting the president." We didn't let the blunt American pressure affect us.

In separate conversations with the respective leaders that afternoon, President Clinton offered each the opportunity to select two representatives on their behalf to engage in marathon secret discussions unbeknown to the other delegation members, and without interfering with the timetable for the negotiations. "We will make a brave and open attempt to conclude the ultimate package which constitutes an agreement on all issues," he told Barak in their meeting. "And if it does not work out, we have lost nothing. We tried."

Barak designated "Amnon or Shlomo and Gilli" to this back channel, Arafat nominated Dahlan and Erekat. Ben-Ami, Shahak and, later, Israel Hasson were let in on the secret. Ginossar, as usual, knew from his Pales-tinian friends about the proposed format, even before he found out from us.

"Use your heads," Arafat said as he sent Dahlan and Erekat off to the secret negotiations. "Bring back a good paper. Just do not budge on one thing: Al Haram is dearer to me than anything else."

At midnight, the four of us were called to the president. Clinton emphasized the importance of the unique event, "You are going off to the most important mission of your lives," he said simply "to bring peace to your peoples. God bless you." Albright gave us each a hug. We felt like we were going off on a special ops mission.

It was pouring with rain outside. The president's bodyguards led us to the central complex in Camp David, Laurel cabin. Security guarded the entrances to the cabin the entire night and would not let us leave. A continuous supply of sandwiches and coffee may not have relieved the fatigue, but it allowed us to continue. In the morning Dahlan tried to leave in order to pray. A loud vocal exchange developed between him and the Americans. I snuck out the side door of the president's office, to shower and change.

The four of us began working at the corner of a huge table in the large conference room. It was the same place where Clinton had launched the summit less than a week ago. The first topic was Jerusalem. As the night dragged on, Ben-Ami and Dahlan worked in the conference together with Israel Hasson who joined them at around 4 a.m., while Erekat and I moved into the adjacent office of the president. A huge portrait of Winston Churchill adorned the wall. There were also a large desk, a computer, memorabilia-filled shelves, pictures, certificates and badges. One black and white picture, in particular, was very touching: Bill Clinton, as a young teenager, shaking the hand of President Kennedy. The photograph was signed by JFK.

I had a long way to go in trying to convince Erekat to put what was already agreed on paper in order to move forward. When we finally started drafting an agreement, it was a draining process, punctuated with short sermons by Erekat about why he refused to write that Israel was a Jewish state, why he would reject any attempt to limit the ability of the future state of Palestine to join international alliances, and a host of other arguments that did little to move us forward.

Slowly, we were nevertheless making progress, as both the negotiations and the drafting were entering a more practical and relevant stage. The changes we made to the text were projected from the computer to the wall in order to make us more efficient. But Ben-Ami and I were beside ourselves when we found out that the Palestinians intended to file a giant lawsuit against Israel for damages caused by the occupation since 1967, explaining in fact why they were avoiding an agreement. At 6 a.m. Erekat decided he must absolutely get some rest. "Are you crazy?" Ben-Ami shouted, bleary-eyed and disheveled. "This is our last chance and you're tired? This is how you work? Don't you want a state? And now you want to sue us for the occupation?" It was only with great effort that he calmed down. Rob Malley intervened, shook Erekat and got him back to work.

Twelve hours after we started, toward noon, we stopped. Meanwhile, we heard other delegation members come and go from breakfast. We had to find a breakthrough. There was, however, no breakthrough to be had. We narrowed the gaps, especially on territory, and went in depth into the issue of Jerusalem. But this was far from being enough.

We reported these developments to the prime minister. Barak presented the concept of this exercise to the other members of the delegation: we were playing with ideas in order to see what a potential agreement could look like.

"The general concept presented last night," Barak said "was as follows: separation from the southern and northern Arab neighborhoods of Jerusalem, and a special regime in the Old City which will be designed in accordance with its holy and unique character. There will be Israeli sovereignty, and complete management by the Palestinians of the Temple Mount. The Palestinians were very inflexible in their response." The prime minister continued, "There is no noticeable Palestinian movement in our direction. Decisions need to be made on both sides. If this is the situation, and this is all we have heard from the Palestinians – we are probably headed toward conflict. This 'intellectual exercise' of Shlomo and Gilli" – as Barak named it – "has no validity or meaning without a Palestinian response."

Dahlan and Erekat's report to Arafat, on the Palestinian side, was laconic and bleak. "The Israelis have not moved forward on anything, except for the proposal to create a special regime in the Old City." They added that Israel demanded to annex four settlement blocs totaling twelve percent of the territory, and demanded control over another ten percent in the Jordan Valley for an additional twelve to thirty years. Sixty-three settlements would remain in Palestinian territory.

At 2 p.m. the sides reported back to President Clinton. The report was loaded and emotional on the Palestinian side, and pessimistic on ours. "There is no package deal," we said. "The Palestinians are holding on to their tactical positions on all issues and are waiting for Israel to make all the concessions. Only then, maybe, under conditions they dictate, will they be willing to present their final positions. Moreover, who will assure us that those seated across from us are able and authorized to commit on behalf of Arafat?" Clinton thanked us for our effort. "I fully appreciate your brave effort. We'll move on."

"God, it's hard," the president said in an interview with the *Daily News*. "It's like nothing I've ever dealt with." Clinton later spoke with Arafat, in a meeting that began with a Palestinian warning. "If the Israelis insist on their demand to pray at Al-Haram, an Islamic revolution will erupt." "You are welcome to present your objections, but if you do not move forward, we will leave here empty-handed." Clinton said. "I think that Barak has in fact moved forward somewhat."

"This means nothing," Arafat replied. "It involves only the distant neighborhoods of Jerusalem, which he wants to get rid of anyway."

Clinton demanded clear answers from Arafat to three questions:

- Will you agree to the Israeli demand to annex 10.5 percent of the territory?
- Will you agree to limited Israeli presence on the Jordanian border?
- Will you agree to an agreement that constitutes an end of conflict, even though some issues remain unresolved?

It was a tense meeting. According to some of the American participants, Clinton actually yelled at Arafat. The president warned that if there was no progress on at least one of the main points, there was no use in staying in Camp David, not even until Tuesday. The Palestinians have another version, claiming the meeting took place in a pleasant atmosphere.

It appeared that Clinton felt justified in placing the burden on the Palestinians, particularly having heard the reports from the two teams that were involved in the "theoretical exercise." According to the Americans, it was the Israeli report that changed the picture, placing responsibility for the dead end on the Palestinian side.

Even so, the Americans viewed this as the turning point in the entire summit and were optimistic that an agreement was attainable and a package deal that would bring an end to the conflict was possible. The agreement on the horizon included a reasonable division of territory with eight percent annexation of settlement blocs and strategic territory by Israel, no Right of Return of refugees to Israel, transfer of the peripheral and distant neighborhoods of Jerusalem to Palestinian sovereignty, and the eastern border – with Jordan – under Palestinian sovereignty. Although an explicit discussion had not yet taken place, security arrangements that would satisfy Israel also appeared attainable at this stage. Danny Yatom noted that it was the first time that a Palestinian proposal was put on the table, which contended that eight to ten percent of the territory would remain under Israeli control. But although Arafat may have said this to Clinton, he was to completely deny it later.

Six days after the summit began and two days before he would leave for Japan, the president felt that he had an opportunity to "seal the deal," and prepared to shuttle between the leaders to ensure there was a concrete basis for this feeling.

It was against this backdrop, that the prime minister convened a brainstorming session on the issue of Jerusalem on the afternoon of July 17. Barak began to systematically peel away at the outer shells and slogans, initiating a process that constituted the beginning of a dramatic conceptual change in the minds of many of the delegation members. Later, it would also mark the beginning of public debate and the adjustment of public opinion to ideas that had not been discussed seriously over the past three decades, since the Six Day War.

"The insight that policy making provides," opened Barak, "involves the ability to foresee and to recognize the wall against which we may crash. Today, the waters might be calm, but the iceberg is nearing. It is possible that a solution to the issue of Jerusalem will bring about the end of conflict and the success of the summit," the prime minister thought out loud. "Is Palestinian autonomy – while maintaining the settlement blocs under our sovereignty – indeed the solution, or will it begin a new problem? Is a painful break preferable to continued ambiguity? In any case Jerusalem is a central and critical issue, and I would like to consolidate a position together with you."

Israel Hasson commented first. "We must aim to perpetuate the existing situation and choose between an alternative of functional autonomy[1] and the option of dividing Jerusalem on the basis of defined sovereign separation," he said. "The components that need to be addressed are municipal Jerusalem, the 'Holy Basin' and the Temple Mount. The greatest danger in functional autonomy is that many questions will become more pointed, and organizations such as the Waqf will strengthen.[2] We should consider mutually suspending the demand for sovereignty in the Old City because the ability to separate or divide is very limited. We have to narrow down to a minimum the area defined as the 'Holy Basin.' Anything that is not demographically clear and simple will not be sustainable. Regarding Temple Mount, it's preferable to talk with the moderates today than with extremist groups such as the Islamic Movement or the 'Hamas' tomorrow," Hasson concluded.

Oded Eran noted that there were 130,000 Palestinians living along the outskirts of Jerusalem. "We have no historic or religious interest in the northern bloc which reaches up to Shoafat; in the southern bloc, east of Har Homa; and in the internal bloc. We have to avoid bringing thousands of Palestinians under Israeli sovereignty. Not doing so would be equivalent to accepting the Right of Return and would cost the Israeli Ministry of Finance US$200 million, annually. Regarding the Temple Mount, in accordance with what our chief rabbis have said, we have no intention of worshiping there. Nevertheless, we must maintain our sovereignty. We cannot divide the Old City into quarters. Instead, we should create a local, internal and common administration to the Palestinians and us. Mount of Olives is – for all intents and purposes – under Palestinian sovereignty. It is where all their national institutions are located, and this is the way it should remain. It is the place from which Arafat has a direct and uninterrupted view of the Temple Mount. As for municipal management, two municipalities and a supra-municipality – the head of which will rotate – should be created."

1 Moshe Dayan was the spiritual father of this term, which meant that Palestinians have daily control of their lives under Israeli sovereignty.
2 The Waqf is a religious endowment, a property giving revenues, as regulated by Islamic law. The revenues from the Waqf finance mosques and other religious institutions.

"For the Palestinians, Jerusalem makes or breaks the agreement," Ginossar added. "There is a complete lack of understanding on their part regarding the significance of the Temple Mount to Israel and to the Jewish people. It's really quite amazing. We must rank our demands for sovereignty in descending order. First, the Temple Mount, followed by the Old City, the circle of adjacent neighborhoods, and finally the more distant neighborhoods." Ginossar warned that even Arafat's closest circle would not support a solution which did not yield some Palestinian sovereignty in Jerusalem, and more specifically, in the Old City.

Dan Meridor recognized that after the principle of an undivided city is violated, "the question is just – how much? It is difficult to draw the final line of withdrawal. If we breach the position of an undivided Jerusalem on the basis of demography, we need to be completely sure we have achieved a Permanent Status agreement. This should be the last step."

"It may be," I offered, "that the nucleus of our position and that of the Palestinian position do not intersect, in which case, the problem would not be solved and there would be no agreement. We could, in such a situation, forget about end of conflict and Permanent Status. If we cannot reach a full agreement, we should try to consolidate an agreed list of issues that remain disputed, and conclude a mechanism for resolving other issues including timetables, as well as the level of continued negotiations. Jerusalem is the main part of the comprehensive package that 'seals' the agreement, and it would be a tactical mistake to discuss and conclude it separately."

"If we do not get the end of conflict, it will be wrong to go ahead with an agreement, both domestically and in terms of what could happen later in our relations with the Palestinians'" agreed Shahak. "It is not simple to explain the issue of Jerusalem or the issue of refugees on either side. We do not know if a deal that will bring about the end of conflict would be acceptable to the Israeli public. But, I would go for it anyway."

"This is one of the most substantial and most important moments that an Israeli prime minister has ever faced, at least since 1967," Shlomo Ben-Ami added. "This entire effort will ultimately fall squarely on the shoulders of Ehud Barak. We said from the onset that this summit is a conference on Jerusalem. Gilead and I could sense that this would solve the entire puzzle. We have made good use of the time that has passed since 1967, while the Arabs have lost and squandered theirs, and not only on the issue of Jerusalem. It is important that we decide today. There will not be a Permanent Status agreement if the Palestinians do not receive something in the way of a mythological element, which is not measured in territory. There will not be a solution without some Palestinian sovereignty in the Old City, or part of it, at least in the Muslim Quarter. We have to change the demographic balance, rather than fall prey or become paralyzed by slogans. Jewish Jerusalem has never been as big, and our control has never been as deep as it is now. Let us finally reach a decision regarding supra-sovereignty, for the sake of Jewish history. We can upgrade the infrastructure and image of the city."

"No to dividing the city, no to transfer of sovereignty," Meridor set off on a speech.

"There will not be an agreement without mentioning sovereignty for Arafat in some area of the Old City," concluded Ben-Ami.

Danny Yatom noted that we all knew how the municipal boundaries of Jerusalem had been drawn. "These are not holy, neither from a religious nor from a national perspective. These are boundaries that received more pomp and circumstance than substance. We need to adopt our real red lines. There must be signs of Palestinian sovereignty in the Old City, and it is important to finish this now – what is difficult today, will not become easier in a few years."

"What is Jerusalem?" Shahak asked rhetorically. "Large parts of the city are not 'my Yerushalaim.' The Israeli interest is to transfer as many Palestinian inhabitants to Palestinian control and leave the least number of Arabs under Israeli sovereignty. We cannot concede sovereignty on the Temple Mount. We cannot give Arafat the Jewish Temple, the cradle of the Jewish culture. But we cannot manage Al Aqsa either. Although I am unsure this will satisfy them, we must find a way of giving the Palestinians a defined area in the Muslim Quarter."

"This discussion is very difficult for me," Rubinstein said. "Legally, things are clear. There is a clear ability to provide for the needs on a human or religious level. But the internal cohesion of Israeli society is important."

Daniel Reisner suggested minimizing the number of areas in which there was division between sovereignty and authority. "Such divisions do not hold over time, look at the case of Hong Kong. We should choose functional solutions. They need sovereignty in the Old City, and therefore this is the only important question. Maybe we should think of sovereignty of both sides in the same area. We should not talk about a joint municipality, because this would then be applicable on the western Israeli part of city. For the Old City, however, a joint administration – subject to both municipalities – for the special regime area could be useful."

Shlomo Yanai made an analogy between Jerusalem and an onion that needs to be peeled. "What is this Jerusalem of ours that we really do not want to divide? The contours of this city allow us to exclude 130,000 Arabs that do not belong to Jerusalem, using a relatively simple definition by dividing sovereignty. We need a peace that will last longer than two days. Therefore, the day-to-day lives in these areas have to be simple rather than dictated by a complex and convoluted regime. Arafat looks at the historic–symbolic meaning, and it appears we can give this to him. As for the end of conflict, I believe we can reach this, although we need a formula, according to which he doesn't lose respect."

Barak returned to the heart of the argument, "I have no idea how we will leave here. But it is clear that we will be united as we face the world, if we find out that an agreement was not reached because of the issue of sovereignty over our First and Second Temple. This is the center of our existence, the anchor of the Zionist endeavor, although this effort was largely secular. This is the moment of truth. We have been sitting here for over four hours, in a discussion that is tearing each of us apart on the inside. The issues are weighty, and we must decide, but not under the duress of fire and blood. This decision is very similar to the one taken on the partition plan or on the establishment of the State of Israel, or even the crisis of the Yom Kippur War. We are seated here, thirteen people, detached from the real world, and we are being asked to decide on things that will have an impact on the fate of millions. Postponing this process further is not an option. Begin understood well the importance of decisions he made in his time. Rabin and Peres knew exactly where certain formulations of Oslo, such as 'Single Territorial Unit,' would lead. Rabin, in his time, took heart-wrenching decisions. I do not see him or any other prime minister transferring sovereignty to the Palestinians over the First or Second Temple. Without separation and end of conflict, however, we are moving toward tragedy."

The prime minister moved on to discuss practical staff work, professional opinions, and preparations for continued work. First, we would examine the mechanism necessary for two coordinated municipalities in the Zone of Jerusalem. After that, we would attempt to assess our minimalist position – which could be acceptable to the Palestinians – regarding the augmented area of Jerusalem. Then we would look into the different aspects of functional religious autonomy on the Temple Mount. Finally, we would work on preparing for separation – the border regime, the possible definitions for sovereignty, and arrangements on the Temple Mount.

With the help of the Ministry of Foreign Affairs and the IDF attorney's office we started preparing for the resolution of serious legal issues related to the framework agreement. The work was based, among other things, on precedents around the world, which focused on ending war, territorial claims, and finality of financial and property claims. In a document entitled "Legal Claims in Regard to a Framework Agreement" precedents were detailed, beginning with the Paris Peace Treaty of 1947, which concluded the war between Italy (among others) and the Allies, through the agreement between Switzerland and Poland of June 1949 regarding financial claims, to the arrangements that were concluded in the agreement between Canada and Bulgaria in January 1966 and even the mechanism for settling mutual claims in the peace agreement between Egypt and Israel. In addition, we had work inputs and professional opinions to prepare regarding:

permanent settlement of the inhabitants of one side in territory under the control of the other side; conflict resolution mechanisms regarding the implementation of agreements between the sides; and anchoring the interests of Israel – both during the transition period between agreements, and in the long term – vis-à-vis the nature of the Palestinian state and its commitments to agreements that the Palestinian side had signed in the past. Our deadline was 11 p.m.

The entire day, July 17, was dedicated to working on Jerusalem. Albright met with Abu Mazen and asked him directly how he would react if a deep disagreement were to emerge between him and Arafat on Jerusalem. "I will not go against him," Abu Mazen responded. "I would quit. You should remember that any concession on Jerusalem constitutes a death sentence for Arafat."

After meeting with Arafat and telling him that "tonight will be the night of Jerusalem," the president began to engage in shuttle diplomacy, marked by a meeting every three hours. Following a discussion with Barak and Ben-Ami, Clinton sensed an emerging possibility of moving toward concluding an agreement, and he wanted to examine if this was indeed so. Ben-Ami with the help of Gidi hastily drafted a document that included suggested talking points for the leaders to refer to. The aim was to clarify whether there was Palestinian willingness to move forward toward a final push. The document was presented as a draft for comments to Reisner, Rubinstein, Yatom and finally to the prime minister. The final version, of course, looked nothing like the original draft.

Concurrently, Ben-Ami and I were asked to move forward with the overall negotiations, on all issues, with Saeb Erekat and Mohammed Dahlan, continuing to collect, integrate and polish the documents, in tandem with the discussions.

An anxious and tired Albright met with Abu Mazen, Abu Ala and Yasser Abed Rabbo. "The Israelis presented ideas, initiated solutions, while you settle for a statement that eastern Jerusalem is yours. This is not a way to negotiate," she contended. "We will not accept a solution that does not include Palestinian sovereignty over East Jerusalem. What do the Israelis think, that they will continue to rule us, and give us only municipal authorities?" Abu Ala asked. "The Israelis cannot go as far as you would like, no one can," Martin Indyk said, adding: "Ben Gurion established the State of Israel without Jerusalem. We can have an agreement in our hands tomorrow." "I'll bet you 10-to-1 that there will not be an agreement." Abed Rabbo said. "We are at a dead end. If we leave Camp David without an agreement there will be violence," Albright replied.

Close to midnight, most of the members of the Israeli delegation were working in the prime minister's cabin. Suddenly, those in the living room of the cabin heard loud sounds from the Prime Minister's Office. There was hard pounding, screaming "Ehud, Ehud" and sawing, siren-like human sounds. Barak was choking on a peanut that was lodged in his esophagus. Yatom and Ben-Ami were chasing after him, tapping on his back, which actually increased pressure on his esophagus. Barak became dizzy and unbalanced, his arms were dangling in the air, and his mouth was open, grappling for air, his eyes wide open. Those in the living room arrived within seconds. Then Gidi grabbed Barak around his diaphragm, lifted him up in the air and brought him down with great force; the Heimlich maneuver. Barak let out a rasping, sharp, strangled shout and reached over to the sink looking for water. By this time the security had arrived and an American doctor was called. Rubinstein wanted to offer a Hagomel prayer. The irony of the foolish, if real, threat of a peanut versus the magnitude of the inhuman stress the prime minister was under was not lost on those present. The rumor about the incident had spread like wildfire throughout Camp David. Yasser Abed Rabbo, upon hearing about this incident, was quoted as saying "he who contrives to feed us peanuts, will choke on them himself. . . ."

Barak was over half an hour late to his meeting with Clinton. The president was furious. His impression was that the positions that were now being presented to him did not match the positions the Israeli team presented to him the day before. The American president who was so familiar with the details, did not find it difficult to identify the areas in which positions had hardened. "I cannot go to the Palestinians with the document you have presented to me," Clinton began his 3 a.m. meeting with Barak. "You have to agree to special arrangements in the holy places, otherwise, I will not be able to reach a compromise between the two sides."

"I cannot allow myself, morally or politically, to go beyond that which is indicated in the document we have presented, on all the issues. However, Mr President, do try to assess what you sense will genuinely create a convergence that will result in an agreement. I ask of you, ensure that Arafat does not document the Israeli position," Barak answered civilly but clearly.

This was the first time that Ben-Ami and I were to witness a process that would repeat itself a few more times during the summit. The fear of being leaked to the press or being documented led to positions being circumscribed and fortified beyond recognition. The mere fact that papers were being commented on by seven or eight reviewers, in addition to the composition of the Israeli delegation to the summit, caused more extreme positions to be presented to the Americans.

Ben-Ami urged Barak to entrust himself to Clinton, so long as the president promised he would not divulge the positions. "There are things that are beyond the mandate I received from the voter," Barak said. "Deviating from this mandate would undermine my moral and political authority to sign any emerging agreement."

The discussion shifted to the issue of Palestinian custodianship of the Temple Mount. Custodianship presented a formula that could neutralize the major reasons why the Palestinians wanted formal sovereignty, including security, archeology and law enforcement. If there were a body responsible for the custodianship, it was possible that the Arab world and international community would support the agreement. As for the Arab neighborhoods of Jerusalem, Barak asked not to discuss the northern and southern suburbs until it became clear whether or not there was an agreement in principle.

Clinton's meeting with Arafat that afternoon was the final blow to whatever energy and stamina the Americans still had. Arafat was clear: "I cannot go back to my people without Al-Quds Al-Sharif. I prefer to die as someone who has been occupied, rather than as someone who yielded and gave up." It turned out that Dennis Ross had presented Arafat with a Jerusalem "package" that deviated from the possible understandings the prime minister had previously presented to the president. Ross's package included: sovereignty in the Muslim and Christian Quarters; custodianship of the Temple Mount under Israeli sovereignty; functional autonomy under Israeli sovereignty in the neighborhoods within the city; Palestinian sovereignty in the neighborhoods in the annexed areas of the West Bank from 1967. "We will not replace occupation with Israeli sovereignty," the Palestinians responded to the offer.

Abu Mazen sharply attacked Dahlan. "You caused the Americans to offer this pathetic custodianship over the Temple Mount," the old leader shouted. The loud exchange nearly developed into a fist fight. This appeared to be the first time Abu Mazen had abandoned the passive and indifferent demeanor he had adopted since the beginning of the summit. His behavior, and to a large extent Abu Ala's attitude, communicated a shrugging of responsibility and entrenchment in extremist positions. This was contrasted by the constructiveness that motivated Rashid and Asfour, and even Dahlan. The two senior veterans were trapped in an approach that constituted a sharp withdrawal from positions that each of them had previously presented.

Within half an hour the Americans would announce the "wrap up" of the summit, unless a real breakthrough was to occur.

The prime minister was between a rock and a hard place: achieving an end of conflict through compromises on Jerusalem that would provide a foothold for Palestinian sovereignty, and further postponing the settling of disputed issues, thus compromising on the finality of conflict and claims. We decided to develop an alternative proposal, according to which a solution in the Old City would be postponed for an agreed, defined period, without prejudice to the claims of either side or their positions on the issue of sovereignty.

An American proposal was being consolidated concurrently, and was presented to the Israelis by Rob Malley. It involved Palestinian custodianship in the mosques and churches; Palestinian sovereignty in the Muslim and Christian Quarters; Israeli sovereignty in the rest of the Old City and the "internal" neighborhoods with Palestinian functional sovereignty; and Palestinian sovereignty in the "external" neighborhoods. This outline was very similar to the one prepared by Reisner and Eran, with one difference, they suggested differentiating between neighborhoods that were part of Jordanian Jerusalem pre-1967, and the other Arab neighborhoods outside these parameters. Regarding the status of the neighborhoods external to the Jordanian city, the two recommended that they be included in the context of the discussion on settlements.

Clinton presented the American bridging proposal to Arafat at around 10 p.m. "This is my offer, and I think it's the best deal for both sides" the president said. "This is a Dennis Ross invention. Albright and Ross are working for the Israelis, not for you," Arafat replied angrily.

Shlomo Ben-Ami and I met with Mohammed Dahlan and Saeb Erekat. The meeting began in a gloomy atmosphere. Ben-Ami said: "This is falling apart. What Arafat presented to Clinton was a slicing up and dividing of Jerusalem without any relationship to rights and obligations – this is completely impossible. Barak returns to Israel in the best possible political situation. He can declare 'I defended Jerusalem with my body.' He will be a national hero, you will be left with nothing.

"Here is our proposal," Ben-Ami continued, while our counterparts where feverishly taking notes. "We will transfer some of the villages outside of East Jerusalem to your sovereignty; at the outskirts there will be Israeli sovereignty, but this is theoretical sovereignty only, since you, meaning Arafat, will receive custodianship of the mosques. For the Old City – there will be a special regime, the details of which will be consolidated together. It could be – and that's the way it looks right now – that these are nothing but our wild ideas, and that Barak would throw us down the stairs when we present this to him – but it's worth trying to discuss this seriously."

"We both know when the lights go out," Erekat began responding, staring directly at us, "but neither of us knows when they will go back on. It could be that Arafat is interested in a crisis, and since we all need more time, we could go back home and continue talking, until September 13. We cannot address everything in eight days."

"This is a completely artificial crisis. Both sides have gone the distance toward an historic possibility of ending the conflict between them," I responded. "Over the past couple of months of negotiations, Shlomo and I have shaken the traditional Israeli positions in order to achieve peace. Our proposals and ideas take into consideration your dignity as individuals and as a nation. You know you cannot possibly get more than this."

In the early evening, Barak met with Clinton and was again criticized for pulling back from Israeli positions that were presented to the Americans in the past. Although his real positions had not changed, he was indeed presenting in a way that made them appear extreme. Barak's standing in the eyes of the Americans – which was impeccable up until then – began eroding. A lot of personal capital and precious time were squandered.

"This situation is tragic," Barak said pessimistically upon his return to the cabin. "We looked beyond the divide, and we saw what truly awaits us. When we return to Israel I will have no choice but to create a national unity government or call for elections." Under the pressure of possible failure, members of the Israeli delegation proposed different ideas, a large portion of which had no basis, in order to avoid a crisis. No one doubted that the Archimedes' point was Jerusalem.

On July 18, while the secretary of state was having a very tough meeting with Arafat, the Palestinian negotiating team played pool in the officers' club, conveying a very clear and intentional message of rejecting the American bridging proposal. "A billion Muslims will never forgive me," Arafat complained to the president, "if I don't receive full sovereignty in East Jerusalem. I do not have a mandate to compromise. It's not me, it's the entire Muslim world." "You are leading your people and the entire region to disaster," Clinton responded, outraged. Arafat formally rejected the American proposals and suggested suspending the summit for two weeks. "I am very disappointed," Clinton said. "You are about to lose my friendship and miss an opportunity to reach an agreement, at least for a few years." "I will not sign without Al-Quds," Arafat replied. "You are coordinating the proposals with the Israelis. If needed, I will wait twenty years. I have to consult with the entire Arab world, not just with the Palestinians." "Why don't you discuss this directly with Barak, and try to find a solution?" Clinton asked. "With Barak everything is words. He didn't offer me anything, except annexing Al-Quds to Israel," Arafat replied.

We were witnessing a paralysis among the Palestinian leadership, as well as personal and structural failings that prevented compromise. The dogmatic and intractable veterans defeated the young leadership. It appeared that Arafat, Abu Mazen and Abu Ala were stuck in their comfortable cradle of international legitimacy as the "victim," and were not interested at all in confronting the problems themselves. And they found a way out: Arafat would blow up the summit because of his unwillingness to compromise in Jerusalem.

The Americans assessed that there was no real chance of reaching an agreement on the basis of the positions that had been heard thus far.

Barak told Sandy Berger that he rejected the American latest bridging proposal but insisted that the president met with him before the official response was conveyed and before he met Arafat.

At 1.30 a.m., shortly after I fell asleep, I was awakened by Ben-Ami. "Gilli, it's scary," he said. "It appears that there's an agreement. Arafat accepted our concept of Jerusalem – the painful division. We are dividing the Old City. We need all our strengths now." My heart sunk. I jumped up awake and tense. There was no joy here. Who knew how the Israeli public would react to this, what it all meant for our history . . . all this passed through my mind in a quick second. My answer to Ben-Ami was short. "This is going to be tough."

In the morning it turned out that it was a false alarm, another deception, more of Arafat's trickery.

News reports from the Territories spoke of venomous incitement against Israel in the Palestinian media. The Tanzim distributed proclamations against soldiers and settlers. Children in Palestinian summer camps were instructed to strike against the "Zionist enemy." The Palestinians had prepared a draft letter to President Clinton, in which they thanked him for his efforts and for convening the summit, and asked to take home the proposals for consultation and to return in two weeks to continue the summit.

"This is the realization of the worst scenario we predicted," Barak determined. "A series of summits, a dispersion which will require us, across a long period of time, to disclose all the components and arrangements to the public without getting the full end-of-conflict picture. We will constantly be on the defensive with our public and the Americans. We need to start preparing preventative measures." He asked Rubinstein and me to prepare a thank-you letter to the president and his team. The letter was supposed to express disappointment from the lack of a real partner on the Palestinian side and from the proceedings that resulted in the Palestinians tragically missing another opportunity. All the proposals, ideas, thoughts that were raised in informal discussion – all of these the government of Israel will announce are null and void. "We expect," Barak added in the briefing, "that the United States will stand by our side. We took political and other risks, in an effort to exhaust the opportunity presented at this summit in Camp David. We must emphasize and warn against violence and unilateral actions," Barak concluded. The letter went out that afternoon, eight hours before the president was to depart for Japan.

Barak instructed Yatom to prepare for the flight back to Israel and to update members of the delegation. We took bets among ourselves on whether the instruction to pack our bags would actually happen or not. In the meantime, President Clinton was busy with belated marathon calls to Arab leaders – Ben Ali in Tunisia, Mubarak, King Abdullah – attempting to convince them to influence Arafat to accept one of the offers on Jerusalem and move forward toward an agreement. He told them about the possibility of postponing a solution on the issue of sovereignty in the Old City, in order to avoid a complete collapse of the process. "I have offered Mubarak and King Abdullah the option to postpone the negotiations on Jerusalem for two years," Clinton said to Arafat. "I ask that you agree, in principle, to my proposal from yesterday. If needed, you may add your reservations to this agreement." "There was nothing new in Barak's proposals. I will invite you to my funeral if you insist on your demands for Jerusalem," Arafat replied. "This is our saddest day." Albright said.

Camp David was bustling with commotion, mostly involving our contact with the outside world in an attempt to avoid a serious crisis. The American team found itself in a perplexing situation. Despite the crisis, Arafat indicated that he wanted to stay to continue the negotiations but Clinton had to leave at 1:30 a.m., at the latest, for the G8 meeting in Japan. However, during lunch the proverbial "cat was let out of the bag" when Abu Ala revealed that Arafat had given a clear order to the members of the delegation that in the first four days they should not budge from their positions. They should listen to what the Israelis offered and then decide. He thus confirmed a concern we had had in the Israeli delegation regarding this possible Palestinian strategy.

"We do not have a partner, in the deepest sense," Barak began after his meeting with Clinton that evening, as we finally prepared ourselves for departure from Camp David. The mood was tense and melancholic. The feeling of an historic mission, which so many of the participants, negotiators, politicians and professionals had embraced – Israelis, Americans and Palestinians alike – gave way to a stinging feeling of lost opportunity. Many of the Israelis were trying to figure out for themselves, what had happened. Most of us did not have a clear and concise answer, beyond the one the prime minister provided. "We have witnessed lack of good faith on the Palestinian side. We are in fact struggling with them over our Holy of Holies, the heart of Jewish culture. No negotiation process will change that. However," Barak continued, "President Clinton would like to see Arafat again, after meeting with me. Something is hanging in the air, on the basis of Clinton's proposals, and he is interested in examining every possibility of seizing it."

Dinner at Laurel cabin had the feel of the "Last Supper" and abounded with such references throughout. We said our goodbyes to everyone at Camp David. Clinton, Sandy Berger and Albright each struck up conversation with one of the participants, in an effort to consolidate something that would leave the package together.

At night we reconvened in the prime minister's cabin. Ginossar began by describing the mood among the Palestinian delegation. "When we parted, some of them actually cried, petrified, suddenly aware of what was going on. They are looking for a way to re-initiate the talks. It's hard for them," Yossi turned to Barak, "that you are always dictating – the mechanism, the summit and its timing, the framework for negotiations.

The American team is almost entirely Jewish, and the Palestinians have no doubt regarding our influence on the president's positions."

The majority of those convened supported staying at the summit, until the president returned from Japan. We also supported a meeting between Barak and Arafat, despite the deep animosity that had developed between them, maybe because of it.

"When the violence begins, we will all have to be persuaded that we did everything to exhaust every effort," someone said. "We will be blamed, even if an American statement comes out saying the opposite," Reisner responded. "There is still a chance. We have to be a hundred percent sure that both sides fully understand the issues the same way." "We came here to reach an agreement. This is the right thing to do for Israel. Nothing has changed this. Arafat probably thinks we can reach an agreement. Otherwise, he would have stood up and left," Shahak said. "What happened here does not constitute negotiations, this was insulting and humiliating. Arafat abused the trust of the president, and we have been relegated to an acrobat who jumps through the trapeze, makes two somersaults, reaches out – and Arafat is still on the trapeze platform . . .," Barak replied. "With oily hand . . .," I added. "And shaking," Ginossar concluded.

Barak turned to Yossi, repeating his position. "I will not meet with Arafat to discuss Jerusalem unless the Palestinians respond favorably to the president's bridging proposal. There cannot be another meeting without a positive response."

I agreed with Shahak and Ginossar regarding the need for a meeting between the two leaders. "You do not have to discuss substance," I told Barak. "Something has started moving over the past twenty-four hours. We assumed there would be a crisis at some point, and we got it. We need to take advantage of this newfound vigor."

Ben-Ami turned to Barak. "The problem is not the positions," he said, "but the cultural gulf between us and them, and between you and him. He is supposedly a leader of a people, but in fact he is a person with a deep need for respect, and he feels that you are disrespectful to him. A large part of his ability to become flexible involves this issue of respect."

At 11.30 p.m., Barak told Clinton he would be willing to stay as long as a certain condition was met regarding a proposal on Jerusalem. Right after, Clinton arrived unexpectedly at Arafat's cabin. "I've decided to ask you to stay," he said, "Secretary Albright will be in charge of continued negotiations until my return. Think of something original on the issue of Al-Haram." "Your words are like an order. I will stay," Arafat replied.

Clinton's luggage and entourage boarded Air Force One, en route to Japan. Our luggage was unpacked.

1 (right to left) Clinton, Barak and Sher at the White House, July 1999.

Source: Photograph by White House photographer.

2 The signing ceremony of the Sharm El-Sheikh Memorandum, September 4, 1999.
Sitting: Barak and Arafat. *Standing (left to right)*: Sher, King Abdullah (*hidden behind*), Mubarak, Albright, Erekat.

Source: Photograph by Moshe Milner, Israeli Government Press Office.

3 The Sharm El-Sheikh Memorandum between Israel and the Palestinian Authority. Negotiator Gilead Sher (*left*), with US Special Mideast Envoy, Dennis Ross.

Source: Photograph by Moshe Milner, Israeli Government Press Office.

4 Harpsund, Sweden: Asfour (*left*) and Sher.

Source: Private.

5 Harpsund, Sweden: Sher (*left*), Asfour and Abu Ala.

Source: Private.

6 A working session in Camp David: (*clockwise*) Albright, Ben-Ami, Sher, Yanai, Shahak, Asfour, Abu Ala, Erekat, Dahlan, Hillal, Indyk, Miller (*behind table*).

Source: Photograph by White House photographer.

7 A farewell photograph of the Israeli delegation before leaving Camp David. *Sitting* (*left to right*): Ginossar, Ben-Ami, Shahak, Gluska (secretary to the delegation), Barak. *Standing*: Sher, Grinstein, Yanai, Yatom, Meridor.

Source: Photograph by Gidi Grinstein.

8 The White House, December 23, 2000 – President Clinton lays out his plan for Permanent Status: (*clockwise*) El Abed, Dahlan, Erekat, Ben-Ami, Sher, Meidan (Grinstein and Yanai *behind*), Miller, Ross, Albright, Clinton, Podesta, Berger.

Source: Photograph by White House photographer.

9 Prime Minister Ariel Sharon (*right*) receiving Gilead Sher's book on the Israeli–Palestinian peace negotiations at the Prime Minister's Office, September 25, 2001.

Source: Photograph by Avi Ohayon, Israeli Government Press Office.

11

ALBRIGHT TRIES TO
PREVENT COLLAPSE

My morning began with a walk in the woods with Dahlan, Hassan Asfour, Nabil Sha'ath and Abu Ala. The Palestinians were trying to convince us to have Barak meet with Arafat and resume the negotiations without preconditions. But Barak would not back down from his position, insisting that before such a meeting took place, Arafat should respond in principle to at least one of the ideas presented to him by Clinton, or that were raised in the course of negotiations. Arafat, on his part, remained stubborn, refusing to give any answer.

After breakfast Albright, Dennis Ross and Sandy Berger went to speak with Barak. "The Palestinians are interested in moving forward," Albright began. "They are interested in creating new committees. They are asking questions. What is the status of the sites holy to Christianity? What is the meaning of a 'satisfactory arrangement' on the issue of refugees? What is the relationship between the water aquifer and security arrangements? What happens to the Palestinians in the Jordan Valley under a period of security control?"

"This is a combination of farce and tragedy," Barak responded. "I will not answer these questions. I will consider answering their questions only after the Palestinians first answer our questions, or after they announce clearly and unequivocally that they accept the ideas of the president. I want an answer, not from Dahlan or Abu Ala, but from Arafat. Yes or no." "We are not here to sit and wait," Albright tried. Barak was determined and impatient. "We allowed the president to propose ideas that were final and maximal from our perspective. Arafat did not react at all. Instead of an answer, he presents questions. We do not intend to turn these ideas into being the opening positions for Israel," Barak replied. "I can come up with questions too – tens and hundreds of them every day!" the prime minister continued firmly. "If the ideas of the president cannot serve as a basis for concluding an agreement – this is a waste of time. If Arafat rejects the president's ideas, I would prefer to disband the negotiations now rather than later. If he doesn't respond to them, the members of the delegations can have informal one-on-one meetings with no records on 'generic' issues such as economics and water."

Albright tried to feel her way through the dead end. "So far you have been so open in your positions and attitude. And now – on a personal level – you are unwilling to meet with Arafat. Isn't this a contradiction?" "I am not willing to give up the principle of symmetry," responded Barak. "Negotiations are not an exercise in asking questions. Obviously, negotiations have to be forced on him. After eight months, eight weeks and eight days, Arafat has not even started to negotiate. I did not come to sell out the State of Israel or bring it to bankruptcy. There is only one test of Arafat's intentions, and that is his affirmative response to the ideas of the president. This is basic decency that is required from the process, and eating Baklava [Arab sweets] together will not help."

It was clear that something had gone terribly wrong in passing on the information regarding the Clinton–Barak conversation from the president to the secretary of state. Before leaving for Japan, certain understandings were concluded between the president and Barak, according to which the Americans would obtain a positive answer, in principle, from Arafat regarding any of the Clinton proposals. Only after Arafat gave such an answer, would the negotiations resume and would a meeting between Barak and Arafat take place. Apparently, this understanding was not conveyed fully and clearly to the secretary of state.

Immediately after Albright and her team left the prime minister's cabin, Barak gathered the Israeli delegation for a tactical discussion.

"The Palestinians folded yesterday," Ginossar said, "you are stepping all over him [Arafat]. He is afraid of you. You can help draw out more flexibility from them through a less coercive and more open environment." Barak, at his end, was offended by the fact that Arafat, who was supposed to be his partner, was treating us like "suckers" and did not even bother to react to the ideas of the president.

In the evening, Secretary Albright apologized about the misunderstanding regarding the agreement Barak and Clinton had concluded, according to which any progress in the negotiations was conditional on Arafat responding to the ideas of the president. Albright accepted full responsibility. "The American document is withdrawn from the table and agenda," she said.

The relationship between Barak and Arafat reached a visible all-time low. In one case, Arafat was about to approach Barak, when the latter entered the Laurel hall. Barak stopped and deliberately did not extend his hand. The two sat on both sides of Secretary Albright, and during the entire evening did not exchange even one word. The situation was embarrassing, uncomfortable and unnecessary. Intentionally ignoring Arafat was interpreted as mixing the personal relationship of the leaders with the hardship and difficulty of negotiations. Understandable as it may be,

it seemed arrogant. And while the delegations engaged in a series of intensive meetings, Barak isolated himself, instructing the members of the
delegation not enter his cabin and holding off the transfer of any phone
calls.

Working tirelessly for a day and a half with the Palestinian and American
teams, Reisner and Grinstein focused on improving the draft. Eran and
Rubinstein met with Sha'ath and Abed Rabbo to discuss the issue of
refugeeism. Ben-Ami met with Erekat to discuss Jerusalem and Yanai,
Hasson and I met with Dahlan and Abu Ala, to mull over security and
territorial issues.

Samih El Abed, the Palestinian map expert, laid out the map, presenting,
for the first time ever, a map that recognized Israeli settlements in the
Territories. But these "blocs," connected by non-existent, "virtual" roads
to the current borders of Israel, looked like stains with thin strands between
them. I asked to look at the second map – that is, not the one that was
prepared to tactically begin the haggling. "This is our second map," Abu
Ala replied, insulted. "You know how difficult it is for me to even look at
it. Our second map notes swap areas, some of which are first priority,
others, which are second."

We immediately pointed to the internal failings of the Palestinian map.
First, the links between the settlements were virtual, and would require
constructing a sort of safe passage between settlements. In addition, the
map accounted only for thirty to thirty-five percent of settlers in 2.5 percent
of the land, which did not even come close to the necessary number of
settlers. Most importantly, the map created an impossible border – not
even a border, but rather strings or laces with what appeared like "marbles"
at the ends. The security and civil reality would be impossible. There
wasn't anything like this anywhere in the world. We presented the Israeli
map, according to which 77.2 percent of the territory would be transferred immediately to the Palestinians. The remaining territory, of 8.8
percent, would be transferred over a period agreed upon by both sides,
thereby leaving Israel with 13.3 percent, and a few percentage points under
dispute. "Now I am convinced that you are not ready for an agreement,"
Abu Ala said. "We will not give up one centimeter without land swaps,
and we will not accept your sovereignty over the Jordan Valley. The entire
Jordan River – from North to South – will be ours."

While satisfactory security arrangements seemed attainable, there was
a sense of a growing Palestinian resistance to what they perceived as
pretended security considerations that would severely damage their sovereignty. Long before Camp David, there were those who supported
presenting an Israeli map that offered the Palestinians more than the sixty-
six percent of the West Bank and Gaza that had been offered prior to
April 2000. This approach would facilitate constructive negotiations and
assure that the other side was not insulted by a low offer and prevent

haggling over Israeli tactical positions, which both sides knew very well, were far from reasonable. It was altogether a mistake to talk about the percentage of territory rather than the territory that was truly vital to us. But considering the impediments that the Palestinians raised throughout the process, we could not present a final outline on the territorial issue without the rest of the issues having reached an equivalent level of fruition.

The components of a Permanent Status arrangement were clear. But invariably, gains on one side of the equation had negative impacts on the other side. We experienced the impact of the grim political reality into which Barak's coalition had sunk, the inability of the American team to contain the process and "close" a deal, and finally the debilitating management and decision-making process on the Palestinian side. All these dictated a slow, heel-to-toe pace to narrow the gaps.

The working group on Jerusalem, which included Ben-Ami, Erekat and Asfour, discussed every possible issue including municipal boundaries, the concept of the Zone of Jerusalem, custodianship in the holy sites, guardianship, shared or divided sovereignty, practical arrangement on the Temple Mount, archeological digs, the status of different neighborhoods, municipal authority and coordination of joint institutions.

During one of our breaks, I met separately with Erekat, who suggested that we conclude the issues in one-on-one meetings and then review all the issues – resolved and unresolved – in groups of four from each side. At midnight Erekat and I met to formulate the draft agreement. We agreed to approach the efforts to narrow the area of disagreement on territory with an open mind. I asked Yanai to prepare a map that included Israeli territorial contiguity mirroring Palestinian contiguity in Jerusalem, including contiguous Israeli sovereignty in the Jewish, Armenian and Christian Quarters, the Archeological Garden, the City of David excavations, a small part of Silwan Valley, and a link to Mount of Olives, the Kotel (Western Wall), and Ras al Amud – a continuous logical web under conditions of peace. In such areas in which Palestinian and Israeli sovereignty collide, Israeli sovereignty would prevail and an engineering or transportation solution would be offered to the Palestinians.

The Palestinians put themselves in the position of protecting Jerusalem on behalf of the entire Muslim world, in essence compromising their own best interests as a possible, reasonable deal was emerging on the other issues – territory, Palestinian state, refugees and borders. With growing religious polarization in Jerusalem in the background, a confrontation on the Islamic–Jewish axis was coming to a head.

On the border of the Jewish and Armenian Quarters of the Old City, one of my forefathers, Baruch Mizrahi, settled around 500 years ago. It was in the mid-sixteenth century, after his family was expelled from Spain and moved to Jerusalem. In his will, Baruch instructed that the estate that he acquired for his family, never be sold, under any conditions, and that it be transferred from father to son, such that with the coming of the Messiah and the resurrection, he would be able to return to live there. This house is no longer in our family's possession, but the language of the will from 1643 states ". . . and I bequeath it to my sons with the books that I have, after my passing, an estate . . . and they will not have permission, not them nor their sons nor their grandsons until the end of the family line, to sell or lease . . . this will be until the coming of the Messiah." This was inscribed in stone on the outer wall of the house.

My mother, Aviva, born Mizrahi, the seventeenth generation descendant of the Baruch Mizrahi family in Jerusalem, was already born outside the walls of the Old City, but her emotional attachment to her ancestral home is deeply rooted.

The Sabbath arrived. Barak was maintaining his self-imposed seclusion, refusing to see anyone nor hear any reports. He was angry with President Clinton for "imprisoning" the sides in Camp David, without getting Arafat to respond to his ideas, if only in principle. Assessing the situation at this time, Barak may have concluded that there would be no breakthrough. For the first time in my life, I fully witnessed the total isolation of a leader during moments of historic decision. At this crossroad of decision-making, Barak was the loneliest person in Camp David.

The internal phone, which connected the cabins, rang in my room. "Come over," Barak said, almost whispering. I took my bicycle, as if for a ride, and stopped at the back porch of the prime minister's cabin. Barak was unshaven. He looked pensive, browsing absent-mindedly through the press clippings that were scattered around him.

"I think today will be crucial for a decision on territory," he said. "What do you think?" The question was very matter of fact, almost technical, but I could sense the gravity and the weight on Barak's shoulders. It was a position in which no prime minister had been since David Ben Gurion. He had to decide on dividing Jerusalem. With all my desire to help him, to share the burden, I knew that the entire responsibility was and would remain his.

Barak was willing to give the Palestinians limited municipal autonomy with a special joint administration in the Old City under Israeli sovereignty. "It is of utmost importance that we secure the right of Jews to pray at the Kotel, the Western Wall, and at the other places permissible by our faith."

It seemed that the Palestinians had adopted a clear tactic of collecting information, positions and flexibilities – and would not make a single move toward our direction. I thought that if we did not reach an end of conflict, we wouldn't be able to justify bending our position on Jerusalem. The other alternative was to leave this explosive, delicate issue for a longer-term discussion within an agreed timeframe and negotiation mechanism.

Barak was convinced that if a solution was reached, in response to which Israel would achieve the end of conflict, it would be endorsed by the Israeli people in a national referendum. His assessment was that the Israeli public was tired of living in endless conflict and of wasting physical and human resources. Indeed, comprehensive public opinion polls pointed to over sixty-five percent of the public supporting a Permanent Status agreement with the Palestinians, which would involve painful concessions, but that would bring about the end of conflict and would return Israel and its divided society into a sound, healthy and reasonable existence.

Barak envisaged a transition period, in which the settlers could transfer from their current "temporary" situation in settlements to a permanent situation of settlement blocs. "Or they can choose to remain under Palestinian sovereignty" he concluded, estimating that the time necessary for the entire process was three to four years and that some 10,000 housing units would ultimately be vacated and made available to thousands of Palestinians to live in.

One of Barak's greatest concerns was the potential military confrontation with settlers who would refuse to evacuate and would take up arms. Could we seriously consider evacuating the settlers of the ultra-Orthodox communities? It was clear that we needed arrangements for worship and security at the Tomb of the Patriarchs. The Jewish settlement in Hebron was another sorely disputed area we had not yet touched on during these negotiations. What should we do with Kiryat Arba? Evacuation would bear difficult political ramifications, while staying at Kiryat Arba meant annexing 0.5 percent of the territory, which would cost us dearly in territorial terms elsewhere, equally vital. Any agreement would also need to acknowledge Jewish property in the city.

President Clinton was due back at Camp David the next morning, Sunday July 23. The basic situation in the camp had not changed since he left. The prime minister was trying to assess if the Americans were focused on reaching a substantial understanding or rather on salvaging the summit with the least damage to the president. There was no answer to this question.

Nothing was moving, not in the committees, and certainly not between the leaders who had no direct or indirect communications between them. What each side could really agree on was nothing like a game of poker in which each player tries to guess which cards his opponent has. Rather, it involved questions each side had to address to itself and to its public. Nevertheless, it seemed the Palestinians were trying to reach informal conclusions in small forums so they would not appear to the president as not having made an effort in his absence.

To boost morale, the Americans organized an evening basketball game in the gym on the base. There was a "local" team, which included Marines averaging nineteen years of age, with imposing bench players, versus an improvised team that included members of the American and Israeli delegations. We lost by one point, primarily because we were out of breath. It was a decent achievement. As usual, the Israeli media reported an "Israeli defeat."

Madeleine Albright later invited the delegations to the president's private screening room for a joint viewing of "U-571" a movie about submarine battles during World War II. There were no real or symbolic similarities to reflect on between the film and our predicament . . .

Despite the stressful, round-the-clock, high-stakes negotiations, one could always take a breather, a walk in the woods, ride a bike, or read a book. "Dahlan's Porch" emerged as a popular hang-out where Yossi Ginossar, Israel Hasson and Amnon Shahak would sit with Mohammad Rashid, Hassan Asfour and Mohammed Dahlan to smoke, drink and talk. These informal meetings, which sometimes lasted into the early hours of the morning, were sometimes more important than the official discussions that took place the day before or the morning after.

Late Saturday night, Barak ended his isolation. He gathered all members of the delegation and asked to hear their impressions of the last two days.

"With a few reservations, they've accepted our concept of security," reported Yanai.

"The issue that's holding everything up is Temple Mount," Amnon Shahak said.

Yossi Ginossar – our emissary with the Palestinians and their spokesman with us – argued that progress was hindered by the fact that the Palestinians didn't fully understand the president's ideas. "They have no idea what 'custodianship' is, for example," he said, adding "They have not internalized the importance of the Temple Mount to us, the Jews, at all." "The Temple Mount has become a 'make or break' of the entire negotiations," agreed Ben-Ami. But Dan Meridor disagreed, arguing that their real need was the Right of Return – to absorb as many refugees as possible into Israel.

"One of the anchors of the agreement," remarked the prime minister, "is the number of Arabs versus the number of Jews. The line that separates the Jewish state from a bi-national state is a number line." Barak was willing to consider a formula whereby, across the life span of the agreement, 20,000 refugees at most could enter Israel proper. At this stage, however, he instructed the delegation that the official position would involve a conditional agreement for a total of between 7,000 to 10,000 refugees, contingent on humanitarian considerations such as family reunification.

Rubinstein believed that the gap in terms of numbers on the issue of refugees was very large and that the Americans were over-optimistic in their belief that they could bridge it.

Danny Yatom was last to speak. "We must focus our efforts toward the Americans, and bring them to put pressure on the Palestinians. Clinton must speak to Arafat."

Barak agreed. "We are at the moment of truth of the Oslo process. Either there is a willingness to discuss a deal to end the conflict, or there is not. Our offer goes further than those extended by all previous governments but it's conditional on a contractual and symbolic end of conflict."

Before midnight, Attorney-General Rubinstein, Daniel Reisner, Dan Meridor, Grinstein and I met to discuss legal aspects of the draft of the agreement, such as: full signature versus initials; jurisdiction and administration; Israeli internal political commitment to a referendum; ratification by the Knesset; release of prisoners – what was required in terms of legal and political procedures; the end of all pretext for claims; Jewish and Israeli property in the Territories; the status of settlers who would remain under Palestinian sovereignty; land swaps and their legal implications; the individual standing of residence versus citizenship; side letters that would be added to the agreement, if signed.

July 23 began with a meeting of the borders and security committee.

"Taking your settlements into consideration, our condition for moving forward in discussing territory is land swaps. What you present is an old map that we saw last year . . ." Abu Ala began.

I told Abu Ala that we appreciated his difficulty as a Palestinian representative to present a map that recognizes Israeli settlements. Subsequently, I suggested that we all take the maps off the table. "We'll remove the fifteen percent map and you remove the two percent map, and let's start to narrow down our differences."

"We will not accept annexation which damages our water aquifer, or which includes Palestinian villages in territory that will be under Israeli sovereignty," Abu Ala replied.

"We agree to the principles," Yanai said. "But every principle has an exception, and water is not related to territory. Let the water group reach an agreement on the issue. Do not confuse it with the issue of territory."

We were aware of the progress in the working group on water. On legal issues such as water rights there were significant differences between the sides. An agreement was emerging on the practical aspects of quantity, management and development of water sources. Moreover, as part of the Interim Agreement, a joint committee on water was actively discussing supply, sewage and the environment.

In our conversations, Abu Ala proposed three percent annexation. In a meeting mediated by the head of the CIA George Tenet, Dahlan offered Yanai 7.5 percent in return for Yanai's offer of eleven percent. "When we start drawing the borders, we will operate on the basis of the principle of maximum Israeli citizens and minimum Palestinians," I said, "but the borders should also be reasonable, simple and not complicated lines that create daily friction."

Both delegations were tense and anxious in advance of the return of the president that evening. Barak held a series of personal consultations with the members of the delegation in order to consolidate a position that would be presented to the president when he arrived.

The issue of refugees is one of the most difficult core problems in the Israeli–Palestinian conflict. The understanding that it would be impossible to end the conflict without a comprehensive and fair solution to the refugees was at the basis of Israel's willingness to contribute to resolving this issue.

Israel did not bear the sole moral, legal or political responsibility for the creation of the refugees problem, but our aim was to participate in the resolution of this issue as part of the permanent peace arrangement. As to the Palestinian claim for the Right of Return, the prime minister held that Israel would consider allowing a limited number of refugees into Israel on the basis of humanitarian considerations or family reunification. The final place of residence of refugees would otherwise be their present place of inhabitance, in third party countries, or in the Palestinian state, when it was established.

We formulated four practical definitions for Permanent Status:

- All persons defined today as a "Palestinian refugee" will receive permanent and equal status, without discrimination, in their place of residence.
- The status of "Palestinian refugee," as defined today, will become irrelevant legally and/or practically.
- Refugees will be rehabilitated or settled in their area of residence, in third-party countries, or in Palestine.
- Refugee camps will be dismantled, rehabilitated or developed, and will become an integral part of the socio-economic-legal system; UNWRA will be disbanded and all its functions and responsibilities will be transferred to the host countries.

The issue of Jewish claims in Arab countries was supposed to be addressed by an international mechanism for resolving the issue of Palestinian refugees. Subject to it, we decided that Jews would have no more claims on assets that were left behind or that were taken from them in Arab countries or in the Palestinian territories in the 1948 war. This statement was important in order to illustrate and emphasize the end of conflict.

It was important that Israel's financial contribution would be final, defined and permanent. Israel would be a full member, with equal rights and obligations, in an international mechanism that would be created and would avoid direct involvement in areas that would result in friction with the refugees and host countries (i.e. the compensation mechanism).

Already, on the first day of the summit, Clinton, Barak and Arafat agreed that one of the four working groups would focus on refugees. During the summit, the working group on refugees met, mostly with two to three people on each side. Our side was represented by Elyakim Rubinstein, Dan Meridor, Oded Eran and Gidi Grinstein. The Palestinian team included Abu Mazen, Nabil Sha'ath, Akram Haniya and Yasser Abed Rabbo. This constellation of participants did not bode well. On the Israeli side there were two individuals with hawkish positions – Rubinstein and Meridor. The Palestinian team was comprised almost entirely of Palestinians of refugee status – Abu Mazen, a refugee from Safed; Sha'ath's family was originally from Safed and Jaffa; and Haniya's family was from Ramle. Haniya and Abu Mazen were well known for their hawkish position on refugees.

The main question, of course, was Arafat's position on the issue. From earlier meetings we knew that Arafat had discussed the distress of the refugees in Lebanon and the need to give them priority in rehabilitation. We also heard general statements regarding the suffering of the refugees over decades. But I, personally – and I believe this is true for the rest of the Israeli negotiators – never heard Arafat himself demand the implementation of the Right of Return for Palestinian refugees in Israel proper (i.e. within the "Green Line"). Arafat was saving his final position on the issue for the last stages of the negotiations.

The Palestinians initially presented radical positions regarding declarations. Israel had to recognize its responsibility for forcefully uprooting refugees and taking over their property, in the course of the 1948 war, and for preventing their return. Consequently, it should bear the responsibility for solving the problem of the refugees. They relied heavily on the writings of Israel's "new historians" to prove their case.

The Palestinian position was that a fair solution of the refugee problem should lead to the implementation of the UN Resolution from 1949, which according to Palestinian interpretation supports the "Right of Return." On the basis of this decision, they argued, every refugee who wants to return to Israel, would be able to do so through mechanisms that would be agreed upon by the sides. They promised that these mechanisms would be built to channel the refugees away from choosing the options of returning to Israel. The exception would be the refugees in Lebanon. They would be allowed – so demanded the Palestinians – to return to Israel soon.

The Palestinians also demanded that Israel compensate the refugees for suffering, uprooting and loss of property. They wanted this category to include the "absent-present" Israeli-Arabs, who may have stayed in Israel but were forced to leave their homes and land. In this context, they did not refrain from using the precedents created by the Jews of Europe in their legal campaign for reparations from Germany.

The Palestinian positions, trapped in declarations and images, were rigid, but not surprising. We realized that, at this stage, the time had not come for Palestinian compromises on this issue. According to many Palestinians, exercising flexibility on the issue of the Right of Return and Israel's responsibility were the last bargaining chips, to be discussed only at the last stages of the negotiations.

In terms of a practical solution, however, there was a substantial area of agreement between the sides, which included an international mechanism that would bear the responsibility for resolving the refugees issue.

On the evening of Friday July 14, at the end of the first week of the summit, the president invited both working groups on the issue of refugees to report on their progress. The meeting took place in the presidential cabin during the late afternoon just before the Sabbath. Clinton, who was dressed comfortably in a jeans jacket, with a cigar in hand, was focused and serious. Elyakim detailed the gaps that appeared between the sides regarding the issue of responsibility and the Right of Return.

Abu Mazen and Nabil Sha'ath differentiated between the right itself, as a principle, and the mechanisms for its realization. In the most dramatic moment of the meeting Clinton asked Sha'ath "How many refugees [who want to return to Israel] are there?"

"Ten to twenty percent," Sha'ath replied.

Clinton looked at him with amazement: "Do you mean that 400,000 to 800,000 refugees would return to Israel?!"

"We do not want to discuss numbers," Abu Mazen silenced Sha'ath.

Clinton summarized: "If an agreement is concluded, I want to bring it before the G8, so that the industrialized nations could contribute to creating a financial package vital for the implementation of the agreement." It appeared that the president accepted the principle of a "cap" on the amount claimed for rehabilitation. He mentioned ten to twenty billion dollars.

The Israelis left the meeting with a good feeling. The president had exhibited full knowledge of the issue, and in summarizing identified a possible area of agreement.

Unfortunately, as far as the mechanism of the negotiations was concerned, there was no methodical follow-up to ensure progress. The refugees committee was left to its own devices, wasting its time in useless and pointless arguments.

On Sunday July 16, the Israeli team presented the Palestinians with a document that detailed Israel's position on all aspects of the refugees issue. This position can be found in the draft framework agreement included as an appendix to this book (see pp. 247–50, Article 6).

It was clear that the Palestinian refugees in Lebanon, both because of their grim living conditions and their isolated position within Lebanese society, required immediate attention of a different kind. As rapid compensation for their continued suffering, we offered each refugee a "personal rehabilitation package" unrelated to the property claim that would be filed.

The document presented to the Palestinians was far-reaching, although it was titled a "Non-Paper" and we clarified that it could not be viewed as an official Israeli position. It was clear, however, to both sides, that if the Palestinians embraced the ideas presented in the document, Israel would not withdraw them. We believed our proposal was a solid basis for further negotiations, but the Palestinians feared conceding before all other issues were resolved to their satisfaction. The sides continued with their endless arguments regarding responsibility, the Right of Return, and the problem of Jewish refugees who left Arab countries, instead of at least making progress on the practical aspects of the issue. Upon his return to Camp David, faced with the bleak outcome of the tiresome and useless discussions on the refugees, Clinton canceled a planned meeting with the working group on borders, and decided to throw all his weight behind a last ditch effort on Jerusalem.

12

EIGHT HUNDRED TIMES JERUSALEM

On the evening of Sunday July 23, President Clinton returned to Camp David and met separately with Barak and Arafat, consequently deciding to initiate two-on-two meetings on the different issues.

Barak summarized once again our basic guidelines of the proposed agreement for ending the conflict:

- An independent, internationally recognized, sovereign, demilitarized Palestinian state with bilateral economic free-trade relations with Israel; a strong police force with naval powers and helicopters; territorial contiguity across eighty-nine percent of the area; a safe passage (above ground) between the West Bank and Gaza; and the right to settle Palestinian refugees in its territory.
- The international community would raise $15–20 billion toward the rehabilitation of the refugees.
- The capital of the state would be Al-Quds and would include Abu-Dis, Al Eizariya and other surrounding neighborhoods, as well as a sovereign passage to the Temple Mount. In some of the internal neighborhoods (e.g. A-Tur) there will be symbolic sovereignty. The remaining internal neighborhoods would be managed by a Quadrant administration, under Israeli sovereignty and the municipal jurisdiction of Jerusalem. These neighborhoods would have a special relationship with the Municipality of Al-Quds in areas such as education. In the Old City there would be a special regime, maybe a separate administration. A defined area, under Palestinian control, would be designated for Arafat in the Muslim Quarter, adjacent to the Temple Mount. The Temple Mount itself would remain under Israeli sovereignty. Jews would have the right to worship, and Palestinians would be given custodianship; both sides would commit not to engage in archeological digs.

Most of us Israelis perceived the benefits of such a framework agreement to be real and tangible: an end to an historic conflict, with permanent borders, enlarging the area of Israeli Jerusalem by annexing Ma'ale Adumim,

Givat Ze'ev and Gush Etzion, and recognizing eleven new neighborhoods that were constructed after 1967 as an integral part of the official capital of Israel with sovereignty over the Temple Mount.

In practical terms, we had to ensure continuity in Jerusalem – including from Mount Zion through the Dormition Abbey, the Jewish Quarter, the Western Wall, the Archeological Garden, the City of David, Yad Avshalom, Mount of Olives, to Ras El-Amud. We also had to examine the passage from Ramot Eshkol to Givat Hatachmoshet ("Ammunition Hill"), Sheikh Jarrah, Silwan, and the Cave of Tzidkiyahu. We had to explore the possibility of relocating – even at our own expense – the refugee camps of Shoafat and Az-Za'ayyem. As for the regime itself – Barak concluded – we must create a coordination mechanism on the basis of parity. There would be two US embassies – one in each capital, and the remaining countries would be invited to open their embassies there.

Moreover, eighty percent of the settlers would be accommodated in settlement blocs, within reasonable boundaries, that would be annexed to Israel, as part of setting the permanent borders. In addition to all these, there were the security arrangements in the Jordan Valley and the West Bank. There would be a gradual withdrawal over twelve years, during which the Jordan Valley would be defined as a Security Zone. Along the Jordanian border, Israel would continue to hold a small section of the Jordan River itself. Above all, a comprehensive plan to end the conflict would be laid out, including cultural programs, people-to-people activities, economic projects, measures to prevent incitement, and education.

These guidelines left room for possible flexibilities and bargaining on: the border with Jordan; the time period for holdings in the Jordan Valley; the final division of territories between us and them; the number and scope of areas in which Israeli presence would remain; the total area necessary for settlement blocs; the timetable for settlement evacuation; the granting of authority in the distant suburbs of Jerusalem and internal neighborhoods, and the size of area that would be transferred to Arafat in the Muslim Quarter of the Old City; the level of coordination at the Atarot airport; and, finally, increasing the number of Palestinian refugees to be granted entry into Israel to 20,000.

At 11.30 p.m. the marathon meetings with the president were launched at Aspen cabin. We began our discussions with the issue of security, followed by territory, refugees, and finally Jerusalem. Clinton sat at the head of the table, with George Tenet seated next to him. Madeleine Albright, Dennis Ross, Rob Malley and Sandy Berger from the American team were in the room. Shlomo Yanai and I represented the Israeli side, while the Palestinian side was represented by Abu Ala and Mohammed Dahlan.

Clinton proposed an agenda for the discussion. We started with a quick review of the issues agreed upon by the sides. He was vigorous and determined to make progress on clarifications, which he hoped would lead to the signing of a comprehensive agreement. Since his return from Japan, he had not rested for a minute.

The first issue to be concluded was early-warning stations. "We agree to only two stations. You do not need three," Dahlan began. George Tenet was angry and did not bother hiding it. "If we do not finalize this simple thing, we get nowhere," he told the Palestinians. "You know exactly where the stations should be, the only question we have to discuss is how to get to the stations and how to protect them." Tenet, who like the president held an extinguished cigar in his hand, appeared to have had his fill of Palestinian excuses. I suspected that Dahlan's remarks were a clear signal of something much deeper than just tactics. Rather, I thought they reflected a Palestinian decision not to reach an agreement, not even on the "easy" issues, and at least not at this stage. "We do not object," was Dahlan's quick response. We then moved to the issue of airspace. Shlomo Yanai clarified that the Israeli position on this issue involved Israeli use but not Israeli sovereignty of Palestinian airspace. "We would have one control system, and maybe one coordinator from your side in the control center. All the air routes would be coordinated, as is the case between the relevant authorities of sovereign states, like with Jordan. It is a simple issue," Yanai concluded. "We did not agree to this," Dahlan replied angrily. "I am not an expert, we have to transfer this issue to the experts. You are creating artificial sovereignty. You do not need either early-warning stations or flights of the Israeli Air Force." Airspace and the electromagnetic spectrum above the Territories are vital Israeli needs. The few miles of "narrow waist" of the country enables the enemy invading our airspace to reach major centers of population within one to two minutes. In order to gain a few critical minutes of early warning, as well as to allow for vital air-force training, Israel therefore needs control of the airspace of the future Palestinian state. Similarly, crowding of the electromagnetic spectrum allows Israel very little flexibility in terms of control and allocation of frequencies. These arguments are clear to those who deal with these issues in Israel, but not so for the Palestinians. Their position was that these security discussions were nothing more than a pretext for perpetuating the occupation and for eroding sovereignty. It is difficult to mitigate these two approaches, but it is not impossible. In fact, Abu Ala had explicitly agreed to our control of the airspace in the Swedish channel talks.

"We have to separate security needs and civilian issues," I proposed.

"We must let the experts prepare a program for coordinating the spectrum, on the basis of mutual respect for both sides," Yanai added.

A similar problem emerged in our next discussion regarding Israel's right to deploy into Palestinian territory in case of emergency as a result of a military threat from the East. Yanai presented the Israeli demand for five areas of deployment in addition to war emergency storage sites.

"Who defines what constitutes an emergency?" Clinton asked. "If I complain about a headache, you cannot tell me I don't have one . . ." "There has to be a certain level of trust between two countries," Yanai replied. "Maybe on this issue we can agree on some sort of American supervision?" Tenet suggested. "On questions of national security we trust no one but ourselves," Yanai answered. In internal discussions, I disagreed with Yanai on this issue because I thought our demand was spiteful, offensive, and without justification. So was the sweeping rejection of the proposed American supervisory force.

Dahlan was quick to latch on to the American proposal. "In these five areas [of deployment] I am willing to have American forces for a certain period," he said. "We are willing to do a lot for an agreement, but what you are asking is very different," Clinton said to Dahlan. And turning to the Israelis: "You must ensure that Palestinian sovereignty is not compromised, and we must clearly define what an emergency situation is. With these two components there shouldn't be a problem," Clinton said.

The next issue on the agenda was establishing a demilitarized Palestinian state: it would not have a standing army, foreign troops could not operate or be established in its territory, and military alliances could not be signed with third parties. "We all assumed that this would be the situation in Permanent Status," Clinton began, "but we must discuss protecting the Palestinian state from an attack by other Palestinians under its sovereignty. We cannot disregard the dangers for a new state with enemies."

"The Palestinians must receive from the US and from Israel guarantees for their security that will be included in the agreement," Yanai replied. "The Palestinian state will have non-military means of self-defense that will be defined. A regional defense agreement is also possible, for example with Egypt, or at least with Jordan," he added.

The Palestinians understood, of course, that the idea was to have a regional agreement in which Israel was party, rather than a military alliance with Arab states that excluded Israel.

"We do not want a military state. We do not need tanks and planes. We want to feed the hungry mouths of our people. We however do not want you – the Israelis – claiming to protect us," Dahlan said. "Let us first define what a 'strong police force' is," I responded. "Yes," Ross followed up. "We must also examine what weapons such a force could have, and what threats, such as terrorism, endanger both sides, and when we – the Americans – should enter the picture."

Deliberations continued over the definition of "demilitarization," and the name of the envisaged police force, which the Palestinians would create and maintain. While it was clear to the Israeli side that, for Abu Ala and Dahlan, taking responsibility for their own affairs and security, and returning with pride to their people, was of the utmost importance, we held steady to the basic tenets of the Israeli concept of security. "We are ready for all cooperation," Dahlan responded, "but we must also show our people that there has been a real change in their lives." "And we are those responsible on our side, not you," Abu Ala was quick to follow.

A similar problem again arose during the discussion on the international passages. From the Israeli perspective, control over the passages would allow for supervision of demilitarization, in terms of the equipment and arms that might be transported through them. "We do not have to do that on the ground," we emphasized, "maybe just observe, or alternatively have a third party operate the passages." Dahlan exploded: "You tested us for six years since Oslo. We are not willing to be tested any longer. You are the ones who should be tested. We will not accept any Israeli presence in the passages. We will however have no problem coordinating everything with you." "If you are not confident we are doing a satisfactory job, we will be willing to consider the presence of a third party at the passages," Abu Ala added.

"The 'trust me' approach is not sufficient in this case," Yanai replied. "We have conceded our original request to control the passages, but this issue is of vital importance to our security." Eager to move ahead to the more substantial issue of the Jordan Valley, the president concluded that the issue of international passages required further work.

Yanai proceeded to describe the plan for Israeli deployment in the Jordan Valley, which included: an electronic fence; ongoing security systems; the possibility of moving west during military operations in the case of a pursuit; visibility of the water surface level in order to identify its crossing at six to ten vantage points; and finally a special security regime in which six companies would operate under two battalions – 800 people in total – for a limited period.

President Clinton feared a "Lebanonization" of the border. Yanai addressed his concern, stating that there would be low-profile Israeli presence for a limited time.

Dahlan was angered again. "Because of different excuses of supposed security, you are causing us not to have a country. Your approach is strangling us. The border with Jordan will be our sole responsibility. We do not want your presence there."

"We could work together to reduce the presence, which would already be very low. In any case, we are talking about a limited period," Yanai replied.

"Our demands in the Jordan Valley are for security reasons only, and do not relate to questions of sovereignty and borders. We will ensure that the wording of the agreement clarifies this," I added.

"In the past you offered an international force with Jordan. And the prime minister himself told me that he would not oppose this. An international force is a condition for achieving an agreement on security," Clinton insisted.

"We'll examine this," I replied to the president, "provided that we are referring to a third party alongside the IDF, and not an independent force."

"Okay, think about it. Since we are about to do a lot for Jerusalem in the framework of this agreement, examine whether Palestinian-Jordanian-Israeli-International force cooperation is possible, for a while, maybe even on both sides of the Jordan River. The Israelis have raised legitimate problems, and the rationale that serves as the basis for their positions is clearer to me now. But I also understand the fear it creates on the Palestinian side," the president summarized.

The meeting ended. Yanai and I felt that we had properly explained the Israeli security concept and that our position could be accepted. We thought that agreements in the area of security could contribute to making progress on the issues of territories and borders. We also hoped that it would help build Palestinian confidence in their developing independence, the major signs of which are an independent and authoritative security force. In hindsight, however, it turned out that for the Palestinians the negotiation on security arrangements was most difficult, and maybe even traumatic and humiliating. A few weeks later they would retract a large portion of the understandings reached in this meeting and the president's conclusions.

We resumed our meeting with the president at 3.15 a.m. He began with a topic-by-topic summary of the security discussions.

Early-warning stations: relatively small sites that are vital to Israeli security "We agree to the demand that these sites should be located on mountain tops, and we do not have problems with the manning and operating of the stations. But we need some form of moral protection when facing our people, in the form of an American or some other representative that will be present there," Dahlan said.

Airspace Clinton told the Palestinians that "there would be one air traffic control because the airspace is small. We must ensure that you are not discriminated against on commercial flights. Moreover, you have the right not to be disturbed by noise or by low-flying planes." I added, "We must ensure that the authorities and responsibilities on securing the airspace, which will remain in Israel's hands, will override civilian ones."

Emergency areas of deployment "Arafat asked for an international force, rather than the IDF," Abu Ala began.

"Please tell the chairman," Clinton replied, "that in this case the Israelis have a justifiable argument. And you," he turned to Yanai and me, "please define emergency."

Demilitarization "The principle itself is acceptable to both sides. Now we have to conclude the composition of the Palestinian force and the weapons in its use. We also have to agree on the name for the force, so the Israelis can present it to their public," Clinton said.

"We want a 'state with limited arms' and not a 'demilitarized state,'" Dahlan replied.

"Think of arrangements at the international passages in the area of customs that allow for an Israeli observer at the passages, and in return, Israel will allow for an observer in its customs stations," Clinton said to the Palestinians.

The Jordan Valley I conveyed that further to consultations with the prime minister and the IDF chief of staff, Israel's response to the proposal of an international force was positive, in principle. Our condition was that the entire security package be accepted on all other issues.

"If I am able to enlist the support of the Jordanian King for this issue, will you agree to operate on both sides of the River?" Clinton asked.

"That really complicates the issue," Yanai replied.

"I do not want anything in common with Israel, with Egypt, or with Jordan. The Palestinian police with the United States is more than enough," Dahlan said adamantly.

Clinton asked the Palestinians to "sleep on it" and think about it again. "Israel agrees to a formula that – to the extent possible – takes into consideration your apprehensions," he told Abu Ala and Dahlan, "and I will not send American forces without being able to protect them. They will draw fire just with their presence, like in East Timor. I sent five hundred people, and then had to send an additional three thousand, to protect the first five hundred . . ."

Feeling that the issue of security was not far from resolution, the president moved to the next topic. Dawn was breaking.

The presidential marathon proceeded. At the end of a session on refugees, that again reached a dead end, the Americans decided to put forward their own proposal on the issue.

The discussion moved on to the issue of territory. We reiterated the main principles of the Israeli concept:

- Annexing approximately 650 square kilometers of the Territories, constituting ten to twelve percent (the exact percentage was a function of the calculation method).
- Accommodating eighty percent of the settlers in settlement blocs that will be annexed to Israel.
- No land swaps.
- Addressing Israel's strategic needs.

- The Jordan Valley as a Security Zone that Israel will have possession of for twelve years, and will accommodate ongoing security. Israel will also hold on to one-quarter of the length of the Jordan River for that period.
- In all calculations of territory, Jerusalem is not to be taken into consideration.
- The borders should be reasonable and protect the access to Ben Gurion international airport.

I laid out the map that presents the distances between various points on the eastern border to the centers of population in Tel Aviv, in Haifa, in Jerusalem, and to the Mediterranean. This map, which Yanai almost always carried with him, again made the point: seven miles from the West Bank to Ben Gurion airport; eleven miles to Tel Aviv; nine miles to Netanya; ten miles from south Mount Hebron to Be'er Sheva. The implications were clear.

In order to sweeten the bitter pill of annexation, on which the scope had yet to be finalized, we offered a valuable economic and symbolic package that included a safe passage between Gaza and the West Bank, rights to desalination plants, an air terminal, and a Palestinian pier at an Israeli seaport.

Clinton started delving into the details. What about evacuated settlements? Where will the 40,000 evacuated settlers be housed? How will the narrow strip along the Jordan River be determined and what will be its depth? How will we overcome the political problem created by a Jordanian fear of a joint border with the Palestinian state? The Americans were concerned about settlement blocs and the problems they created from the Palestinian perspective. "How do you minimize the number of Palestinians included in annexed blocs, under the assumption that the final situation in terms of territorial division is ninety percent, more or less?" Dennis Ross questioned. Ben-Ami suggested a technical solution, physically linking the Palestinian villages with the Palestinian state.

"Will you agree to an arrangement similar to the one in the Jordan Valley, or to the same arrangement on the Palestinians' western border with you? That is, the settlement blocs will not receive sovereign standing in Israel?" we were asked.

I replied that we would not. "This relates to our permanent borders and to the strategic depth that we need."

The president remarked that he doubted we would be able to achieve more than we presented. "I once got Arafat to agree to annexation of eight percent," he added, "but this was subject to certain land swaps." Under the assumption that we would have a breakthrough on Jerusalem, he believed the issue of territory could be resolved.

Following the Palestinians' presentation of their positions on the issue of territory, the president decided against convening a joint meeting for both sides, opting to try to bridge the gaps in the proposal the Americans decided to put forward.

At a meeting with Barak on the issue of Jerusalem that afternoon, we were joined for a short consultation by Reuven Merhav, the former director general of the Ministry of Foreign Affairs. Merhav was adamant about the need to provide the Palestinians with sovereignty somewhere in Jerusalem, but took into consideration opposition in the Christian world to Palestinian sovereignty in areas with sites holy to the Christian faith. In the past, no national/religious connection had been made between the Palestinians and Jerusalem. "If we provide Arafat with secular symbols – such as a flag or guest house – on the Temple Mount, it would turn him into a kind of king," he argued. He also noted that there were no flags on mosques in any other Muslim country, including Iran.

In the Bible, Jerusalem is mentioned over eight hundred times as "Jerusalem" or as "Zion." In the Koran, it is not even mentioned once. Over sixty years ago, at the end of the 1930s, Ben Gurion was willing to give up Jerusalem, turning it into an international zone under joint Jewish-Arab control. Later on, he changed his mind, largely under the influence of other Zionist leaders, who viewed the compromise of dividing the city as the only way of maintaining Jewish sovereignty in its western half. In 1949, Moshe Dayan suggested dividing the city between Israel and Jordan and allowing international forces to supervise areas such as the Mount of Olives and the Jewish Quarter.

Dr Moti Golan, an historian at Haifa University, studied the retroactive Zionist fervor for Jerusalem. "Until 1937 there was no Zionist claim to Jerusalem," he said in a lecture. It was actually in the Revisionist circles of Jerusalem, that the idea of dividing the city was originally raised. In 1932, the Revisionists wanted to grant autonomy to the Jewish neighborhoods in the city. Most of the Jewish neighborhoods, with the exception of Talpiot, the Jewish Quarter, and Mount Scopus, were on the western side of the city. In 1947, it appeared that the temporary agreement to concede Jerusalem to internationalization was a price Zionism was willing to pay for the creation of an independent State of Israel. Since being exiled from Jerusalem by the Romans two thousand years ago, the Jewish presence in Jerusalem had dwindled, but the religious and emotional ties to the city, for the Jews in the Diaspora, remained throughout the centuries of exile.

In the year 2000, there were more than 600,000 inhabitants within the Jerusalem municipal boundaries, out of which 240,000 were Palestinians. Of those, 30,000 resided in the Old City. According to Barak, in areas in which Israel must maintain control, the number of Palestinians would not exceed 12,000. Among the "internal" neighborhoods were Sheikh Jarrah, Wadi Joz, Salah A Din (or Bab Az-Zahra), Sultan Suleiman, Musrara, As-sawana, A-Tur, Ras Al Amud, Silwan, Abu Tor. Within the outer perimeter of Jerusalem we identified Israeli interests that included Atarot airfield, Atarot industrial zone, the IDF's Central Command headquarters, Ma'ale Adumim-Ramot intersection, Givat Hatachmoshet ("Ammunition Hill"), the police academy, the Shepherd Hotel, the Tomb of Simeon the Just, the Tomb of Maimonides in Sheikh Jarrah, the monument of the convoy to Mount Scopus, Rockefeller intersection, the museum, and the Hadassah center in As-swana.

In the evening, Clinton called Ben-Ami and Erekat to his cabin to discuss, and hopefully reach some agreement on Jerusalem. Ben-Ami pointed out Barak's significant deviation from his campaign promises regarding Jerusalem, hoping to underline the kinds of compromises that are necessary, and expected, in order not to miss this historical opportunity to resolve our tragic century-old conflict. Erekat acknowledged Ben-Ami's remarks, using uncommonly hard words to express deep frustration at Arafat's indecision. There were still no answers from the Palestinians except for their insistence on sovereignty over the entire Old City, barring the Jewish Quarter and the Western Wall.

The president proposed three alternatives:

- Postponing conclusions on the entire or part of the issue of Jerusalem for a later date (maybe in five years). Postponement could include the "Holy Basin," only the Old City, or all of Jerusalem.
- Palestinian custodianship on the Temple Mount alongside residual Israeli sovereignty; a special regime in the Old City, and decreased Palestinian sovereignty in the "internal" neighborhoods. Or finally:
- Functional Palestinian autonomy in the internal neighborhoods; full Palestinian sovereignty in the outer neighborhoods; the Old City divided; the Muslim and Christian Quarters for the Palestinians, the Jewish and Armenian Quarters for Israel.

Clinton asked that Arafat, through Erekat, convey a response to the proposed alternatives. Ben-Ami left the meeting with little hope.

In the evening there was a feeling of crisis. It appeared that we had exhausted all the possibilities. Shahak, Ben-Ami and I recommended to Barak that he approach Arafat, in a final attempt to examine, informally, the positions that were close to our real "red lines," and concurrently, to work with Mubarak to convince Arafat. The prime minister listened attentively, but no action followed. At dinner, the American team was discouraged. They claimed that the president had used up all his credit and time. He could invest no more in this process. In conversations, accusations were made against the "Old Man," Arafat. He was difficult, he was stubborn, and he would not move.

Rob Malley said that the Americans were very disappointed by what the sides presented in the meetings on borders/territory and refugees. The positions were still provisional and no progress had been made. They expected more. As did we.

The history of Israeli–Palestinian negotiations shows that when both sides want an agreement, it can be reached directly. This was the case in the DOP in Oslo during 1993, and the Beilin–Abu Mazen Understandings. When one of the sides, however, did not want an agreement, American involvement was critical. But for the mediation to successfully move the parties toward closing such a dramatic "deal," the process must be clearly defined and extremely strict. A rigid, binding agenda from which the parties cannot be allowed to deviate is needed in order to ensure progress. Unfortunately, the business-like, practical atmosphere that had marked the beginning of the Camp David summit quickly dissipated and returned only sporadically. There was no follow-up on the "assignments" given to each of the sides after the initial presentation of their respective positions at the start of the summit. The process was mismanaged, unclear and disorganized, leaving the delegations without a map, so to speak.

Still, the Americans knew where the gaps were and where the areas of agreement lay. I urged Rob Malley, and the rest of his team, to stay the course as mediators and force the sides to talk within the confines of the issues that were now clear. We raised the possibility that the president issue a one- to two-page paper, with instruction for further activity.

On Tuesday morning, July 25, the members of the Israeli delegation gathered in Barak's cabin. There was a feeling of an end, of goodbyes. We took pictures to remember the moment.

"I bear the full responsibility for the delegation and the results of the summit," Barak opened. "We engaged in a serious effort to make peace with the Palestinians – but not at any price – not by compromising Israel's vital interests. The developments of the past twenty-four to forty-eight hours thoroughly clarify that we do not have a partner. The process stopped with the other side's demand to transfer sovereignty over the Temple Mount. Even Clinton's proposal, in which we would have inconspicuous sovereignty on the Temple Mount and the Palestinians control over the mosques and on the ground, was rejected by Arafat."

Amnon Shahak agreed. "The State of Israel did everything to reach a positive result. We have not been successful because of Arafat's position."

"We touched our – and their – most sensitive nerves over the past two very special weeks," Ben-Ami said. "Although everything is null and void, we received a conditional agreement to annexing Arab land with eighty percent of the settlers. It was an historic breakthrough in deep-rooted Arab positions. Our negotiating partner had to make an historic decision – it turned out that he was unable to."

"Our main problem now is how to avoid a violent confrontation and keep the dialogue alive," said Shahak. "I suggest you meet with Arafat," he turned to Barak.

"We have to create a situation of co-existence, knowing that we are divided on the principle issues," agreed Israel Hasson.

Barak was agreeable to the idea of a possible meeting with Arafat. The meeting never took place.

I was entrusted with preparing the main public messages. For the Israeli public we would have "full disclosure" of what we did at Camp David. In the United States we tried to convey Israel's commitment to Jerusalem and to its holy sites. In our message to the Arabs, we would focus on Israel's willingness to end the conflict even at a painful price, and on our commitment to acknowledge the Palestinian national aspirations, address their needs regarding Jerusalem and find satisfactory resolutions to the plight of the refugees.

Clinton, Barak and Arafat parted formally from each other, with a warning. "We must do everything to prevent the region from deteriorating into a disaster," Clinton said. The two others nodded. The disappointment and fatigue was evident on all three.

In hindsight, with Camp David now another milestone in the complex, turbulent history of the Arab–Israeli conflict, I have no doubt that Arafat – as a national leader – acted wholly irresponsibly. After decades of leading the Palestinians toward such a deciding moment, he failed once again to lead them to peace. He missed seizing the point after which the Palestinians could start living their lives as a people in their own sovereign state. Arafat simply damaged the long-term cause of the Palestinian people, thus determining the short-term fate of the people of Israel.

The Palestinian leadership was not homogeneous. There was the "young group" which consisted of second-generation Palestinian leaders, including Mohammad Rashid, Mohammed Dahlan, Hassan Asfour, and to a somewhat lesser extent, Saeb Erekat. Each was trying to push forward the gospel of compromise through treacherous waters, with the understanding that insisting on "all or nothing" would leave the Palestinian people stuck – with nowhere to go for a long time to come. But they were confronted with Abu Mazen, Abu Ala and Akram Haniya, who encouraged Arafat to adopt uncompromising positions that proved unrealistic.

The beginning of the violence and hostilities in September 2000 – the madness that has accompanied the religious fanaticism, the vicious and cruel Palestinian incitement, and the total collapse of trust – have all diminished the chances that those within the Palestinian leadership who supported compromise would continue to push for an agreement.

The speed with which the Americans dismantled the summit was yet another example of the American organizational efficiency that stood in sharp contrast to the summit's substantive management inefficiency. In less than an hour, the base was emptied, with no remnants of the American teams or the logistical set-up.

The president went off to a concluding press conference. Barak prepared for a press conference immediately after, in which he stated:

> The government of Israel, and I as prime minister, acted in the course of the Camp David summit out of moral and personal commitment, and supreme national obligation to do everything possible to bring about an end to the conflict . . .
>
> Israel was prepared to pay a painful price to bring about an end to the conflict, but not any price. We sought a stable balance, and peace for generations to come, not headlines in tomorrow's paper.
>
> Arafat was afraid to make the historic decisions necessary at this time in order to bring about an end to the conflict. Arafat's positions on Jerusalem are those which prevented the achievement of the agreement.
>
> I, as prime minister, bear overall responsibility for the Israeli positions presented in the course of the summit, just as I would have stood behind any overall agreement, difficult as it may have been, had it been achieved.
>
> Q: Mr Prime Minister . . . you have failed in the Syrian track and now in the Palestinian track, is Ehud Barak a disappointed man today?
>
> A: Of course . . . but the primary responsibility of the Israeli government is to turn every stone to ensure there is a way to reach an agreement with our neighbors that would strengthen the security of Israel and to reach this agreement, if possible. But two are needed to tango . . . there is no way of forcing it on the other side.

Some members of our delegation remained in Camp David to document conclusions and prepare for departure. The Palestinians seem to have vanished. In the afternoon, we left Camp David in the president's helicopter. Half a dozen American officers conducted a short and emotional military review for Barak, and saluted farewell.

On the flight back to Israel, members of the Israeli delegation were more cooperative than ever with the press, explaining what had happened, detailing discussions and contacts, and describing events at the summit. After two weeks of an almost complete media blackout, both the negotiators and the media were craving contact. The next day, the newspapers were filled with articles, analysis and editorials. A great number of reports described the course of events at Camp David quite inaccurately.

13

THERE IS GOING TO BE
A CATASTROPHE

Camp David improved Israel's standing vis-à-vis the Palestinians in the international press and diplomatic corps, but the support quickly dissipated as the region flared up with a new cycle of violence and Israel's positive peace-seeking image was transformed overnight to that of a monstrous superpower that slaughters and fires without mercy on a civilian, weak, rights-deprived population. The media portrayal of our reality was twisted and manipulative.

For now, however, Israel was perceived as having striven toward peace, proposed far-reaching ideas, and adopted brave positions. Barak was praised for having "delivered the goods" politically, while Arafat turned out to be an unworthy partner. The Palestinians were viewed as having sabotaged the summit by failing to move from dogmatic to pragmatic positions. Clinton was very clear, although he did not explicitly blame Arafat, "I think the people of Israel should be very proud of him [Barak] . . . I think he took a big risk . . . he came over here to do what he thought was right for the people of Israel, and . . . he would never do anything to put the security of Israel at risk."

The struggle over the world's public opinion took place across five continents. Envoys were sent to China, Japan, India and Indonesia, to Europe, North American, Jordan and Egypt to describe how events had unfolded at Camp David and to explain the Israeli position.

Some members of the Palestinian leadership were lamenting their inflexibility at the summit and the missed opportunity to reach a Permanent Status agreement. Still, Erekat was optimistic. "I believe that by September 13, we will reach a comprehensive Permanent Status agreement with the Israelis. The possibility of reaching such an agreement after Camp David is stronger and greater than ever before," he said.

Our goal was to resume negotiations on the basis of understandings that were concluded at the summit and a Palestinian agreement to President Clinton's ideas. It was vital that the Palestinians postpone a looming Declaration of Independence from the target date of September 13 to at least January 1, 2001, to prevent negotiating under the threat of a unilateral declaration. Equally important was forming an Arab coalition in support of Arafat signing an end-of-conflict agreement – Arab support was deemed one of the most critically missing components at Camp David. Finally, we wanted to return to the "Swedish code," which would allow us to quietly consolidate the maximum possible understanding in advance of another summit. We anticipated that another summit would convene only if and when the majority of a drafted agreement would be agreed upon, leaving a limited number of issues for the leaders to decide.

In their analysis of the political forces that were at play at the summit, political scholars and analysts drew comparisons between the first and second Camp David summits and between Barak and Menaham Begin. Begin who "sacrificed" the Sinai Peninsula in favor of an historic peace agreement with an Arab nation, was viewed as a gifted negotiator with a shrewd sense of political timing. Barak was viewed as courageous and determined but arrogant and aggressive, resolute on dictating the rules of the game, which is why Arafat rejected his proposals.

Although Barak's personal behavior and management skills may not have been without fault, they had in fact little influence on Arafat's positions and strategy. A more accurate historic analogy may be the one between Barak and President Jimmy Carter who in 1979, during his third year in office, became embroiled in the collapse of the Shah's regime in Iran and the American hostage crisis. In the midst of the 1980 presidential campaign, Carter focused his full attention on saving the lives of the American hostages, convinced that his heartfelt dedicated efforts to bring forth their safe release would have more influence on the voters than the usual rhetoric of a presidential campaign. In November 1980, the American voters sent Carter home, and elected Ronald Reagan to the White House.

Similarly, Barak was convinced that he was doing the right thing for the nation, that the justifications for the process were clear and that the majority of the Israeli public recognized that his actions were driven by a deep sense of responsibility for the security of Israel, political vision and courageous leadership. This absolute confidence in his political strategy and in the ability of the public to recognize and understand the logic behind it, left Barak removed from political reality. He was sure that if he was able to deliver an agreement with the Palestinians, the public would support it and that if he failed, the public would recognize that he was not the one to blame and would thus still support him. Equally as damaging was his failure to create a mechanism that would ensure continued political process in case the negotiations fail. As a result, Barak found himself without a political foundation that would have helped gain support for an agreement in the case of success or keep him in his position as prime minister in the case of failure.

Having received a convincing mandate from the voters, Barak formulated his political strategy by relying primarily on his own unwavering logic, neglecting to take advantage of the extensive collective knowledge and experience of fellow Labor Party politicians such as Shimon Peres, Haim Ramon, Yossi Beilin and Dalia Itzik. When he did seek political advice, it was from people whose talent and experience in no way matched those of these politicians.

Barak's plan for his four-year tenure as prime minister was to carry out negotiations with the Syrians and/or the Palestinians for a year and a half, spend six months preparing the necessary legislation for a national referendum, and be left with two years to begin to implement the agreement. By implementing an agreement he himself concluded, Barak hoped to avoid the fate that previous agreements had suffered, namely, having to be executed by a different government from the one who signed them initially, resulting in stagnation in the good case, and total rejection in the worse. Such was the case with Netanyahu and the Wye River Memorandum, which Barak viewed as problematic because it forced Israel to concede assets without any real returns. Projecting further into the future, Barak anticipated that in the last year of his first term, with the re-election campaign in full swing, the public would already be enjoying the benefits of the agreement, such as improved security, better relations with the international community and Arab countries, economic prosperity and being able to make foreign investments. The timetable in the agreement would release him from the obligation of having to evacuate settlements immediately, leaving this most difficult part of the agreement to be implemented during his second term.

From the outset, Barak anticipated that the political process might erode the wide coalition he formed. It was not unlikely that the NRP (Mafdal), for example, would abandon the coalition, but an unexpected Shas–Meretz crisis that culminated with Shas leaving the coalition was not a scenario he had considered. The sad truth was that, even if Camp David had ended with an agreement, it was doubtful Barak would have had the "political credit" necessary to see his ambitious agenda through a national referendum and implementation. It is difficult to say, in hindsight, if insightful and reliable political advice would have given him the tools necessary to tackle the complex conflict he was resolved to bring to an end. It would have certainly broadened his perspective and made him more aware of the magnitude of the difficulties ahead, allowing him to prepare accordingly. Barak did not often receive this kind of advice, ultimately becoming a prisoner of his own approach and actions.

Immediately following Camp David, the international community was mobilized to salvage the negotiations and prevent the crisis from escalating into a violent confrontation. Egypt assumed the lead, introducing a host of political initiatives and mediation efforts in hope to bring the sides back to the path of Permanent Status negotiations.

Upon his return to Gaza, Arafat was greeted with cheers, "You are the champion, the hero, defender of our people's rights!" He then went off on shuttle missions to eight Arab capitals.

The Egyptians and Palestinians wanted to resume the negotiations immediately. The Americans wanted to develop new initiatives for arrangements on the Temple Mount before launching into a new round of talks. Our position was that the first stage of the discussion on Jerusalem would focus on practical arrangements, while the discussion on the sovereign-religious-legal issues, which were perceived as the major reasons for the failure of Camp David, should be postponed for the later stages. We felt that gradual progress on the technical and practical issues would facilitate discussions on the emotional, controversial and symbolic issues of principle. The message from Mubarak was that the sides had to find a solution for the mosques, which would ensure that, if Muslims wished to do so, they could arrive from Mecca to pray at Al Aqsa without having to be stopped and inspected by Israelis. This would allow for Saudi support. To us, this was a positive and encouraging sign that stirred up a certain level of optimism. Mubarak was focused on the mosques, not on the entire Temple Mount. However, as a rule, the Egyptians supported the Palestinian claim for sovereignty on the Temple Mount, and expressed no understanding of our aspirations. "No single person in the Arab or Islamic world can compromise on East Jerusalem or Al Aqsa Mosque," was how Mubarak put it in an interview in Alexandria.

The Americans seemed to support the Egyptian initiative, but were still waiting for an ideological shift among the Palestinians before resuming negotiations. They viewed Abu Ala as a destructive force in the process and wanted Saeb Erekat – whose star was rising as far as Arafat was concerned – to continue the ministerial level negotiations with Ben-Ami. Another summit, they said, would be possible in mid-September or early October, as long as it would be almost certain that an agreement could be reached, particularly on the issue of Jerusalem.

Barak assessed that secret negotiations were the best way to proceed. He directed Ben-Ami and me to meet Erekat and Dahlan to explore whether there was a chance of reaching an agreement by postponing resolution for the Temple Mount. I met with Erekat on July 31 in a corner of the YMCA building in Jerusalem. Exactly a year had passed since the day we both began negotiating the Sharm Al Sheikh Memorandum. Our aim was to consolidate the understandings reached at Camp David, and to bridge the gaps on the issue of Jerusalem. "We have August," Saeb said, "and if we need – we also have September. We will address the core issues, the generic issues, and the drafting." In order to ensure the secrecy of our meetings and assure their success, Erekat suggested that the sides maintain a public channel, which would consist of Oded Eran and himself.

We agreed that it was important to involve Egypt and Jordan, maybe through joint briefings of both sides. We were both unsure of the desired scope and extent of American participation.

In meetings I had with Ambassador Indyk, we discussed several formulas for combining sovereignty, custodianship and a special regime on the Temple Mount. We thought that the solution lay somewhere in the legal and political ambiguity surrounding concrete arrangements.

Over forty comprehensive, detailed negotiating meetings had taken place from the end of the Camp David summit through September. Both sides maintained a tight media blackout, keeping the press mostly unaware of the developments that were taking place in these meetings.

The Palestinian feeling was that the Israeli side was acting as if it were bargaining in a flea market. Even those among them who supported compromise, had difficulty convincing their colleagues that Israel had reached its "red lines." There was always someone who would press to wait just a little longer; perhaps Israel would budge a bit more. The Palestinians interpreted the absence of Ben-Ami from most of the meetings following Camp David as an Israeli intent not to achieve real progress and to leave them with most of the blame for the failure. The truth was simply that Ben-Ami, minister of Foreign Affairs and Internal Security, was overloaded with extensive diplomatic duties and public relations efforts.

From our perspective, the Palestinian negotiating team had no real decision-making authority. Erekat was restrained. "I do not know, until now, if Arafat accepts what I presented to him at Camp David regarding Jerusalem," he said bitterly. The mandate he and Dahlan received from Arafat, in the presence of President Clinton, had no real value without the backing of Abu Mazen or Abu Ala. He was unable to reconcile substantial issues. Regardless, Arafat would have no difficulty to completely renounce what his representatives agreed to.

Mediation by the American team became even more difficult. Dennis Ross had lost the Palestinians' trust and was no longer a welcome guest among them. Any idea he proposed automatically rejected. As a result, the center of gravity shifted from the State Department to the White House.

Ross, who had led the American team since 1989, was dedicated, focused, congenial and calm. His ever-pleasant demeanor was arguably a minus as in order to move the stubborn parties toward an agreement he may have needed to pound fists on the table, or even turn it over.

There was also the issue of Abu Mazen's involvement, which some of us viewed as a critical component in the success of the negotiations. Abu Mazen and his assistants were partners of Yossi Beilin and his team in consolidating their self-titled understandings in late 1995.

In February 1996 renowned security columnist Ze'ev Schiff of *Haaretz* reported the details of these understandings:

Israel shall extend its recognition to the independent State of Palestine, demilitarized.

Large areas such as Ariel, Ma'ale Adumim, and the parts of Gush Etzion will be part of Israel. Most of the settlers will remain in Israeli territory. The Jewish settlers in the settlements that will not be annexed into Israel and for whom mandatory evacuation is not imposed shall be able to remain as permanent foreign residents in the Palestinian state, whichever they choose.

In the area of the Jordan Valley under Israeli control, three battalion sized military zones shall be established along with early-warning stations that shall remain throughout the transitional period. Thereafter, authority over the border crossing points shall be transferred into the hands of the Palestinians in 2007 if the test of intentions period has been maintained.

The present municipal boundaries of Jerusalem shall be expanded, and the Parties agree to maintain one Municipality for the "City of Jerusalem." The Arab Eastern part of the city, under Palestinian sovereignty, to be "al-Quds" will include the villages of Abu Dis, and Al Eizariya. The other part, the capital "Yerushalayim" will also include Ma'ale Adumim. The State of Palestine shall be granted extra-territorial sovereignty over the Haram ash-Sharif. No agreement was reached on the status of the Old City, and that question remained open.

Refugees: Israel will contribute financially and in other ways to the repatriation of refugees outsides its borders. The Palestinians will continue to morally claim the Right of Return for refugees, but Israel does not have to accept this position.

The drafting of the Beilin–Abu Mazen Understanding, which bears striking similarities to the agreement draft that had emerged at Camp David, was completed on November 1, 1995, three days before Prime Minister Rabin was assassinated.

When the final document and maps were presented to the Israeli and Palestinian leaders, Arafat's first reaction was that it would be difficult to approve the details of the agreement. Abu Mazen, however, believed that the agreement could be approved within a month, if the government of Israel supported it. Prime Minister Peres was doubtful from the outset. Peres vehemently opposed transferring control of the Jordan Valley to the Palestinians, even though the document stated that the full transfer to the Palestinians would be set only in 2007.

It was a shame, in hindsight, that the Beilin–Abu Mazen Understanding did not serve the American team as a point of reference for the Camp David summit; it was disappointing to deal in Camp David with Abu Mazen who shamefully retracted from his previous compromises.

In his position as head of the Israel Desk at the PLO since 1983, Abu Mazen was consistently clear on one issue: "The Palestinian Authority," he promised Israelis he met with, "will act to prevent violence on the ground, at any price. If not, we will have a catastrophe." The hope that Abu Mazen would become the point man and serve as the point man for a breakthrough and a possible signing, did not materialize. At the end of the day, he did not act as a leader, let alone as a strong "number two."

Jerusalem, which serves as a microcosm of the Israeli–Palestinian conflict, in the most extreme and impulsive way, continued to occupy our time. The Israelis had made ten years worth of progress in a week. They realized that the motto "Jerusalem cannot be divided," which had overshadowed the lives of Israelis for over a generation, could be interpreted less strictly, to allow for the development of creative solutions that would give sufficient expression to the national aspirations of both peoples. In the area of Jerusalem, two capitals for two sovereign states could definitely be considered, each homogenous in terms of the composition of its population.

The Arab world and the Palestinians began to accept the special emotional–religious relationship that religious and secular Israelis alike have with their capital. Leaders in the Arab world understood that neither the issue of refugees, nor even territorial disagreements, would prevent the sides from reaching a Permanent Status agreement; but the issue of Jerusalem would. Everyone was looking for creative solutions and breakthrough formulas.

The sanctity of Jerusalem in Islam is based on the story of the nightly voyage of the Prophet Mohammad on the flying horse "El Burak" from Mecca to the "Farthest Mosque" (Al Masjid al Aksa). Following Islamic traditional and common interpretation of the Koran, the Sacred Mosque is the Prophet's Mosque in Mecca while the "Farthest Mosque" is a certain place on the Temple Mount in Jerusalem. Although the story in the Koran is legend and most researchers are convinced that Mohammad was never in Jerusalem, the belief took root and has become historical fact in the eyes of Muslim believers, solidifying the sanctity of Jerusalem in Islam. Interestingly, the name Jerusalem does not appear anywhere in early Muslim writings. When there is reference to the city, it is referred to by its Roman name, "Aelia Capitulina," so named in response to the failed second Jewish ("Bar Kokhba") rebellion, in a clear effort to eliminate all Jewish connotations.

On the evening of Saturday August 5, Barak invited Professor Ruth Lapidoth to his home in Kohav Yair to examine the legal basis for the proposals in Jerusalem. A reputable expert in international law, Professor Lapidoth is a member of the team that examined these issues at the Jerusalem Institute for Israel Studies, and former legal adviser of the Ministry of Foreign Affairs. Lapidoth detailed the possible approaches to

the term "sovereignty," starting with the traditional classic view of territorial sovereignty as something that cannot be divided, and continuing
with the concepts of "spiritual sovereignty," "joint (condominium) sovereignty," "functional sovereignty," which draws on maritime law, "limited
sovereignty," "relative sovereignty," and "suspended sovereignty" as in the
case of the South Pole. Lapidoth stressed the distinction between *de jure*
and *de facto* sovereignty, which would make it possible to leave responsibilities that have not been divided between the sides in the hands of the
formal sovereign.

Lapidoth and her colleague, Dr Menahem Klein, a member of the
Jerusalem Institute, drew on their vast research to present a practical resolution whereupon, even without recognition of sovereignty claims of one
side by the other, all practical–logistical governance issues are arranged
between the sides. They recommended that arrangements should be developed from the bottom-up by first dividing responsibilities and implementing
practical arrangements on the ground, and only thereafter tackling the
issue of definitions. This was indeed the approach Ben-Ami and I had
taken in order to avoid the potential dead end of a conceptual legal clash.

The next morning, the prime minister hosted another discussion on
Jerusalem with the head of the Shin Bet, Ami Ayalon, the head of AMAN,
Amos Malka, Matti Steinberg, an expert of Arab affairs, the prime
minister's military secretary, Brigadier-General Gadi Eizencot, Ben-Ami
and me.

We were all in agreement that the Saudi Arabia–Jordan–Egypt–Morocco
axis should be strengthened. The Arab countries, headed by Egypt, were
not interested in a holy war and were turning a cold shoulder to the
Palestinians. We thought the Palestinians understood that without another
step forward on their part, there would be no progress. Arafat had to
move away from the extreme position he had taken at Camp David.

We also discussed the significance of the term "Waqf," a religious concept
that refers to the dedication of property in trust for a pious Muslim purpose.
According to Islam, there could be no foreign sovereignty over its holy
sites. To dissolve the constant friction that Israeli sovereignty over Temple
Mount would cause, the younger generation within the Palestinian leadership – Dahlan, Asfour, Rashid – was looking for other solutions, such as
international sovereignty. The Americans raised the idea of entrusting
sovereignty on the Temple Mount to the Security Council, which in turn,
would transfer sovereignty to the organization of Islamic states, which
subsequently would entrust sovereignty to the Palestinians.

We wanted to remove the religious connotations that Arafat introduced
into the discussions toward more political language and discuss the day-
to-day activities, rather than the religious issues relating to the Temple
Mount. On the Palestinian side, however, the negotiations resurrected old

fears of a supposed Jewish takeover and destruction of the mosques on the Temple Mount.

One of the proposals discussed previously seemed to gain some momentum: based on the special status of the UN in Jerusalem, Israel and the PLO would present their demands for sovereignty over the "Holy Basin," but both sides would recognize that the UN and the international community would view the "Holy Basin" as part of the area that was designated as Corpus Separatus under the management of the UN. Both sides would ask that the UN recognize, on behalf of the three religions, the division of sovereign responsibilities that would be detailed in the agreement. The aim of the proposal was to solve the issue of sovereignty while preserving reciprocal claims and recognizing that the UN was the sovereign authority in this area, which is sacred to the three monotheistic religions.

In our proposal on Jerusalem, we expanded the description of the division of responsibility in the "Holy Basin" and the Temple Mount. The use of national symbols in the "Holy Basin" would be minimized and would be defined in detail within the context of the comprehensive agreement. With the exception of the entry points, no flags would be raised on the Temple Mount. In the area of the "Holy Basin," national institutions would be prohibited; only religious–administrative bodies would be permitted. A joint committee or municipality would be created and would be responsible for managing the "Basin." The respective government institutions of Israel and Palestine would be equidistant from the Mount. Security and public safety would be addressed through special arrangements on the basis of cooperation and coordination. The Palestinians would be responsible for public order in the site of Al-Haram Al-Sharif. Muslims would enter the Old City through "Palestinian" entry points, while Israelis would enter the city through "Israeli" entry points. All entries of Jews to the Mount would be carried out in coordination with Palestine. Within the "Holy Basin" there would be free movement of people, although there would be special arrangements on the Temple Mount. Law and order would be applied on the basis of a person's legal–civil–personal standing rather than on the basis of location. The freedom of access and worship would be ensured. The "Holy Basin" would be recognized as a world heritage site, its architectural and design characteristics would be preserved, and excavation or building on the Temple Mount would be strictly prohibited. Israel would have residual authority over the Jewish and Armenian Quarters and the Palestinians would have residual authority over the Christian and Muslim Quarters. The UN would supervise the implementation of the arrangement.

The main issue was – and remained – the expression of Israeli and Palestinian sovereignty on the Temple Mount. To this end, the concepts of guardianship, custodianship and trusteeship should be incorporated. Israeli authority in the Israeli–Jewish site would mirror Palestinian authority over the mosques.

The benefit of this proposal involved our ability to anchor it in international legitimacy. The Palestinians could show that according to international law, the sovereign in the "Holy Basin" was actually the UN, and therefore it had the ability to "break up" sovereignty into its components and transfer them to both sides.

Jerusalem. August 9, 2000. Arriving straight from a meeting with Arafat, Erekat declared that the political survival of the Palestinian regime was contingent on concluding an agreement. He asked that Abu Ala be part of the picture and that the teams be changed to a format of three-on-three meetings. We agreed to meet again daily, and that Ben-Ami would join us once he returned from his diplomatic missions in Europe. In the meantime, Israel Hasson and Mohammed Dahlan could meet to discuss security issues. A follow-up meeting on the morning of August 11 was dedicated to a theoretical exercise on what daily life would look like in the "internal" neighborhoods. Hasson and Erekat analyzed the maps and aerial photographs. Two days later we found out that Abu Ala would not participate in the meetings. He departed for a week-long trip to India. This appeared to please Erekat, who again was in the lead. After reviewing our agenda, we assessed that six to eight weeks were necessary to reach a framework agreement.

Arafat, in a stopover in the region before his trips to Russia and Iran, would hear from the British envoy, Michael Levy, that "Barak committed political suicide for peace." "I am still 'wounded' from the meeting on security at Camp David," said Dahlan in one of the bilateral meetings. "We did not reach any understandings, although I understood your needs. Know this – Arafat wants an agreement, one hundred percent. Like Barak."

Among a non-negligible portion of the Israeli population, the negotiators and the prime minister himself were portrayed as traitors who had betrayed all that was dear to the people of Israel. These opinions were usually the result of a lack of information regarding the negotiations, as there is nothing more frightening than the unknown. The right-wing circles heaved a sigh of relief when the summit failed. Nevertheless, during the entire period of the negotiations, I never encountered any signs of personal hostility. I personally received a great deal of support. People I did not know sent me touching letters and faxes expressing hope and thanks.

"I'm from a die-hard Likudnik family," a shop owner in the main street of Rehovot grabbed my arm, "and I'm telling you, bring home an agreement! Enough, I'm tired of wars. Give them what they want, and that's it." Five people around him nodded and patted him on the back. An industrialist friend who lives about an hour away from my home in Jerusalem offered to come to my home every morning to drive my children to and from school to free me to concentrate on the negotiations. There were plenty of "thumbs up" and "good luck" signs from people at traffic lights. Gideon Avrami was the deputy manager of the King David

Hotel in Jerusalem, where many of our negotiating meetings took place. Gideon, who was a company commander in the army reserves while I was the battalion commander, would stop by almost every meeting to check in to see that everything was all right. He smiled, shook hands, and left. I could sense that he too was hoping for the success of the talks.

The failure of the discussions at Camp David did not kill hope. On the contrary, the fear that another opportunity would be missed just strengthened our resolve as well as our feeling that we were close – within reach – and that we could not let the effort go.

And we did not let go. Even at home, in the few moments that I was there, it was the only issue I discussed. Exhausted, I had to continue discussions with my wife and children on the issues of refugees, borders, settlers and the fear of disastrous deceit, until I fell asleep.

The internal political situation was deteriorating. In analyzing it, Barak suggested: "place a 'wall' in front of Arafat in order to force him to give answers. Time is running out, we have to move forward despite the solid majority opposition in the Knesset. According to the law, if we cannot pass the budget, the Knesset will be dissolved and there will be new elections. As the date of the budget vote draws near – and if there is not any significant progress with Arafat – we will have to create a broader coalition, which means ending the current political process [with the Palestinians]." The "evaporation" of the Camp David Understandings, the erosion of Israeli achievements, and the missing anchor for continued negotiations concerned us.

On August 16, Dahlan, Erekat, Ben-Ami and I met again to discuss the issue of Jerusalem, focusing on the practical aspects. We laid out the maps and the aerial photos and discussed the smallest of details – roads, intersections, law enforcement, zoning and construction, access to holy sites, transportation and territorial continuity, points of tangency and problem areas. The Palestinians had reservations regarding our demand for a wider passage east, from Jerusalem down to the northern part of the Dead Sea. They rejected the idea of relocating Az-Za'ayyem and the refugee camp Shoafat, which created a real physical obstacle going east.

Moving on to security, Dahlan repeated the mantra, "We refused and continue to refuse Israeli military presence in our land." "The minutes of the Camp David session on security do not leave anything open to interpretation, or wishful thinking," I said. "As long as nothing else has been concluded, this is the basis for discussion. Our mutual goal now is to present our convergences, rather than our arguments. An agreement that is acceptable in terms of security will provide stability to the region and allow for joint living." Dahlan was furious. "You will not present me with a fait accompli," he screamed. "We cannot go back to 'square one.' You, Dahlan, are a man of truth, and so is Gilead," Ben-Ami replied, shouting. "We cannot deal with interpretation." After a vocal exchange, we decided to involve the Americans in the hope that their objective notes would reflect what had been agreed upon, and serve as a basis for continuation.

My thoughts wandered. There seemed to be a huge gulf between Israel's basic wish for peace – through its ups and downs over the past decade – and the feeling among the Palestinian leadership and in Palestinian society. Under Rabin and Barak's leadership of the Labor Party, and also under Begin, Israel searched for a political resolution. It pushed for a plan and channels of dialogue to promote peace despite intense political and public difficulties. It is true that the politicians failed to enlist public support in policy making. But they still made efforts by working on examining positions, consolidating strategies, conducting debates, meetings, dialogue, creating plans, maps and analyses, and preparing briefing papers for different alternatives.

"Why are we always the 'A' student while the Palestinians are always lying lifeless on a stretcher," I used to say to my friends. Israeli activity contrasted strongly with the passivity with which the Palestinians managed their policy making. Without outside pressure they lacked initiative. It was always either the Israelis – Rabin at Oslo, Cairo and Taba, Barak at Sharm Al Sheikh and Camp David, and later in Taba – or the Americans, or sometimes even the Egyptians or Jordanians, who put a proposal or an initiative on the table. The Palestinians never presented a long-term initiative or practical political plan that did not reflect a position of "all or nothing."

Israel too had its faults, particularly under the administrations of Shamir, Netanyahu and the first years of Sharon. Lacking a plan or any political initiative, they dug in their heels, biding time, concerned primarily with their own political survival. The three and half years of the Netanyahu administration were particularly destructive to the peace process. They perpetuated in the eyes of every Palestinian the feeling that the occupation could last for ever. It was during such periods that sound, moderate Israelis and Palestinians as well as think-tanks in the US explored ways to break through the political stagnation with initiatives. The Geneva initiative led by Beilin and Abed Rabbo, the Peoples Voice led by Ayalon and Nusseibah and finally a Comprehensive Disengagement Plan drafted in 2002 by General Sagui and myself at the Van Leer Jerusalem Institute are the main examples. It is obvious that those non-governmental, unofficial processes contributed to the public debate and ignited the political processes within the government.

Ross was called in from his private vacation in Israel. Indyk also arrived. Erekat and I presented the large differences we had in understanding the Camp David conclusions on the issues of refugees and security. "Your help is needed," Erekat concluded. It sounded like we were appearing before a tribunal to determine who was right, or worse yet, like two gangs that the school principal has to break apart.

"We do not have any official notes from Camp David, only impressions, based on the conclusions of the official meetings with the president, and on the informal meetings we had with each of the sides," Ross replied. "Therefore, for example, on the issue of territory and borders we have answers from each of the sides that go much further than the formal positions, but we will not compromise the trust you have put in us." Ross skimmed through his notes, which were much closer to the Israeli notes than the Palestinian ones. He concluded that everything was more or less agreed, except for Israeli presence for a period of time in the Jordan Valley. Dahlan was quick to disagree. "On all issues on which I have not committed myself in Camp David," he argued, "I continue to negotiate."

Ben-Ami and I reported back to Barak. "How do we bring Arafat to understand that this is the end of the road, and that it is time for him to make a decision?" the prime minister asked. "We must have a positive plan of action. The lives of millions will be condemned because of Arafat's misjudgment. If we do not reach an agreement – Arafat will move toward conflict. We must bring concrete pressure on Arafat from Europe, the US, and Russia. But we must also advance a unilateral disengagement plan. We will not implement it, unless we are forced to do so," he concluded.

On the following morning of August 24, we had another meeting with Ross and Indyk. Erekat asked for clarification of Israeli positions. "We are discussing the 'what' not the 'why,'" I replied. "We finished the conceptual arguments and lectures. Now it's time for conclusions." A very harsh argument erupted, in the course of which we tried to pressure Erekat into acknowledging the conclusions from Camp David as a basis for discussion. I suggested that Erekat mention to Arafat that Israel could also engage in unilateral measures, some of which would be irreversible. The conditions that were being offered were the best he could get. If he continued to refuse, a right-wing government would surely come to power in Israel. "Let us act as if guided and directed by a desire to reach a solution, not by history and justice," I tried to convince Saeb.

Erekat proceeded to present the Palestinian package. The US would be responsible for the security of the Palestinian state and for control of the Jordan Valley and Jordanian border. There would be coordination between Israel and Palestine regarding airspace, with certain considerations for the needs of the Israeli Air Force. Territorial division would be on the basis of "real," specific, Israeli needs, while avoiding the inclusion of Palestinian inhabitants in the annexed areas, and preventing damage to the aquifer. Israel should evacuate Kiryat Arba and the Jewish settlement in Hebron.

In Jerusalem, the Palestinians proposed that the vital interests of Israel in the Old City and its surroundings would be preserved under Palestinian sovereignty, while the Jewish Quarter and a quarter of the Armenian Quarter would be under Israeli sovereignty. The Palestinians would have sovereignty over the Muslim and Christian Quarters. With regard to refugees, Erekat demanded the Right of Return, using the refugee population in Lebanon as a "pilot" for implementing the agreement. Refugees there could choose between returning to Israel or other alternatives.

"On which issues do you see solutions?" asked Ben-Ami. "We have come to you in an attempt to reach an agreement on what is possible. The Right of Return is not possible, because when a country is established it does not demand the return of its people to another country. Regarding Jerusalem, let us try to use the wording as a tool to advance the issue."

Erekat offered a "deal": the end of conflict for the Right of Return.

"All we can do now," Ben-Ami responded, "is present principles. Don't act like we are haggling in a bazaar."

We returned to discuss security. Erekat proposed a revolutionary idea. The sky above Palestine would be free of any air force. In my reply, I again detailed the Israeli perception of security. "This approach is not open to negotiations. These are our basic demands," I added. Indyk proposed that the Americans carry out separate conversations with each side, especially on the issues of security and refugees. The aim was to consolidate a memo on these issues. I opposed the proposal. The basic Israeli approach was that the negotiations would be carried out as a "package" with a comprehensive trade-off mechanism that avoided leaving unresolved issues of potential explosiveness.

Ben-Ami left for Europe where he demanded from his counterparts to "stop cajoling Arafat." "The Dutch and the English are beginning to press the issue of the settlements," he said in one of his calls to Israel. It was not easy for Ben-Ami to reconcile his two political positions. On the one hand, he was a negotiator, one of the leaders of the process; on the other, he was on the public relations front. The messages conveyed in these two forums – in the negotiations and in public – were not reconcilable.

In Israel, in the meantime, not everyone responsible for public opinion activities had deep knowledge of the issues, and not everyone who appeared in the press knew enough about the issues to accurately comment on them. Quite often, an envoy on behalf of the prime minister would update the leaders in the region after being briefed – often hastily – by Barak. The envoy would then update Barak, who didn't necessarily pass the reports on, creating a sense of confusion and lack of coordination. Differences in the versions conveyed by the different envoys were a useful tool for the Palestinians and served as leverage for the Americans.

Toward the end of August 2000, the American team was expanded. It accompanied Erekat and me in our drafting efforts, and at our negotiations meetings at the King David Hotel in Jerusalem. This was the third time we sat to draft the same exact chapters that were supposedly concluded by the negotiators in May – through the "Swedish channel" – and that were re-opened by the Palestinians at Camp David.

14

TWO STATES FOR
TWO PEOPLES

President Clinton and Mubarak were very interested in promoting a formula for the Temple Mount in the hope of moving quickly forward toward concluding the package. The precondition was an agreement on Jerusalem. A small summit was considered for the following week in New York. The American effort focused on convening a full summit – for conclusion and signature – by November 15. From now on, each of the sides would work with the Americans. The problem with this format was that the positions of the sides would harden. Each side knew that it must present a position that the "fair mediator" would have to "wear down" even before it was presented to the other side. Moreover, if negotiations were to suddenly stop, each side would want the remaining documentation to leave as much room as possible for future flexibility with the resumption of negotiations.

The negotiation meetings on August 30 and 31 were dedicated to drafting the introduction and articles 1 (the purpose of the framework agreement) and 2 (relations between states). Erekat proposed that the Palestinian wording "financial claims for the occupation" would be replaced by "Israeli civilian aid to promote good neighborly relations." Erekat and I read to each other the paragraphs on the issues of territory, settlements and borders. We were guided by the mutual interest of formulating logical, practical solutions, and expressing fairness both in territorial and security arrangements.

While the Israeli text on Jerusalem met with a few reservations, the Palestinian text reflected a rigid, dogmatic position that was substantially backward relative to the progress we had made in the discussions. The Palestinians focused on the concept of an "open city" – a theoretical model which had no practical possibility of being implemented. It was a bleak meeting. We had no idea how to reconcile the contradictions between the positions of the sides on the issue of Jerusalem in general, and on the Temple Mount in particular. Saeb proposed that I meet with Abu Mazen and discuss with him the Beilin–Abu Mazen Understandings. I agreed, wondering why the Palestinians were not willing to accept the chapter on security from the 1995 document, as a basis for continued negotiations. There was no answer.

The discussions continued intensively in the days prior to the prime minister's trip to the UN General Assembly in New York. The Palestinians were trying to create a link between the end of conflict and the implementation of the agreement. In relation to the finality of claims, they demanded to detail the full list of claims in both the framework and comprehensive agreement, most likely because of their intention to file claims compensating them for the occupation. This outrageous intention, which is a bold-faced contradiction of good faith negotiations toward peace, first came up in a casual conversation with Erekat at Camp David. One could describe the process we were experiencing as a conveyor belt, in which a fine product comes out of the manufacturing line, only to be damaged and destroyed by someone time and time again.

The chapter dealing with relations between states was mostly completed. There were conceptual gaps on some issues that we could not resolve in the drafting process. For example, we did not reach an agreement regarding prohibiting representation of communities or individuals of one side by the other side. This demand was meant to prevent interference by the Palestinian state in the internal affairs of Israeli-Arabs. This was at the heart of the concept of "two states for two peoples." It turned a set of demographic and national arrangement into binding legal commitments between two neighboring countries.

The Americans were considering either another attempt to address the entire package, which was perceived as too ambitious, or taking the risk of a focused effort on the issue of Jerusalem, which if it failed would leave us with nothing. We offered two alternatives in planning the meeting in New York, suggesting that Clinton agree with Barak and Arafat on six to eight key phrases for the continuation of negotiations or alternately, that the president, Barak and Arafat develop "guidelines for negotiations," based on the work of the American team, which would be presented to both sides. We offered the Americans an opportunity to coordinate with us the texts of the president, with a commitment, that if the Palestinians were to accept them, Israel, on its part would also agree.

In preparation for this round of discussions, we tackled issues that had not yet been addressed thoroughly, including the Jewish settlement in Hebron, Palestinian enclaves in Israel and Israeli enclaves in Palestine.

"The Israelis and Palestinians are working on two different timetables," noted Shahak. "Arafat will not 'close' until he feels he has completely exhausted all the time available. His political longevity is unfortunately much shorter. It is preferable that you meet with him as early as possible. The Palestinians do not understand you," he turned to Barak "not even after Camp David. Your personal relationship is very important to the success of the process." Fearing that Erekat and Dahlan may have not even reported our last series of talks to Arafat, I agreed a dialogue between Arafat and Barak was essential.

Although Barak believed that good relations could help, he did not think that this would be the determining factor in whether an agreement was finally concluded. "After thirty years, Arafat needs to make a decision. It is not a coincidence that the two 'Abus' [Abu Mazen and Abu Ala] are not by his side at this time. They do not want to be responsible for concessions or compromises. The most difficult steps are ahead, we have to be careful and completely even-handed in terms of allocating any type of sovereignty on the Temple Mount. We could possibly reach a full agreement without finalizing the issue of Temple Mount."

The next morning I spoke to Erekat in this spirit. "In my opinion, you have not internalized either the real timetable for the negotiations or our political constraints. We are at the final stages of the negotiations, and you are not there. You haven't even started the endgame. There are issues we will not be able to negotiate because they deal with our fundamental positions, the real core of our existence. Until you understand this, we cannot move forward."

It seemed the Abu Ala–Abu Mazen axis was strengthening, while Abu Mazen and Arafat were disconnected from each other. Everyone attacked Erekat for supposedly giving in to his tendency to go into the details before the principles were agreed.

The center of political gravity shifted to the "Millennium Conference" at the United Nations headquarters in New York. Our hope was that Arafat's speech would be in the spirit of his Stockholm speech of October 1998, in which he presented his logic for peace, including important phrases regarding a vision of peaceful co-existence of two states for two peoples, in good neighborly relations, and paying special attention to the issue of security. I urged Barak to give a speech geared toward peace, presenting to the entire world the clear and lucid political agenda of his government. We discussed possible components of the speech including Jerusalem, refugees, borders, security; a call for an historical compromise by both leaderships; the vision and logic of peace; the moment of truth for Zionism and the Palestinian movement together; the Rabin legacy.

Despite recognizing the critical stage of the negotiations, and the rare opportunity in an international political forum, Barak delivered what many considered a disappointing speech:

> Jerusalem, the eternal capital of Israel, now calls for a peace of honor, of courage and of brotherhood . . . Jerusalem will remain united and open to all who love her . . . the opportunity for peace in the Middle East is now at hand . . . May we muster the inspiration and the fortitude to bequeath to our children a better world, a brighter future, a more secure life. It is in our hands.

The Prime Minister's Office prepared equally for the possibility of a breakthrough in New York and for the possibility of failure. If the first, more optimistic, scenario was realized, the peace administration unit would be responsible for planning the transition period between the framework agreement and the comprehensive agreement, preparing certain components of the agreement, and supporting the negotiations for a CAPS.

The "peace administration" was asked to prepare a comprehensive action plan for the implementation of Interim Agreements. The National Security Council, headed by Major-General Uzi Dayan, was instructed by the prime minister to prepare a joint action plan with the Palestinians for "the day after." Professor Matti Steinberg, special adviser to the head of the Shin Bet, was asked to map the power structure within Palestinian society, and to propose a plan for "marketing" the agreement – if signed – to the Palestinian public.

The international arena was the responsibility of the Ministry of Foreign Affairs and the political adviser. We had to prepare for a comprehensive public relations campaign in Europe, and to mobilize the international donor community in aiding the implementation of an agreement. It was also necessary to coordinate the relevant aspects of the agreement with Jordan. With regard to the remaining Arab countries, we were hoping to enlist the support of the moderates, including Saudi Arabia, and the North African and Gulf territories, and to consolidate a plan to prevent hostile states, such as Syria, Iran and Iraq, from sabotaging the process.

While we appeared to be nearing some path toward resolution, we did not disregard the possibility that the negotiations could fail. Staff at ministries and at the peace administration prepared for this scenario as well. They were asked to examine alternatives, such as a transitional agreement, bridging agreement, unilateral declaration or unilateral disengagement.

It was an ambitious work plan that required massive preparations. The prime minister considered nominating a senior minister in the Prime Minister's Office to oversee the staff work. We also discussed creating a special team dedicated to Jerusalem in the Prime Minister's Office headed by Haim Ramon, the minister for Jerusalem affairs. The team would include a former city engineer, a person of faith, a security expert and an international jurist.

We received information indicating that as the incubation period for the different initiatives on Jerusalem and the Temple Mount grew longer, Arafat grew cognizant of the fact that he would not be able to get full sovereignty on the Temple Mount. But Arafat did not want to make the decision on his own, and searched for support in the Arab world. It was in this context that Clinton again suggested that sovereignty of Al-Haram Al-Sharif would be transferred to the UN Security Council. It appeared to everyone that if a Jerusalem formula were found, the rest of the issues would be resolved. But Barak was in doubt, as were Shahak, Uzi Dayan and I.

Barak and Arafat did not meet formally in New York, although they bumped into each other accidentally, near the elevators, while the delegations were scrambling around the halls of the UN building.

On the evening of September 10, right before Barak was to return to Israel from the Millennium Assembly, he was visited at his hotel by President Clinton, Sandy Berger and Madeleine Albright. The unofficial and unplanned visit followed an outrageous interview by Arafat on CNN. It was an angry interview, in which Arafat told the interviewer, Christiane Amanpour, "You have to remember who you are speaking to. You are speaking to Yasser Arafat ... you forget everything." He then disconnected the microphone and left the studio in the middle of the interview.

This was not the only time Arafat would act in this manner during the visit. He rejected all the American compromises, returning to one position – full Palestinian sovereignty over East Jerusalem and Al-Haram Al-Sharif. The "flexibilities" he presented to Secretary Albright amounted to establishing an Islamic committee sovereignty over the Temple Mount, through a Jerusalem committee headed by Morocco, which would grant the right to worship to all religions, including Jews.

"How can you raise the idea that Israel will give up sovereignty over the site where the Great Temple stood?" Albright asked.

"A lot happens in history, this still does not mean sovereignty. Can Italy demand sovereignty over Gaza because of archeological remains from Roman times?" Arafat replied. When Albright used the term Temple Mount, Arafat responded, "when you meet with me, it is not the Temple Mount, it is Al Aqsa." He got up, furious, and walked out of the room.

Under these circumstances there was no point anymore in talking about a meeting between Barak and Arafat in New York.

"I don't know if Arafat has decided to reach an agreement," Dennis Ross began his meeting with Ben-Ami and me on the morning of September 12 at the Park Lane Hotel. "The president, in any case, is interested in presenting the best package." Ross said the president was very determined in speaking to the Palestinians, who in turn urged him to initiate progress in the drafting process. "There is no point to this, as long as no real progress has been made on the question of Haram and refugees," Clinton told them. "Israel will not be able to change its demographics or its national character."

Ross detailed the American understanding of Palestinian positions. On territory, they would be willing to agree to an annexation of seven percent of the West Bank in return for two percent in land swaps near the Gaza

Strip. On security, the Palestinians would agree to three early-warning stations. The Israeli Air Force could use Palestinian airspace as long as "heavy" guarantees were provided that Israel would not make use of Palestinian airspace to attack other Arab countries. In Ross's opinion, the Palestinians accepted the Israeli position on the need to seize territory in an emergency situation within the Palestinian state, but they wanted to limit this in terms of size and duration. As for demilitarization of the Palestinian state, the Palestinians asked for a "state of limited arms" (as opposed to the term *demilitarized*). They would not be willing to accept IDF presence in the Jordan Valley or along the River. For deterrence and supervising the fulfillment of obligations they requested the forces of a third party.

Ross continued with the question of refugees. He said the Palestinians "could live" without the Right of Return to Israel, as long as refugees from Lebanon would be given preference in returning to Israel within a framework of family unification or humanitarian considerations. They would agree to criteria that would limit the number of Palestinians allowed to return to Israel. They demanded, however, that the theoretical option to return should exist – for their public.

As for Jerusalem, the Palestinians demanded sovereignty over the Arab neighborhoods, "internal" and "external," but would agree to certain limitations of this sovereignty in the internal neighborhoods – those that were part of the Jordanian Al-Quds before 1967. In the Old City they saw themselves as sovereign over two and a half Quarters, but they understood that above or below this sovereignty there would be a special regime. The Palestinians also understood, according to Ross, the importance of the Mount of Olives and the City of David to Israel.

In turn, I presented Israel's comments on the Palestinian position. First, we needed an area that would accommodate eighty percent of the settlers. As for security, we demanded that demilitarization and a commitment to preserve it be mentioned explicitly in the agreement. On security, I responded specifically to the issue of airspace. We would fly above the Palestinian state under the same conditions and with the same constraints to military flights above Israel. As for Jerusalem, an option to be considered was that neither side received sovereignty over the Temple Mount, but rather that sovereignty be transferred to the Security Council, which would in turn appoint an international body with the authority, mandate and conditions defined in the agreement. Each side would have powers and obligations. Excavation would be strictly prohibited.

The next day Ben-Ami, Ambassador Ivri and I heard additional details about the meetings between President Clinton and Arafat from national security adviser Berger. "I have never seen more embarrassing meetings than the ones the president had with Arafat at Camp David," he said. There were however positive steps since the summit. World opinion had changed, favoring Israel. Other Arab nations may not help, but they would not interfere in reaching an agreement.

"The only alternative is that an American document be presented. We do not know who is authorized to negotiate on behalf of Arafat, and there is a huge difference between what we hear about their impressions of Camp David and what we know actually happened," Ben-Ami said.

"We intend to recalibrate Camp David," Berger said. "In the next ten days we will try to prepare what we consider a 'package.' As far as we are concerned it will be very rigid and not open to negotiations."

I returned to New York from Washington for a short meeting with Dahlan and Erekat. Saeb, as usual, was smoking a cigar, in his non-smoking room. He was asked, with the proper American assertiveness, to move to another floor, or stop smoking. Well aware of how high-end hotels operated, he moved to another floor. "Abu Mazen supports our positions one hundred percent," they said. "Abu Ala will take part either on Arafat's side trying to convince him, or in the negotiation itself. The rest of the Palestinian leadership, and Arafat himself, decided they want an agreement – and this is why we are here. Arafat asks for intensive work, in the US, Egypt, or in the region."

In the evening, Ben-Ami and I met with Albright and Ross for dinner. We had no illusions about the way forward. Everything depended on Arafat. If he wished, there would be an agreement, and if he refused, who knew where this would lead.

Although the following day was September 13, the deadline for a Palestinian UDI, the day passed uneventfully. Ben-Ami and I met with the American team, headed by Ross. Ross brought updated positions from the Palestinians. They asked that we reduce the size of the annexed settlement blocs, so their country would not be "carved into." They also asked to discuss refugees the following week. In the meantime the UN Secretary-General Kofi Annan and his representative in the Middle East Terje Larsen were brought into the picture. Although we disagreed, the Americans believing that Arafat was under enormous pressure, we both shared the view that we should not approach him too soon with a package that was not yet watertight.

Upon our return to Israel, we were on the brink of what appeared to be the two most important weeks in the peace process. During this period it would finally become clear whether or not Arafat was going to finally move toward agreement. The prime minister feared that the American package would be introduced, but would not be coordinated with us or would be timed in a way that would prevent us from affecting it. We needed to organize our work in order to support all aspects of the negotiations, to move forward with integrative drafting, to process the essence and substance that hid behind the general title "special regime" relating to the Old City, to check the legal implications of Palestinian inhabitance in the settlement blocs, and to define the necessary changes within the PLO when an agreement would be signed. Hebron had yet to be addressed. Work was in full swing but time was short.

Negotiations resumed with Erekat and Dahlan repeating their usual arguments. Dahlan called on us to work together to move from hate and hostility toward friendship. "We silenced the groups that oppose the agreement, including the Hamas, with which I started a dialogue," Dahlan told Hasson and me. "But you want to reorganize your control over us, according to your old approach of occupation. We understand that we cannot be a state with military capabilities. But you can achieve the same results without using the word 'demilitarized.' Do not worry, we will protect the settlers ourselves as long as they are in our territory or until they are evacuated."

"Hostility exists on both sides," I replied to Dahlan, "the conflict between us is multidimensional. It is not just a border conflict like we had with Egypt. We need to create a new reality. Both sides have serious fears about this reality. We do not have hidden goals of perpetuating the occupation. But we know that we are not welcome in this region. We must uphold our right to self-defense and general security. On drafting the understandings and agreement," I emphasized, "there are far fewer gaps than it appears."

Erekat did not give up trying to accumulate points on marginal issues in the hope that this would eventually constitute a critical mass for the Palestinians. Thus, for example, he continued to argue against the limitations on military alliances for the Palestinian state. "My dilemma, as a Palestinian Arab," he said, "is how not be thrown out of the Arab League, and at the same time sign a peace agreement with you. I cannot be your ally, but I will not join those who attack you."

Dahlan emphasized that his presence at the talks was conditional on the acceptance of his objections to the Israeli demands on the issue of airspace and the Jordan Valley.

We agreed that during the week to come, we must make progress with a draft that included agreed points as well as issues on which the sides still disagreed. The American proposal should, in time, focus on the differences that remained at the end of this stage.

Erekat reported that in his conversations with the Americans it appeared that they would conclude their proposal for a package within the next few days, and would present it to the political leaderships within two to three weeks. Another round of negotiations may be necessary, in the context of which the ideas of the "package" would be presented to the negotiation teams. He suggested that both sides engage in an intensive negotiations round in the United States, but had reservations regarding Ben-Ami coming along, probably fearing that reciprocally he would have to include Abu Ala.

The second half of the meeting was dedicated to the issue of security. Dahlan presented his very thorough and organized comments. His approach, he claimed, was based on a transition from the logic of conflict to the logic of a partnership of interests and cooperation. "To my disappointment, the positions that you have presented – continued presence of Israeli forces in Palestinian areas, control and use of Palestinian airspace – embody continued control of Palestinians and 'interim period' thinking." He emphasized the Palestinian strategic commitment to combating terrorism, as reflected by the unequivocal efforts of the PA institutions to combat the Hamas. He did understand that to satisfy Israel's security concerns, Palestine would have to serve as a buffer between Israel and threats from the East. The Palestinians would agree to a temporary and limited presence of international forces in the Jordan Valley that could therefore move into Palestinian territory parallel to a gradual withdrawal of Israeli forces. The Palestinian forces would serve as a guarantee for Palestinian national security and would supervise the implementation of agreements. The Palestinians agreed that the international force would report directly to Israel. Dahlan demanded that we agree on the status and number of Israeli soldiers present in two early-warning sites, which the Palestinians agreed to – two as opposed to the three that we had asked for and that they had ultimately agreed to, they were now reneging again. In light of the above, concluded Dahlan, he did not understand the demand to place 400 Israeli soldiers in military facilities on Palestinian land.

"We accepted your demand that Palestine will not have military capacity to attack Israel or ally itself with other countries that wish to do so," Dahlan continued. But in addition to the land and maritime components, to which Israel agreed, Palestine needed aerial capabilities for combating terrorism, transporting the chairman and other transportation activities. The Palestinians wanted an air force without combat planes and would agree not to import or produce weapons prohibited for use by the Palestinian forces. Except for the Palestinian police force, the Palestinian state would not allow people to carry weapons; this included the Israeli settlers. Dahlan demanded Palestinian sovereignty over the airspace and electromagnetic spectrum. Under this definition, experts from both sides should be allowed to mull over the details for coordination and cooperation, but the Palestinians opposed the use of their airspace by the Israeli Air Force.

In hindsight, there is some irony to these discussions (in which Dahlan vigorously argued about the definition of demilitarization and the proper name of the Palestinian police force) taking place just two weeks before the Al Aqsa Intifada erupted. Palestinian police joined the violent hostilities and used their weapons against Israelis. It was neither law enforcement nor public order they were concerned with, rather sustaining the Palestinian terrorist uprising much like a national militia.

We were not that naive. Even during the argument we knew violence could erupt at any time, effectively putting an end to all our efforts. Nevertheless, we were convinced that our mutual duty requested exhausting all the efforts to negotiate.

It was clear that the perception and interpretation of security arrangements were as important to the Palestinians as the actual substance. They therefore examined every possibility of "stretching" the period during which Israeli military forces would gradually withdraw to military sites, and Israeli Air Force free access to Palestinian airspace would be maintained. They also looked into the options of creating the foundation for regional arrangements. In this way, the Palestinians could present the Israeli withdrawal as an achievement, while we could present the fact that it was gradual. During this period an effort would be made to promote regional security arrangements, primarily with Jordan. In addition, we could request that the presence of international forces be substantially extended to twenty-five years, with an option for another extension, and the creation of meticulous supervision and verification arrangements. We could address the Palestinian concern that their airspace would not be used to attack other Arab countries, and show generosity insofar as Palestine would be the only Arab country with access to a corridor in Israel's airspace, between the West Bank and Gaza. With regard to the Jordan Valley, it was clear at this stage that Israeli presence in the Jordan Valley would not contradict Palestinian sovereignty or Palestinian plans to develop the area, and that the areas of deployment in the Valley would be under Palestinian sovereignty. Use of these areas would be limited to emergency situations.

On the core issues of security, however, including the Jordan Valley, use of Palestinian airspace by the Israeli Air Force, and emergency deployment, there were formal gaps that could not be ignored. The Palestinians continued to try to erode the Israeli positions, not realizing, or rather refusing to accept, the fact that maintaining our military capabilities was an integral part of the end-of-conflict package, an indispensable component in Israel's strategic approach aimed at preserving the region's stability.

15

WALLS OF
MISUNDERSTANDING

The prime minister had to make decisions on issues that were nearing the point of resolution in the negotiations:

- Settlement blocs – the current approach to settlement blocs, which will result in the annexation of thousands of Palestinians under Israeli sovereignty and the special status of permanent resident, has far-reaching long-term internal and legal implications.
- Presence of an international force in the Jordan Valley – there are substantial doubts outside the security establishment regarding the necessity of "designated areas" and the need to make use of them in an emergency situation. A discussion regarding the presence of an international force is proposed as an alternative to the long-term presence of our forces in the Valley and the "designated areas".
- The use of Palestinian airspace for use of the Israeli Air Force – this is an uncompromising demand by Israel, which includes some symbolic aspects that are difficult for the Palestinians. It is suggested that we discuss the substance of the request and the manner in which it will be included in the agreement.
- Hebron and the Jewish settlement – slight border corrections north of the Gaza Strip.
- Territory – does our position require control of fifteen percent of the Jordan River permanently? Does this request extend to the northwestern bank of the Dead Sea? What are the reasons for the one-to-seven ratio in the final division of the "gray" territories?
- Jerusalem and the regime around the holy sites – should we appoint a commissioner? Do we create a committee to manage the holy sites? What are the rules of the special regime in the Old City? What is the meaning of the concept "open city"?

We addressed all these issues in coordination with the "peace administration," the Israeli National Security Council, the IDF and others.

I asked the prime minister to urgently convene a discussion on the strategy for negotiations and its mechanisms:

- Examining the substance of our positions; the framework for continued negotiations (explosion/dead end/intensive negotiations with the leaders/Americans/meeting between the prime minister and Arafat . . .).
- Consolidating a position in relation to an American package (rejection/advancing/conditions); participation of American representatives as observers in the discussion; continued negotiations in the United States (time, composition, structure, etc.).
- Internal division of labor to update Egypt, Jordan, Americans and Europeans.

At this stage the staff work was accelerated in parallel to the negotiations. We needed to complete work on the following issues:

- Bringing in line the work of the negotiations team on the "core" issues with the working groups dealing with economics, water, legal affairs and other civil spheres.
- Preparing an array of spokespersons and briefings in advance of another summit (based on our lessons from Camp David).
- Putting in place/resuming a program to deal with public opinion in general, as well as specific sectors (settlers, Shas, ultra orthodox, Israeli-Arabs, Russian immigrants).
- Completing staff work for preparing the American aid package, and preparing the bilateral understandings necessary between Israel and the US.
- Consolidating an action plan for the Jewish communities.
- Coordinating interfaces, Israeli and international guarantees with the Jordanians.

Seeing no progress on the Palestinian side, Barak announced that he had instructed the team to stop the talks for a while. Erekat, who never lacked a sense of drama, accused Barak of "abandoning the peace process," and denounced the decision. The Prime Minister's Office tried to wriggle out of it: since there were no negotiations, they said, there was nothing to stop.

I was asked to respond. "Since Camp David," I said, "we have had thirty meetings. Unfortunately, we have not identified any substantial movement on the Palestinian side on the core issues, not even a symbolic response to the American proposals that were raised during the negotiations. Sometimes, there are situations in which we, like other sides, are asked to make an assessment, and we have taken a time-out for that purpose."

Ben-Ami, who was in Paris at the time, told President Chirac, "It is just a technical–methodological break . . . there are enough dramas in the conflict itself, there is no need to create artificial ones."

I met with Erekat on September 20, 2000, a day after our planned meeting was canceled. "We have requested a time-out to assess the situation internally. This is natural and normal, and in your reaction, you have caused it to appear as if we suspended discussions. You have blown the situation out of proportion," I told him. "The prime minister intends to continue to work toward understandings that will lead to peace. We cannot, however – neither you nor us – avoid making difficult historic decisions. Thus far, we have not seen any significant movement from the chairman in this direction. Rather, we have seen repeated requests for external intervention that would force the conditions of the agreement on us. The next time one of the sides cancels or reschedules a meeting, it would be better not to use extreme words in the press. It fosters an artificial crisis and erects walls of misunderstanding. And now, let us be practical and continue with the drafting."

Most of the discussion was dedicated to reviewing the characteristics of the special regime in the "Holy Basin" of Jerusalem, especially in the Old City. "The working assumption is that the area in question is so small and limited that its physical separation becomes ridiculous and impossible," I said. "We can declare that one Quarter, the Jewish one, is under our sovereignty, and one Quarter, the Muslim one, under your sovereignty – but the entire Old City would be under the 'umbrella' of a special regime. The characteristics of such a regime would include preservation through special planning and construction laws, special identification for residents, defining the holy sites as world heritage sites, and an unarmed special police force that would focus on tourism and securing freedom of worship. All these and the status itself are supposed to protect us from the madness of extremists and ensure stable political control in areas that are prone to violence, and which constitute religious symbols for billions of believers around the world."

For the first time ever, Saeb was willing to put these principles on paper. He told me that he asked Danny Abrams to organize a one-on-one meeting between Barak and Arafat, and suggested that he and I prepare it. "It cannot fail," he said. Danny Abrams, an American-Jewish billionaire, was one of the largest contributors to the Democratic Party, in general, and to Bill Clinton, in particular. He was also willing to use his money and time to support the peace process. More than once, before and after the beginning of the Al Aqsa Intifada, he assumed the responsibility trying to form a bridge between the leaders. At different stages of the negotiations he even proposed drafts of his own to the agreement.

We continued to discuss in detail the disagreements on security. I reported to Barak that no Palestinian movement was visible toward the Camp David conclusions on this issue.

The following day Dahlan, Hasson and I had another detailed discussion on the principles of territory and security. "I understand that you want 650 square kilometers for 'your needs,' supposedly, and you say this is 10.5 percent of the land. What would you say if I prove to you that all your needs do not exceed three percent?" Dahlan said defiantly.

"I'll prove to you, along the same line of reasoning, that as a Palestinian state you have no need for sovereignty on Temple Mount," I responded. "But beyond demagoguery, you already know that the requested annexation is not meant to address only the settlement needs, but Israel's strategic interests in the long term."

"I completely reject this exaggerated demand. But for the sake of discussion, show me how many Palestinian villages would be included in these blocs, how many Palestinian roads and paths, and everything on a map that we can discuss," Dahlan replied.

Such a map was already in our hands. It was prepared for the purpose of discussions at Camp David. The Israeli team tried to minimize the number of Palestinians – inhabitants and villages – that would be included in the annexed blocs. Because we were frustrated by lack of Palestinian willingness to bring their own proposals, reasonable maps and initiatives to the table, we were not thrilled about returning to the usual format of an Israeli offer, a Palestinian rejection, and so on. It was true that lately the Palestinians had revealed some openness in this channel of discussion, and even a willingness to discuss an innovative outline for the negotiations – from details to the principles. But on the disputed issues, they did not move forward at all.

Our time-out shook up the Palestinian system just a bit and caused Arafat to somewhat reconsider his delaying tactics. It did not, however, have an impact on the negotiations. The possibility that an agreement would not be reached, and that the incredible, extensive effort would not only end with nothing, but would also possibly end with violence and deterioration in the region was again raised in the internal Israeli discussions. Even the American "package" was not expected to benefit Israel. Ben-Ami noted that the dialogue at the staff level – as differentiated from the leaders – was causing erosion in Israeli positions. "As long as there is no tête-à-tête between Barak and Arafat, the process cannot end. Each additional person that is introduced to this circle, like Abu Mazen, just makes us pay somehow or somewhere else," Ben-Ami argued. He believed that the American document would be preferable to anything achieved through direct negotiations.

I disagreed. "We will not benefit from an American document. We are negotiating with the Americans, at the expense of our own positions. This is a process that has gone on since Camp David." On one issue we were in complete agreement. The "two-on-two" channel had been completely exhausted. To reach an agreement we had to arrange meetings between Barak and Arafat. This would undermine Arafat's usual negotiations tactic and would clarify whether he was moving toward an agreement through brinkmanship or, as we tended to assess, toward conflict. "Arafat pretends he wants an agreement," we told Barak, "but in order to find this out you need to speak with him directly." Amnon Shahak emphasized that the last months, since Camp David, had damaged the thin layer of trust between the sides. "Meet, speak about what you want – anything in the world – but you have to meet," he urged Barak.

"I should meet with him," Barak concluded, "even before receiving any document from the Americans. But at the same time, he needs to hear from the international community that the offers he is receiving improve his condition. And he needs to understand we have reached our limits in the negotiations."

Against our recommendation, Barak decided that the two-on-two channel of dialogue would continue, even if we were treading water, just as long as Israel was not accused of stopping the negotiations. Ben-Ami was sent to update Mubarak.

Erekat and I met again, this time with the Egyptian ambassador. The Egyptians started to promote the idea of a joint DOP – not an agreement – with a few lines on each issue. Thus, for example, Bassiouni offered – although not of his own accord – that the principle of "annexation of maximum Israelis and no annexation of Palestinian inhabitants" appear instead of the percentage of the total territory annexed.

Also on that day Ambassador Martin Indyk was suspended from his position because he was suspected of using his laptop in violation of security regulations. We spoke briefly on the phone; I attempted to console him but he sounded depressed.

The poet Yehuda Amihai, a personal friend and a client of my law firm, passed away. He was the clear expression of Israel's secular aspiration for peace. Amihai was invited by Rabin and Peres to the Nobel Peace Prize ceremony in 1994. I could not attend his funeral, but later visited his wife, Hannah.

The White House believed that the best way to achieve progress was through negotiations between Ben-Ami and Beilin on one side, and Abu Mazen and Abu Ala, on the other, with Osama El Baz present. Concurrently, Erekat and I were supposed to continue our meetings. The American idea was to work on the basis of the Beilin–Abu Mazen Understandings, which would be fleshed out in the presence of the "founding fathers." This idea had no chance. Barak and Ben-Ami were not prepared to actually incorporate Beilin in the negotiations, concerned by his alleged tendency to go beyond his principal's guidelines. Abu Mazen refused anyhow to be publicly and personally identified with Beilin with regard to the Understandings.

The Americans thought that after completing a round of negotiations, keeping in mind our progress on mapping disagreements, we could decide how to move forward. Should we convene another summit? Should an American initiative to present a bridging document be launched? Finally, should we move to a less substantial alternative to a Permanent Status agreement, in the form of a DOP or guidelines?

The president's team assessed that the Palestinians could live with seven percent annexation of territory from the West Bank to Israel in exchange for land swaps totaling two percent of the territory of the West Bank, in addition to a safe passage from Gaza to the West Bank.

On security, Washington believed that the Palestinians would agree to their state being limited in terms of armament, but would not accept Israeli military presence in the Jordan Valley or its control of the River. They would agree to three early-warning sites. The timetable for withdrawal was eighteen to thirty-six months. They predicted that the Palestinians could agree that the Israeli Air Force would use Palestinian airspace, in return for guarantees that it would not attack Arab countries and with understandings regarding noise and flying levels under an agreement of civil aviation. They were under the impression that the Palestinians would accept the principle of emergency IDF deployment, but would want to limit the area and duration.

On refugees the Americans prepared a formula, according to which a limited number of refugees would return to Israel without using the words "implementation of the Right of Return of refugees to Israel." UNGAR 194, however, would be mentioned.

As for Jerusalem, the Americans believed that the Palestinians would not settle for anything less than sovereignty over the outer and inner neighborhoods, including access to the Shoafat refugee camp. They would be willing to accept arrangements in inner neighborhoods. In the Old City, the Palestinians would demand sovereignty over two and a half Quarters, with the rest under Israeli sovereignty, under a special regime in the Old City. They understood the significance of the City of David and Mount of Olives for Israel.

Our impression was that the Palestinians would undermine any progress in the bilateral negotiations in an effort to bring the Americans to present the "package" to both sides.

Erekat, Hasson and I met on September 24 to prepare for a meeting between the prime minister and Arafat and for the expected trip to the United States. Erekat said that Albright had requested that two teams come to the US – in secret – for three working days, beginning on the morning of Tuesday September 26. He proposed a meeting between Barak and Arafat in Ramallah or in Kohav Yair. The small working teams would leave for Washington right after the two leaders met.

We hoped that the meeting would help jump-start the negotiations and return them to a more positive track. The conditions for success were clear. We needed a clean slate, a joint vision for both the short and the long term, a limited number of key principles for continued negotiations, and a safety net in case of failure.

The most important part was supposed to take place in a "one-on-one" session. In the scenario we planned, Barak would start by saying: "We are stuck . . . we could miss an historic opportunity . . . Dahlan and Erekat and our team are doing great creative work, and want to reach an agreement ... but our leadership is necessary to consolidate the principles on the basis of which the negotiations will take place; the American package will be less beneficial for both sides; a solution which comes out of the region is preferable ... we are at the moment of truth ... we have a few days in which to work together; I want to reach an agreement with you that will lead to the end of conflict ... you are the only one who can ensure the future of the Palestinian people ... we have time ... we will organize the government or go to elections and come back ... we are committed to the peace process ..."

In the second part of the conversation, Barak was supposed to build a joint vision with Arafat. "... Our vision – a Palestinian state with Al-Quds as its capital, existing in economic and civil cooperation with all its neighbors; arrangements in Jerusalem, that would reflect its universality and its sanctity to the three religions; security arrangements that would ensure Israel and the Palestinian state's national securities; we must end the refugees' plight through physical rehabilitation, settling all claims in this regard, and ensuring equal personal status to all."

At this stage, we hoped, Barak would be able to achieve the necessary breakthrough. He had to agree with Arafat on the conditions for continued negotiations. The two leaders would agree on a few statements that would enable the negotiations team to enter a new round of discussions, in which the details would be fleshed out.

It was hoped that the Palestinian side would agree to the following statements. The framework agreement – under the assumption that sufficient guarantees for its implementation would be provided – would constitute the end of conflict; the 1967 lines would be changed in order to ensure sovereignty over eighty percent of the settlers in settlement blocs that would address mutual needs; a gradual withdrawal of Israeli forces from Palestinian territories, subject to the provision addressing Israel's security needs and deployment of the international force; the Right of Return of refugees would be implemented first and foremost in their homeland – the Palestinian state.

In return, we proposed that Israel clarify that the framework agreement would be based on UNSCRs 242 and 338, and would lead to their implementation; there would be sufficient guarantees to implement the agreement; to the extent possible, Palestinian cities, towns and villages would not be under Israeli sovereignty; Israel, on the basis of its sovereign considerations, would allow the return of an agreed number of refugees to its territory, within the framework of family reunification; implementation of the framework agreement would be recognized as implementation of United Nations General Assembly's Resolution (UNGAR) 194; finally, Israel would commit to creating a free-trade area that implemented a comprehensive program to develop water sources.

Barak and Arafat were supposed to agree that the arrangements in the "Holy Basin" would reflect both the universal importance of the site to Islam, Judaism and Christianity, and the opposing demands of Israel and Palestine for sovereignty and functionality.

Finally, they had to agree to a "safety net," in the case of failure. If the negotiations failed, Barak was supposed to say to Arafat, "we will find a way together to settle the issues of the creation of a Palestinian state and subsequent mutual recognition, to transfer the three villages near Jerusalem, and to implement the Third Further Redeployment as agreed in March (ten percent in two stages), to release more prisoners, and to continue with the negotiations."

Erekat suggested that Barak should appeal to Arafat's emotions, along the lines of "I don't know what went wrong on our side, but I ask that you realize that I respect you very much and am interested in reaching an agreement with you. We must find formulae that satisfy you and that do not leave Israel at a loss."

Initially planned for September 25 at Abu Mazen's home, the Barak–Arafat meeting, mediated by Danny Abrams, was moved to Barak's home in Kohav Yair. The feeling was festive. Abrams was very excited: "this is the first day of the end of the conflict," he said as he reached for a glass of water, "we have two to three weeks to realize the historic opportunity."

The entire Palestinian leadership was present, including Abu Mazen, Abu Ala, Nabil Abu Rudayna and Erekat. On the Israeli side Ben-Ami, Shahak, Hasson, Yatom and I were all there.

We were seated in the living room. Arafat opened with words of thanks. "We thank you from the depths of our hearts for the opportunity to be here. What is important is that we make peace for our children. I say to the people we are sending to the United States – do all you can, and *inshallah* we will succeed."

Our bags were in trunks of cars that waited outside to take us to the airport. We intended to leave for Washington early that morning. Dahlan would join us later.

"We are on the verge of reaching a formula on all the issues that will allow every Palestinian to receive what he deserves," Barak said. "To every Israeli we say – it is painful, it is difficult, but it is fair. We have all fought together, cumulatively, perhaps two hundred years. This is an effort that the future generations deserve."

Arafat knew that we were concerned about the "length of the rope" he gave his people to negotiate on his behalf. Without being asked he remarked, "my representatives have a full mandate. I hope they succeed together with your representatives. We are linked with each other, this is our destiny."

Hasson, who was not planning to fly to Washington, was surprised when

Barak said to Arafat that he was part of the team leaving that night for the United States. Being experienced with unexpected missions, he improvised quickly. A suitcase waited for him on time at the airport.

Nava Barak came in, welcoming those present, introducing herself to each person, and acquainting herself with those she had not met. Barak and Arafat went out into the garden arm-in-arm, alone, without the help of bothersome note-takers. They sat outside for about an hour, speaking in English. There was no remnant of the estrangement that had characterized their relationship during the second half of the Camp David summit. We did not know if anything of the scenario we had proposed actually took place.

Ben-Ami and I sat with Abu Ala; Shahak spoke with Abu Mazen. It was a relatively comfortable and pleasant atmosphere. At the end of the evening, Barak parted from Ben-Ami, Hasson and me. "You are off on an historic mission," he said, shaking our hands.

We left the meeting in Kohav Yair for another round of negotiations in Washington that included Ben-Ami, Hasson and me, on one side, and Erekat, Dahlan and Akram Haniyah on the other. My assistant Gidi Grinstein along with Raith Al Omari, a Jordanian jurist who aided Erekat, rounded off the teams. The feeling on both sides was that the meeting between Barak and Arafat could constitute a benchmark in the negotiations. Arafat described the meeting as "familial."

Both the Israelis and Palestinians stayed at the Ritz Carlton in Pentagon City, just south of Washington DC, in order to facilitate coordination and save time. This was the "hotel of choice" for many in the Palestinian leadership when they visited Washington. Erekat only ever writes with the hotel's blue pens – no matter where he is. It was always difficult for me to reconcile the national Palestinian struggle with its refugee camps and hardships, on the one hand, with the fancy suits, high living and luxurious cars on the other.

The first meeting was with the Americans. "We have not been able to bring Abu Mazen and Abu Ala into the negotiations," Dennis Ross began. "We concluded that we needed to bring our own package to the table, to promote progress."

I repeated the principles of the agreement, especially on the territorial issue: "Eighty percent of the settlers would be accommodated in settlement blocs annexed to Israel, as few as possible of these being Palestinian villages and towns. The borders agreed would be the permanent borders, and they would need to be reasonable and frictionless. Though not particularly fond of the issue of percentages, you have heard us proposing an Israeli percentage of 10.5 percent. However, from the Palestinians, the Arab world, and from you, the proposed percentage was nine percent. We must reach an agreement that will be possible for both sides."

"Will you be willing to consider a 'peace park' or leasing, somewhere along the border? And on the issue of security, would you agree that they not be completely demilitarized? That is, you would not forbid them from joining a coalition, like in the Gulf War?" Ross asked.

"You are confusing two issues," I replied. "There must be demilitarization. Prohibiting military alliances or having an army outside of their country – that is another issue."

Ben-Ami proposed a creative solution. "A limited number of refugees could be settled on Israeli land, within the Green Line, as part of the land swaps."

On the following day, September 27, we had another meeting with the shuttling American team. They described "a new feeling" in the mood and approach of the Palestinians. Dahlan and Erekat participated in part of the meeting and repeated that Arafat genuinely wanted an agreement.

The day was dedicated to a detailed review of all the issues and to pressing phone calls back to the region regarding Member of Knesset Sharon's planned visit on the Temple Mount. Ben-Ami, in his capacity as minister of internal security, and Hasson had spoken to Jibril Rajoub, who assessed that the event would not get out of hand if Sharon would not enter the mosques themselves. The visit was meticulously coordinated with senior officials of the Israeli police force. Barak did not consider canceling or preventing the visit. According to his legal advisers, headed by Attorney-General Rubinstein, there was no solid legal ground for a prime ministerial decision to prevent the visit, in the lack of a clear and imminent danger to public order. In Israel, Member of Knesset Rubi Rivlin continued with preparations for Sharon's visit. The organizers were unwilling to postpone the event, even if asked to do so by the police.

Questions were raised in our discussion about the Western Wall, the City of David, the national institutions of the two states and their location, demilitarization, and settlement blocs and their rationale. The issue of refugees was identified as the main problem at that stage, and it was on this issue that Ben-Ami and I urged the Americans to make their own value judgment. "We will not commit national and political suicide," Ben-Ami warned. "You must return to the Palestinians and tell them – you have a possible deal, which on many issues such as Jerusalem and the Jordan Valley, stretches Israeli positions very far."

The American team was supposed to meet with the president just one week later, with its final recommendations. It appeared that they would unequivocally recommend to the president that he present a "package" to the sides, and that he use his political influence to impose it on them.

Toward the end of the round, both sides could identify the outline of the developing American "package." Our impression was that the Americans would accept our position, that signing the framework agreement would constitute the end of conflict between the sides, and would bring about a finality of claims.

On the issue of territory, we thought the Americans intended to propose that Israel annex between seven to eight percent of the West Bank in return for transferring an area equal to two to three percent of the West Bank in the framework of a land swap, some in leasing agreements or under a joint regime (i.e. "peace park"). We mentioned Issawiya in the context of land swaps, since part of it was included in the Israeli enclave of Mount Scopus as part of the 1949 Armistice Lines (that is, it was under Israeli sovereignty even before 1967).

In relation to the settlement blocs, the Americans were going to adopt the criteria of accommodating eighty percent of the settlers in blocs. We presented the considerations guiding the outline of blocs, emphasizing permanent borders, security needs and areas of community development. Our impression was that they accepted these considerations, but that they did not agree with our demands in terms of percentages. They also made it clear that they would not support annexation of areas inhabited by thousands of Palestinians. They argued that they knew how to sketch a map that included eighty percent of the settlers in five percent of the territory, with only 4,000 Palestinians. According to their calculations in moving toward blocs constituting eight percent of the territory, the number of annexed Palestinians increased to 60,000, although we spoke of 45,000 Palestinians in 10.5 percent of the area. They also did not support our request for a corridor of Israeli sovereignty from Jerusalem going east.

The American approach on Jerusalem declined in clarity as we moved from the external neighborhoods to the neighborhoods inside the Old City. It was clear that the external neighborhoods would be completely transferred to Palestinian sovereignty. With regard to the inner neighborhoods our impression was that the Americans would support the creation of a special regime with limited Palestinian sovereignty. We assumed that their proposal would include territorial continuity and roads. Our impression was that they had yet to consolidate their offer in relation to the Old City and the Temple Mount. We thought they would support the division of sovereignty in the Old City on the basis of two Quarters for the Palestinians and two for Israel, or even worse, on the basis of "Jewish interests – to Israel, the rest to the Palestinians." They also examined the possibility that sovereignty would be realized only in a manner compatible with the rules of the special regime, with limited Palestinian sovereignty. We emphasized that Israel demanded sovereignty over the Jewish Quarter, the Western Wall, and places sacred to Judaism (Mount Zion, the City of David, the Tombs of the Kings, Mount of Olives), and that the special regime would not apply to the Western Wall and the rest of the "Holy Basin" under Israeli sovereignty.

Regarding the Temple Mount, the Americans had doubts about how to reconcile the area on which the mosques were built, the space underground and the Western Wall. We emphasized our demand for a complete balance in the regime that would apply to Al Haram and that which would also apply to the Western Wall, as well as to the space underneath. At that stage it did not appear that they were leaning toward presenting a package that explicitly included Israeli sovereignty over the Western Wall and the space underneath. In the formula "Israel will have sovereignty over the Western Wall and the structure that the Western Wall was part of," they tried to hint at Israeli sovereignty over the area underneath (meaning the remnants of the Second Temple that are deep underground). They were also going to propose an "advisory council," appointed by the UN secretary-general and empowered by the Security Council, which would monitor the arrangement.

On the issue of refugees, the developing American proposal mentioned the Right of Return using the formula "Right of Return to the homeland" together with details that included entry into Palestine and entry into Israel under specified criteria. We demanded that "Palestine" would be specifically mentioned after the word "homeland." Alternatively, we proposed considering the use of a unilateral Palestinian statement that expressed their belief in the existence of the Right of Return but acknowledged the impracticality of its implementation. With regard to entry into Israel proper, the Americans suggested an annual number that would be examined after fifteen years, according to criteria defined in the agreement. We emphasized that the number of those returning to Israel must be defined and final, that it was under Israel's sole discretion, and that Israel's financial contribution must be limited and final.

Before the Americans presented the "package" they wanted to ensure that either side would not reject it. But there were still substantial differences between the formal positions of the two sides on most issues. The guidelines for a solution had yet to be consolidated on the Temple Mount (a formula of sovereignty in the area, underneath, and the Western Wall), in the Old City (dividing sovereignty into Quarters), and on territorial division (percentages, Israeli eastbound corridor, Palestinian "islands" in Jerusalem, etc.).

The Americans wanted to ensure that by using bridging formulae, the "package" that would be presented would be "reliable" in Palestinian eyes and would be very close to the Israeli red lines. They pressured us to reveal our red lines and real areas of flexibility, claiming we needed to arm them with convincing arguments. This was the focus of the visit to Washington, as far as they were concerned.

Our assessment, after the meeting in Washington ended on September 28, was that the president would present the "package" to Barak and Arafat after Yom Kippur (October 9, 2000), at the latest. We thought that if one of the sides rejected the "package" the Americans would try a "soft" approach, of consolidating guidelines and principles for continued negotiations and relations between the sides, while postponing the Permanent Status agreement.

The consolidation of the American "package" and its expected presentation were supposed to move the negotiations close to the final stretch. It was clear that the components of the American offer, if presented by the president and accepted by the two sides, would be the basis for an agreement in the future.

Looking ahead, we suggested to the Americans that Clinton call Arafat for a meeting to discuss the end of conflict and the future of the Palestinian state as an ally of the United States.

We hoped to organize a meeting between Barak and Arafat right after the Jewish New Year, on October 2, to discuss either territory or security. Further to the results of the meeting, and depending on whether a breakthrough was evident in the direct negotiations, we could consider a week-long intensive negotiations round right before Yom Kippur. It appeared that the internal disagreements among the Palestinians had vanished. Dahlan and Erekat appeared as if they wanted and were willing to achieve an agreement, and they also indicated that Arafat and Abu Mazen held the same position. They preferred direct negotiations. They did not believe in the ability of the Americans to "connect the dots."

On Friday afternoon we left Washington seated in a cramped space in back of a small plane. The latest reports we received from Israel indicated that Sharon's visit to the Temple Mount did not spark unusual events. "Only" five Palestinians were injured from rubber-covered bullets. Sharon, with all the Likud faction Knesset members, and surrounded by dozens of policemen and security officers, stuck to the plan that was agreed upon with the Palestinians. There were thousands of Palestinian protestors on the Temple Mount screaming "Sharon the murderer," "with blood and fire we will liberate Jerusalem." Even so, the visit ended with relatively few injuries, and no fatalities.

Twenty-two Arab countries condemned the visit as an "attempt to harm the holy places of Islam." All members of the Meretz and the Labor parties emphasized that every Israeli citizen had the right to go to the Temple Mount, while criticizing the provocative nature and the timing of Sharon's visit.

Ben-Ami was focused on nominating the new inspector-general of the Israeli police force. He was supposed to announce his decision the next morning in Israel and was preparing his speech for the event. Our minds were focused on the next stage of negotiations. The decisive moment was nearing.

The reality into which we landed was completely different.

The Israeli media could not have foreseen the implications of Ariel Sharon's visit to the Temple Mount, and almost completely disregarded the visit just days before. The intelligence services of both the Shin Bet and the IDF failed to predict the severe implications of the event. The visit received very little press coverage, commentaries and analysis. Instead it was reported rather laconically as a regular news item, buried in the back pages of the newspaper. Of the big newspapers, only *Yediot Ahronot* dedicated a whole page to the visit in the Friday paper.

The Al Aqsa Intifada had erupted and would change the face of the region.

16

HEAD OF A GANG,
NOT A LEADER

Years from now, historians will wonder whether Sharon's visit to the Temple Mount served as an excuse for Arafat to order the outbreak of violence in the Territories – which he had devised and planned in advance – or whether the visit led to a spontaneous uncontrollable eruption of violence that Arafat had no choice but to support.

Another question, equally important, involved Ariel Sharon's motives for the visit. There were journalists who argued that Sharon was disappointed by the decision of the attorney-general not to put Benjamin Netanyahu on trial for the "presents" scandal. This would allow Netanyahu to run for office in the upcoming elections, if they were to take place in the next few months.

Others claimed that Sharon's visit was much more than an internal political maneuver. They argued that Sharon planned to destroy Barak's achievements in the international arena and to torpedo the political negotiations, especially because of the issue of Jerusalem.

Ben-Ami himself, who had just appointed Shlomo Aharonishki to the position of police inspector-general, did not anticipate these developments. Ben-Ami, brilliant and compassionate, was overburdened by his commitments as acting minister of foreign affairs, minister of internal security and as a senior negotiator. He consequently failed to predict the miserable chain of events that led to the escalation. With closer monitoring by the police command, it might have been avoidable.

The sight of Israeli policemen, shooting into the Al Aqsa Mosque – shooting that was totally unnecessary given the circumstances – infuriated a billion Muslims around the world.

In protests that took place the morning after Sharon's visit, five Palestinians were killed and dozens were wounded. About sixty people from the police force and border patrol were wounded. The Territories were set ablaze. Joint Palestinian–Israeli patrols ceased after an Israeli border policeman was murdered by his Palestinian crew partner.

Within ten days, the popular outbreak deteriorated into an organized and murderous armed conflict. Starting with ambushes using light weapons, the Palestinians progressed to mortar shells, explosives, booby-trapped cars and suicide bombers. Marwan Barghouti, who became a central figure in initiating the riots, argued that if the Israeli security forces had not shot at the Temple Mount, the violent riots would have subsided after a few days. As it was, the diabolical and poisonous incitement in the mass media and the public sermons of the muezzins extended beyond the borders of the PA, becoming the bread and butter of broadcasts in Arab news stations in the Middle East and the Persian Gulf.

Measured and balanced as the IDF's response was, it photographed badly. Against the backdrop of a difficult, complex reality, these images determined the fate of Israel in the media. The heart-wrenching pictures depicting the tragic death of the child Mohammed Al Durrah in the arms of his father, as he was caught in the crossfire in Gaza, were broadcast on every news channel in the world. To this day, he is identified as the symbol of the Al Aqsa Intifada.

IDF Chief of Staff Mofaz, Dichter (Shin Bet), Yatom and Central Commander Major-General Eitan met with the West Bank and Gaza security chiefs, Rajoub and Dahlan respectively, in order to bring about calm – to no avail. Barak spoke to Arafat on Saturday evening, September 30, and was promised the riots would be calmed. But the situation actually got worse.

Joseph's Tomb in Nablus – one of Israel's weakest military points in the heart of the Palestinian population – was under siege. The soldier Madhat Yusuf was injured and died of his wounds. His body was later evacuated only thanks to the personal involvement of Jibril Rajoub. Most alarming was the spillover of the riots to the Israeli-Arab population. "Death to the Jews" calls were reverberating in the Arab villages of the Galilee. Violent demonstrations spread out to Arab capitals across the Middle East.

The instant violent outburst of the Israeli-Arab population brought back into focus the forgotten two-sided equation to the confrontation in the region. No longer "Israelis" and "Palestinians," but "Jews" against "Arabs." Thirteen Arab citizens of Israel were killed in riots and confrontations with the police. Jewish citizens were beaten, public property was vandalized, and structures and installations were destroyed. My friend Rami, a symbol of tolerance and co-existence, was nearly beaten to death on the way home in the Upper Galilee, and was evacuated to an emergency room by an Arab resident of the area. Israel was in flames.

At the end of the Jewish New Year, on October 1, after two days of violence, Barak convened a meeting to assess the situation. Everyone at the discussion suggested to Barak that he meet with Arafat before American or other international involvement was forced on us. Ginossar arranged a meeting between the two leaders, but Barak never went ahead with it. In the meantime, Arafat grabbed on to the American initiative to restore calm. With Albright and the UN secretary-general in Paris, it was proposed that Barak and Arafat meet there. "If we have Paris – we do not need Gaza or Ramallah," Arafat stated.

Bloody battles continued at Joseph's Tomb on the following day, October 2. Military helicopters shot into the Netzarim Junction in the Gaza Strip. Israeli visitors to the nearby settlement had to be evacuated by helicopters. An Israeli soldier and a civilian were killed in the Territories, seven soldiers were wounded and ten Palestinian protesters were killed. Five Israeli-Arabs in Um El Fahm and Nazareth were killed by the police. Among them was seventeen-year-old Asil Asallah, from the village of Arabe, a remarkable and charismatic activist in the "Seeds of Peace" movement, an organization dedicated to Arab–Israeli peace, co-existence and tolerance. Asil was shot at close range in his neck, without having taken part in the protests.

A small delegation that included Barak, Shahak, Ben-Ami, the Deputy Chief of Staff Moshe "Boogie" Ya'alon, Yatom, Ginossar and me, left for Paris. On that same day, Palestinians fired on the southern neighborhood of Gilo in Jerusalem for the first time. The IDF responded by positioning tanks near to the Mar Elias Monastery at the outskirts of Jerusalem, overlooking Beit Lehem and Beit Jallah, where the Palestinian fire came from.

Whether he had actively planned the riots or not, Arafat benefited from them as his position in public opinion worldwide had improved. He showed that he was unwilling to compromise on Jerusalem, and he strengthened the Palestinian claim, in the name of all Muslims, for sovereignty over the Temple Mount. The French president greeted him with open arms.

Meeting at the residence of the American ambassador in Paris, near the Elysee Palace, the Israeli delegation found itself under attack with allegations of physical military abuse. Upon further investigation, it turned out that in each one of the alleged incidents there was a malicious distortion of the truth, in some cases going as far as blaming the IDF for something the Palestinians did themselves. This did not prevent the Palestinians – particularly Nabil Sha'ath – from disseminating stories of Israeli "war crimes."

"The meetings here are critical," Albright urged. "We must find a way to end this dance of violence, to restore calm, and to return to a mindset of peacemaking with an agreed mechanism. The goal is an announcement by the end of the day."

The first meeting, which lasted for two hours, was carried out under a feeling of urgency. The atmosphere was tense and nervous.

"For the first time," the prime minister said, "I am unsure that Arafat wants to put an end to this. We will have to act. Arafat must not be allowed to gain anything from this violence. We cannot reward violence. We are sure he can stop it immediately. We have clear evidence that the leaders of the Tanzim believe that Arafat wants the riots to continue, at least in the next few days. We are witnesses to blatant and continuing violations of the agreement and the rules of the game by the Palestinians. The Palestinian police continue to fire. The Tanzim is out of control, and its weapons have not been seized. Arafat must control the weapons, their distribution and operation, especially with the Tanzim – he acts as the head of a gang, not a leader.

"It breaks my heart to watch the painful and tragic pictures of Palestinian funerals," continued Barak, "but we must ask ourselves who initiated this wave of violence, and for what purpose. We have a reasonable peace agreement within reach, instead, Arafat is 'playing with fire' in order to gain favor with the world public opinion. Cessation of violence is a prior condition for any continuation in the peace process. We will stop shooting the minute they stop attacking us. The choice is his."

"The problem is the loss of Palestinian control," George Tenet said.

"There is no loss of control," Barak answered. "Arafat can and should make the two phone calls necessary to stop this within twelve hours."

"I want to meet the heads of security to discuss the mechanism necessary to neutralize this. My main concern is the Hamas," Tenet added.

"The violence erupted after a meeting between Marwan Barghouti and Arafat," remarked the deputy chief of staff, General "Boogie" Ya'alon. "The open channels we have to their heads of security, General Majayda and Jibril Rajoub, are worthless. They cannot fight the Tanzim. This is an armed gang of the Fatah. Their leaders get their orders directly from Arafat. He is the only one who can stop them. There is no point in speaking of a ceasefire. We are just reacting to their attacks. We are not using live fire on innocent people, but our civilians and military posts are being attacked with live ammunition."

"Seems like the right wing was 'right' after all," remarked Barak. "We should never have given guns to a militia of terrorists to whom an agreement means nothing. It is possible that we are observing a failing of an entire decade of peace negotiations. If at the critical moment, Arafat is unable to make a decision, we will know how to interpret this."

"Arafat has a political problem," Albright said. "How does he return to calm after the death of over seventy people? Maybe we could propose a temporary international presence, like TIPH (Temporary International Presence in Hebron), in hot spots like Netzarim or Joseph's Tomb."

Barak was very skeptical. "If the Tanzim is not disarmed, all the peace efforts of the past decade will appear absurd. Arafat uses blood in an effort to raise international support. A clear order must go out which will lead to the cessation of violence." "The US must try to stop this killing . . . this is only getting worse. We will clarify to Arafat that he is not the victim of gangs, but that he has the ability to control," Albright insisted.

"It is easier for me to negotiate than to fight," Barak said, "but I will fight if I have to. I will not give in to blackmail."

"If you do not address the root cause of the violence – it will return within days, weeks, or months," remarked Amnon Shahak. "This is the result of Sharon's political frustration. His provocation was not against the Palestinians, but against our government, which he perceived was about to make far-reaching concessions in Jerusalem."

Albright, as if predicting what was about to come, turned to Barak. "We, the Americans, are willing to tell Arafat what is necessary. But we are alone, and you will realize this when you speak to Chirac. The pictures of helicopters firing missiles into apartment buildings are horrible. Sentiment is against you. If there is calm, President Clinton is willing to meet with the negotiators on Tuesday."

The Israelis were whisked to Elysee Palace in a protected convoy and were led into one of the halls where President Chirac, Foreign Minister Vedrine, political adviser Jean-Marc de la Sabliere, the EU envoy Miguel Moratinos and officials from the Elysee and the Foreign Ministry sat on one side of the table.

"We all know the events," Chirac began without introductions. "The past should not concern us, but the next few hours should. I met with Arafat this morning, I spoke to Clinton, and I met with Albright. The goal is to reach a ceasefire, a withdrawal of Israeli forces, especially tanks and heavy weapons, and to launch an international inquiry. If we cannot reach an agreement on these three points today, France will find it very difficult to participate in a trilateral meeting. I insisted that Arafat fly to Sharm Al Sheikh right after we finish here."

"The entire Israeli peace camp is on the defensive as a result of Arafat's reckless maneuvers to gain international support and applause . . ." Barak replied, composed. "Cessation of violence must be the first step in any process that is supposed to bring about calm, examination, and the re-opening of a negotiating path toward an agreement. The attacks are not two-sided. These are Palestinian attacks, with people accompanied by policemen and the Tanzim attacking isolated Israeli posts. We are firing only in places in which we are being fired upon . . . control over posses-sion of arms is a legitimate request for a national entity leader who wants to become a head of state. He does not look like a head of state, rather as a gang leader. It is important that at such a vital crossroads, Arafat – who it appears has not yet decided where he is headed – will not receive signals that there is a reward for violence. We are therefore obviously opposed to an international inquiry. After the cessation of violence, each side should conduct its own self-examination, then meet with the Amer-icans and devise a mechanism that will increase coordination and prevent the recurrence of these incidents."

Chirac did not appear impressed by the lecture. "Your account of events does not match the impression of any country in the world," he said. "At Camp David, Israel did in fact make a significant step toward peace, but

Sharon's visit was the detonator, and everything has exploded. This morning, sixty-four Palestinians are dead, nine Israeli-Arabs were also killed, and you're pressing on. You cannot, Mr Prime Minister, explain this ratio in the number of wounded. We cannot make anyone believe that the Palestinians are the aggressors." The eyes of the professional translator were filling with tears, in the face of the sharp attacks on Barak and Israel, but she nevertheless went on with her work as Chirac continued: "When I was a company commander in Algeria, I also thought I was right. I fought the guerrillas. Later I realized I was wrong. It is the honor of the stronger, to reach out and not to shoot. Today you must reach out your hand. If you continue to fire from helicopters on people throwing rocks, and you continue to refuse an international inquiry, you are turning down a gesture from Arafat. You have no idea how hard I pushed Arafat to agree to a trilateral meeting."

"Our soldiers are involved in self-defense, Mr President," offered Shahak. "Where are the wounded Palestinians? At Joseph's Tomb, which is a Jewish holy site. There are a dozen soldiers at an Israeli weak point, completely surrounded by Palestinians. The IDF chief of staff has avoided entering the site forcefully to rescue a wounded Israeli soldier, to prevent causing dozens of casualties on the Palestinian side. The other place is Netzarim Junction. There, they fired machine-guns from high buildings on the post. This prime minister and this government are determined to achieve peace. An Israeli policeman has never turned his weapon on his Palestinian partner. The opposite indeed happened, more than once. The reality that has been created will make continued negotiations more difficult. Therefore, from here, from Paris, we need a ceasefire. We can do this by talking to a few key people. Everyone knows their name, and where they can be found," Shahak concluded.

"We have to find something – some gesture on your part, the Israelis – to bring about positive results today," Vedrine said.

"Albright asked that I come to Paris, and that in meetings with you and Albright, Arafat will be given an opportunity to return from the limb he is out on," Barak turned to Chirac. "Another gesture will encourage him to promote violence and terrorism instead of stopping it."

Chirac was short-tempered. Things were not going according to plan. "History will be written later," he said. "We have to try and express support for both sides."

Barak wanted to finish the conversation on a positive note. "I thank you again. Your involvement in the details of the issue is very important. When the day comes for writing history, we will remember."

Later on that day, Albright met with Barak and Arafat at the residence of the American ambassador in order to draft a joint statement. Albright initially planned to present the statement at the end of the day, and have it signed the following day in Sharm Al Sheikh, in the presence of President

Mubarak. The process was slow and tiring. During one of the breaks, an angry Arafat started leaving with his aides toward the front door, and from there to the outside gate. Determined as a football linebacker, Albright chased after them, barking at the security guards "Don't open the gate!" then grabbed Arafat, taking his arm in hers, literally dragging him back, trying to appease him. It turned out that Arafat and his aides were left alone in the conference room, thinking that Barak went out for a consultation and would return shortly with an answer. Unaware that Arafat was waiting for a response, Barak actually took a break from the intense negotiations. As time went by and Barak did not return, Arafat, deeply insulted, decided to leave. Barak apologized for the misunderstanding and after some more American pleading, Arafat was appeased and the meeting was resumed. The short, one-page document was read to Arafat in English, and translated word-for-word into Arabic. The two leaders agreed, in front of Albright, that the document was completely acceptable, that they would initial it that night, and that they would sign it in full the next day, as planned, in Egypt.

From the early evening, President Chirac started calling every half hour, and as the hours went by, every ten minutes, to find out what was going on. Upon completing the draft, someone proposed that we honor our host, Chirac, by reporting to him on the day's achievements, and then return to the American ambassador's home to initial the document.

Rule number one of any negotiations: *never* leave the negotiations table without signing the agreed-upon draft.

At around midnight the leaders and their delegations arrived at the Elysee Palace, where they were joined by UN Secretary-General Kofi Annan and Terje Larsen. Albright began with a briefing on the progress that had been made. "The two leaders have just called the heads of the security establishments and instructed them, starting tomorrow morning, to begin calming the situation on the ground and to regain order. We prepared an agreed-upon document that details a mechanism that will bring about calm. We intend to initial the document immediately after we finish here. On Tuesday, in less than a week, President Clinton will host the Israeli and Palestinian negotiators in Washington."

Chirac asked just one question – the major stumbling block in the discussions, which was removed only with great effort in order to facilitate an agreement: Is there going to be an international inquiry? Barak explained politely but firmly: "Creating an international inquiry is a mistake. It would be better if an American body, or a highly respected American official lead this investigation. But we cannot resolve this dispute in the current forum." Arafat grabbed onto the opportunity to begin a confused speech, the brunt of which was that the peace process is based on UN resolutions and therefore UN Secretary-General Kofi Annan should head the inquiry. Albright, who was short-tempered, clarified that the purpose of the discussion was to restore calm and stop violence on the ground. "If we focus on the inquiry, we will not be able to focus on the substance. Of course we must discuss a fact-finding commission, and we intend to consult with the secretary-general and with you," she turned to Chirac, "and the president of the EU, among others, but not right now." Chirac was not convinced. "There is a need for an inquiry. A reliable committee must be formed, and the role of the secretary-general is to help with this," he said – in essence burying any prospects of ending the violent, explosive crisis in our region before it develops further.

Upon returning to the residence of the American ambassador to initial the document that was agreed before the meeting at the Elysee Palace, we learned that Arafat had decided to return to his hotel and sent Nabil Sha'ath and Saeb Erekat to initial the document in his place. Albright was fuming. "We will not go to Sharm until that man comes here to sign. What are we, puppets?"

Erekat and Sha'ath were deeply embarrassed. But even after several attempts they could not bring Arafat to the ambassador's residence. While all this was taking place, the members of the Israeli delegation crashed on the sofas and carpeted floors of the Ambassador's residence trying to get a few minutes of sleep after an intense twenty-four hours. At 4.50 a.m., Dennis Ross arrived to brief Barak. "The Palestinians will maintain their commitments on security, as they were communicated orally," he said. "It is difficult for them to see this documented. They might want to get more in Sharm. Arafat is on his way there." Barak told Ross he would agree to go to Sharm only if Arafat's promises proved themselves on the ground.

A few weeks later, one of the French diplomats would tell me, in a random conversation, that historic research has shown that no agreement signed at an embassy or foreign consulate on French soil has ever lasted.

The violence did not stop.

On the following day, October 5, there were shootings toward the Jewish settlement in Hebron and Tel Haras. Two Palestinians were shot dead trying to climb up the IDF post at the Netzarim Junction. At the Beit Lehem–Jerusalem Road, IDF forces killed two Tanzim militants who threw Molotov cocktails at Israeli cars. One Israeli citizen was slightly wounded from rocks thrown at the Karmei Tzur road. There were more shootings toward homes in the suburb of Gilo. On Friday October 6, the violence continued with riots on the Temple Mount. This time, however, following lessons they had learned the previous week, the police force was evacuated, to prevent confrontation with the Palestinians. At the end of prayers, the Palestinians raised the PLO and Hamas flags on the Temple Mount, and hurled stones down onto the area in front of the Wailing Wall. The riots spilled over to the Muslim Quarter. The police station at the Lions Gate was torched. Ten soldiers were trapped inside, as they suffocated in the burning station. In the north of the country, close to Mount Dov, the

Hezbollah abducted three soldiers. Joseph's Tomb was pillaged, destroyed and torched by Palestinian protestors hours after it was evacuated in the early morning of October 7 by the IDF. The religious strife and incitement were further fueled in the Territories and in the Arab media. Two days later the body of Rabbi Hillel Lieberman was found. He was on his way to Joseph's Tomb after he heard of the evacuation. At a shooting incident at the Rafah terminal, nine workers were wounded. A few days later, Barak decided to close the Dahaniya Palestinian airport near Rafah.

Upon returning to Gaza from Europe, Arafat blamed Mofaz, the IDF chief of staff, for intentionally targeting places holy to Islam. The UN secretary-general met with Ben-Ami in Tel Aviv, and later with Arafat in Gaza. In the latter meeting, a Hamas representative was included for the first time in discussions with the Palestinian leadership.

Over Yom Kippur, there were dozens of violent clashes between Israelis, Jews and Arabs, in Nazareth, Tiberias, Carmiel and elsewhere in Israel. Two Israeli-Arabs were killed and three were badly wounded in Nazareth. The Palestinians intensified the violence with roadside explosives. Shootings at Israeli communities and private vehicles became part of the daily carnage.

For some months Barak had been pressing me to assume the prime minister's chief of staff position. I was reluctant, for a multitude of reasons, not least of which was that I preferred concentrating on the political effort to bring about a negotiated agreement with the Palestinians. The historic conflict between Jews and Arabs being situated at a decisive crossroad required a far-reaching attempt to bring about an end to the conflict through an historic compromise. I humbly felt that contributing to ensure the most fundamental interests of the State of Israel – its existence as a Jewish, Zionist and democratic state – was the most significant role I could have. However, the eruption of the Al Aqsa Intifada and the ongoing erosion in the government's political stability finally made the decision for me.

Upon entering the office, I requested that two photographs be hung. The first picture was of the 1994 signing of the Interim Agreements in Cairo: Arafat can be seen in the picture, refusing to sign the agreement; Yitzhak Rabin looks at him in wonderment, detached, almost in despair; Mubarak is cursing at him. The second picture was from the protests on Bar Ilan Road in Jerusalem, in which an ultra-Orthodox Jew is pushed aside by a policeman on horseback. It reminded me of the fragility of the framework within which we live.

The following commentary appeared in a *Haaretz* article entitled "A Sher in Peace," by Akiva Eldar:

> There are few cases in which a decision in a matter of staff can teach as much about policy as the appointment of Gilead Sher as the prime minister's chief of staff . . .

The Palestinians have learned to read Barak. Sher's appointment excites them far more than the threat to send the peace process on furlough. They know that it is possible to count on the fingers of one hand the number of people in Barak's inner circle for whom peace matters so much in their hearts.

In any case, Sher's appointment is the best news we have had recently concerning the peace process.

On October 12, in the Ramallah police station, two reservists – Vadim Novesche and Yossef Avrahami – were murdered, in front of an excited mob.

In a telephone conversation Barak asked Egyptian President Hosny Mubarak: "Use your influence on Arafat to make the two phone calls necessary to the heads of the Tanzim, to stop this atrocity. We cannot tolerate bodies being dragged, like dogs, after a lynching. There are pictures that no public, no person, can bear. Do all you can to get him back to the negotiations table, to stop encouraging perpetration of violence by his people under the table and saying the opposite in public."

On the evening of October 12, the political-security Cabinet convened in the Ministry of Defense in Tel Aviv. It was my second day on the job. The pace of events did not allow me time to draw breath.

The ministers arrived to the meeting shocked by the intense cruelty and bestiality of the mob in Ramallah. Barak asked the Cabinet to allow him, and two or three other ministers, to authorize targeted activities that would send clear warning signals to the Palestinians. A sharp and painful discussion ensued. Some ministers recommended measures that were more drastic than those that were ultimately adopted. In this and future similar Cabinet meetings, Barak, recognizing the limits of military reactions and retribution, steered toward more moderate decisions. He left room to return to the sanity of dialogue, but he did not bar targeted action. Barak's double duty – as prime minister and as minister of defense – was a huge burden on one man and his ability to move forward calmly and responsibly through a barrage of criticism on the one hand, and acts of violence, on the other, was admirable.

Air force helicopters attacked the Ramallah police station in which the lynching took place and the nearby Voice of Palestine radio station. In Gaza they attacked the Tanzim headquarters and coastguard vessels. The attacks were broadcast around the world, immediately erasing any memory of the lynching.

Blurred as the overall picture was during this second week of violence, the danger of quick and uncontrollable escalation to a wide, full-scale confrontation was clear.

Clinton phoned Barak. "A government in the Middle East that does not respond to such a lynching loses all legitimacy," said Barak, "both in the eyes of its own people and in the eyes of others in the region. Arafat is double-tongued, he speaks peace with world leaders, and supports and encourages violence with his people – the lynching in Ramallah is the result."

Referring to the terrorist attack on the USS Cole in the port of Aden, Clinton said "We lost fifteen boys on board. It's awful. We have to immediately meet at Mubarak's – you, Jordan's King Abdullah, Arafat and me – and reach a ceasefire within forty-eight to seventy-two hours." Barak was willing to participate only if Arafat unequivocally instructed the hostilities leaders Barghouti and Hussein A-Sheikh to put an end to the violence.

Palestinians torched the old synagogue in Jericho.

The next phone call was from President Mubarak. "They torch holy places, Mr President. This is madness." Barak said. "I understand that it is difficult for them to enforce orders on their people," retorted Mubarak, "but you need to be wise and even-tempered. I am telling you this after seven or eight phone conversations with Arafat. We must be patient." Barak insisted on a precondition of a seventy-two hour ceasefire before convening the leaders in Sharm. "And don't believe the numbers the Palestinians give you – there are no dead as a result of IDF actions following the lynching in Ramallah, and the number of wounded is low."

Barak formulated the conditions for attending the ceasefire summit in Sharm Al Sheikh: signing the "Paris document"; setting a time in the very near future to resume negotiations on the basis of the ideas raised at Camp David; immediate cessation of terrorism and violence; resuming security coordination; and re-arresting Hamas and Islamic Jihad terrorists that Arafat had released from prison. Barak supported American management of the summit. On October 15, it was agreed that the summit would be convened without preconditions, but with an informal understanding that components of the Barak's conditions would be included.

An IDF reservist officer, Colonel Elhanan Tennenbaum was kidnapped in Europe by Hezbollah.

Barak began to speed up negotiations to create an emergency unity government. An agreement for the Likud to join the coalition was apparently near but fell through after the Sharm summit when Sharon announced that he was ending the talks.

October 16, 2000. During the morning hours of the summit at Sharm Al Sheikh, the political leaders held small meetings mostly among themselves. Barak met with Mubarak, Kofi Annan, King Abdullah and President Clinton. Only in the afternoon, after a small opening session, did everyone converge for a joint lunch.

Mubarak intended to bring about a withdrawal of Israeli forces and removal of the closure within a few hours. "We have a very difficult problem with public opinion, and on Saturday the Arab Summit is convening. The fanatics among us threaten peace in the entire region," he said.

King Abdullah agreed: "The current cycle of violent conflict has put an end to the Israeli–Palestinian dialogue. It has turned it into an Arab–Israeli issue. We have to rebuild the peace camp and to neutralize the risk that we will face on Saturday, at the Arab Summit in Cairo."

Barak demanded that Arafat make a commitment to return to prison Hamas and Islamic Jihad members that he had released back and that Arafat give clear orders to the heads of the Tanzim and the Palestinian police to stop the shootings.

"Sharon is the cause of all this trouble," snapped Mubarak.

Amnon Shahak tried to explain that Sharon's visit to the Temple Mount was targeted toward the prime minister and the government itself, and not toward Islam, the Palestinians or Arabs. The Egyptians did not appear convinced. "The Israeli government does not have the authority to stop the leader of the opposition or any other person from going to the Temple Mount," added Ben-Ami. "We will not discuss events within Israel in this forum," concluded Barak.

Clinton was practical and focused as usual, detailing the security steps necessary to separate forces and produce a ceasefire. The first step would involve withdrawal of IDF forces, and then, removing the military circles around the Palestinian cities.

At the full assembly, Mubarak delivered harsh words, meant for the Arab audience:

> The grave situation and tragic developments in the Palestinian land and the acts of aggression inflicted on the Palestinian people over the past two weeks prompted me to take the initiative for convening this meeting ... provocative actions and oppressive attempts against an unarmed people designed to crush down its will and undermine its dignity ... This is a situation which we must face with all our power and determination because it will have such grave consequences that no party alone can tolerate, regardless of any power or supremacy it might think it possesses ... and allow all parties to move forward balanced and comprehensive peace that gives the Palestinians their right to self-determination.

The Israeli delegation held itself back.

President Clinton tried to be more optimistic. "Our goals are to end the violence and restore security cooperation. We hope to achieve agreement on an objective and fair, fact-finding process ... and we want to get the peace process going ... remember before these terrible events how far we have come since September 13, 1993."

After the plenary, on the ground floor of the hotel, Erekat started to make a speech with demagogic enthusiasm. Ben-Ami yelled at him, "This is not CNN, we are speaking about the facts, and you can calm down – there are no cameras in this room ..." Albright tried to calm the heated meeting of the foreign ministers, with only little success.

Back in my hotel room, after midnight, I watched Egyptian television broadcasting continuous, ugly and blatant songs of sedition, against the background of close-ups of wounded Palestinians, some en route to the ambulance – unedited. "This is hardly an environment for bringing about calm," I thought to myself.

At 2 a.m. Barak was called to meet Clinton. The president proposed an action plan in advance of completing the drafting of his morning statement. He looked for a balance between steps in the area of security, and the convening of a committee to examine the events. Barak saw a direct link between the two, "We signed many agreements with Arafat – he either did not respect his commitments at all, or he turned a blind eye to their violation by his people. Palestinian Authority bodies that are supposed to combat terrorism are cooperating in violent actions against us. We cannot agree to the international aspect of the proposed committee."

Clinton pressed. George Tenet detailed the immediate steps that would follow after forty-eight hours: a joint declaration regarding the cessation of violence and the resumption of security cooperation; the opening of international passages; withdrawal of IDF forces, tanks, and others to their pre-September 28 positions; removing closures; collecting illegal arms; convening a high-level joint security meeting.

Clinton then invited the whole Israeli delegation into the room. "I know that these past few weeks have been hell for you, and I don't know how you have been able to live with it," the president said. "I really expect that this time the Palestinians will make an effort that will work. If they keep the military understandings secret – it will work, just as they were able to maintain calm a year and a half after the Wye Summit. Everything was addressed with the security committee."

The events in the Territories casting a heavy shadow over the summit, the delegates' fatigue, and the tension between the sides made for a closing ceremony that was anything but festive.

Mubarak summarized. "Although the results which we have reached in this meeting may not be up to the expectations of our people ... what our peoples will be looking forward to in the upcoming days is how far both parties will be committed to thoroughly implementing points already agreed upon and how far they are willing to push forward the peace process ... Our ultimate goal should and will always be to reach a comprehensive and just peace ... We should avoid backtracking ... and help reach a peace agreement within the framework of full respect for sanctities and the right of peoples to live in peace and stability."

President Clinton followed suit. "Our primary objective has been to end the current violence so we can begin again to resume our efforts toward peace . . . Toward this end, the leaders have agreed that the United States would consult with the parties within the next two weeks about how to move forward . . . We should have no illusions about the difficulties ahead."

On our return from Sharm on October 17, the prime minister made the following statement:

> Detailed security understandings were formulated on all related issues. These understandings were deposited with the United States, which will monitor their implementation . . . As obligated thereby, upon my return to the country, I ordered the security forces to do everything required to implement the Sharm declaration. They will contact their American and Palestinian counterparts in order to act jointly to achieve this goal forthwith while strictly upholding our obligation to defend Israel's citizens and soldiers. I would like to emphasize that the IDF and Israel Police will take great care to halt the violence and prevent additional loss of life. They – and only they – will assure the security of Israeli citizens . . . In recent weeks, violence has surged in our region and Israeli and Palestinian lives have been lost. We regret this. We now have before us an additional opportunity to get back on track toward stability, co-existence and cooperation. I expect that our Palestinian neighbors share this hope with us.

At this stage, everyone still hoped not only for a reduction, but a complete cessation of violence. We believed that it was still possible. But after continued unsuccessful efforts to return to the ceasefire formula developed at Sharm, the phrase "reduction in violence" became a more common goal, replacing the former, more ambitious one.

The Al Aqsa Intifada was part of a deep historic shift. While we strove toward a continuing dialogue that would stop the tragic tide of violence, the deep crisis of confidence between the two sides was likely to prevent the process from recovering in the foreseeable future.

In accordance with Israel's commitments in Sharm, the prime minister instructed Avi Dichter, head of the Shin Bet, and Yanai, head of AGAT, to resume security coordination with Dahlan and Rajoub. He also instructed the military secretary Eizencot to follow up on the opening of international passage, removing the encircling of Palestinian cities. He then met with the leadership of the Settlers' Council to explain the understandings that were reached.

And he began counting the forty-eight hours of calm.

Out of a comprehensive view of the nature of the conflict, and the need for practical alternatives that are independent of the auspices of third parties, Barak initiated work on unilateral disengagement, a complicated undertaking that would have an effect on all aspects of Israeli life. Unilateral disengagement was based on a strategic concept, which claimed that the State of Israel and the Palestinian state should be separated, living side by side in peace and good neighborly relations. It would be preferable if the separation would be the result of a negotiated agreement between the sides, on the basis of principles defined in the framework of the agreement. In the absence of an agreement, however, the separation would be initiated by Israel. It would be implemented on the basis of a defined program. Implementation would be gradual and would be phased in over a few years. During implementation, the door would remain open to resume the negotiations process.

The practical components of the separation plan included:

- Creating settlement blocs under Israeli sovereignty in Permanent Status, with eighty percent of the settlers of Judea and Samaria: Gush Etzion, Ariel-Kdumim bloc, Alei-Zahav-Heshmonaim bloc, Hinanit-Shaked bloc, the broad road circumscribing Jerusalem and additional changes along the Green Line; a broad security zone would be created in the Jordan Valley, and from Mehola southwards along the Dead Sea; security and law enforcement presence will be increased in East Jerusalem and surrounding areas.
- In the immediate stage of implementation, isolated settlements would not be evacuated. When the time was right, these settlements in distant areas beyond blocs and security areas, would be transferred into the settlement blocs or into Israel.
- Separation arrangements would be examined in all the government offices, including economic, environment, and utility and infrastructure (electricity, water) issues. These arrangements would require large investments – or we so believed – especially water desalination.

Government ministries, the IDF and other official agencies worked thoroughly and vigorously on detailing the plan components, and examining its physical, legal, sovereign and political implications. It involved comprehensive staff work, which with time developed into a comprehensive vision. But the plan was tucked away for the time being, awaiting the point where all other options had been exhausted.

The assessment of the decision-makers – especially at the operational level, such as the general staff of the IDF – was that a confrontation with the Palestinians would be drawn out. The probability of a regional deterioration was increased accordingly. "We are not to blame for the escalation," Barak would say in private conversation, "and we cannot punish ourselves." Nevertheless, international terrorism, Islamic fundamentalism, the terror attacks, the serious incitement among Israeli-Arabs, the Palestinians, the situation in Lebanon, the Hezbollah, and the unclear situation in Syria – all had the potential danger of bringing about, under certain conditions, a complete deterioration. Only our willingness to consider far-reaching ideas on the path to peace could prevent the realization of the dangers that Barak was observing. "Arafat decided to bring about a deterioration in the situation through violence and blood," Barak said in a telephone conversation with the British prime minister, Tony Blair, on October 24. "I am completely serious about creating a government that would receive a mandate from the public to address this situation ... Look, Tony – if you and others in the world, do not say to Arafat that violence does not pay and is unacceptable – the entire region will become a conflict area with global dangers. Any other position would be like surrendering to blackmail. The minute Arafat feels he has lost international support – he will act differently."

Paradoxical and infuriating as it was, international public opinion, which was fed by quick and superficial pictures, was clearly against Israel. None of the main networks bothered to confront the roots of the conflict in general and the current cycle of violence in particular. The foreign correspondents in the Territories settled for pictures depicting Israeli reactions to terror attacks and violence. CNN was especially manipulative and hostile, systematically ignoring the facts and broadcasting non-coincidental mistakes, violating accepted rules of journalism. Together with Alon Liel, the director general of the Ministry of Foreign Affairs, we prepared a comprehensive and detailed analysis of their coverage. Senior network officials arrived in Israel for meetings and clarifications. For a short period pursuant to the meetings, CNN was clearly making a concerted effort to balance its reports.

Barak's political life was facing several difficult fronts – the threat from the north, the kidnapping of the three Israeli soldiers (being held by Hezbollah), the Palestinians, Israeli-Arabs unrest, international public opinion, internal politics, and the domestic and international media. The Knesset was to convene November 7 and 15, with planned no-confidence votes threatening to potentially topple the Barak government. Feeling that establishing an emergency government was a national necessity, Barak began maneuvering in that direction. But risking his personal/political survival, he nevertheless continued to emphasize his steadfast commitment to Israel's security and to the quest for peace through negotiations.

17

A SINGLE POLITICAL BULLET
IN THE BARREL

Abu Mazen, who after Arafat's death four years later, became in January 2005 the first truly democratically elected chairman of the PA, vigorously supported the American initiative of "all or nothing" – rejecting any attempt to bring the Europeans into the picture. He saw a need for land swaps at a ratio of one to one, and in Jerusalem, a division according to the principle "what was Israeli to Israel and what Arab to the Palestinians." The Muslim area of "Al Haram Al Sharif" would be under Palestinian sovereignty, and the Temple Mount, in its Jewish sense – under Israeli sovereignty. "All that is needed," Abu Mazen told his counterparts, "is a creative formula." He would not give up the Right of Return or mentioning UNGAR 194 but he was leaning toward a mechanism that would sterilize the right, through a committee comprised of the US, Israel and the Palestinians. In contrast to what many Israelis thought at the time, Abu Mazen did not oppose announcing the end of conflict and signing a FAPS. However he was not willing to take the reins in his hands and undertake the personal risk involved.

The forty-eight hours necessary to implement the Sharm Understandings had passed. Israeli hikers were attacked in crossfire for hours on Mount Eival in Samaria. On October 22, Barak announced a political "time-out." His decision was attacked from every direction. Arafat lashed out again: "We are proceeding to Jerusalem, the capital of our independent Palestinian state," he said. "Whether Barak accepts it or not – he can go to hell!"

Tunisia and Morocco announced they were breaking off diplomatic relations with Israel. The Egyptian foreign minister was quoted as saying: "The peace process has ended ... we must support the Palestinian uprising." If Cairo did not want an agreement now, there was no point in putting pressure on Arafat.

Our assessment was that without a significant political achievement (establishment of a Palestinian state, internationalization of Jerusalem, or confidence-building measures toward Permanent Status) the violence would not cease. Although the term "Interim Agreement" was absolutely unacceptable to Barak, he began to seriously contemplate the possibility of phased negotiations. Moderate forces within the Palestinian camp – headed by Abu Mazen – were searching for a way to return to the negotiations table, but with reduced or more "balanced" American intervention. The Barak government had "one bullet in the barrel": every political step that would require a Knesset approval would require going to elections.

October 30 was a particularly violent day. Two security guards were shot to death in the social security branch in East Jerusalem. The body of a resident of Gilo was found with signs of violence. Shells were fired toward the casino in Jericho. Air force helicopters attacked Nablus, Ramallah and Khan Yunis. The prime minister delivered a political message to the Knesset regarding the developments:

> Over the past sixteen months, especially in Camp David, we were willing . . . to consider a far-reaching compromise with the Palestinians . . . Let the Palestinians know that we were ready to allow for the realization of some of their dreams even at a heart-wrenching price. But let the Palestinians realize we too have dreams. We too have national interests that we cannot compromise – the security of Israel, unity of Israel and our sacred values.
>
> . . . The path I chose tested the willingness of the Palestinian leader to achieve a Permanent Status agreement of peace and end of conflict . . . namely in Camp David . . . Unfortunately, the other party did not pass . . .
>
> Time is not in our hands . . . In a few more years, one of the more extreme Arab states could have nuclear capabilities, or worse yet, the whole region could be swept by wave of terrorism.

After a meeting between Amnon Shahak and Arafat on October 31, 2000, Shimon Peres suggested to Barak the idea of introducing the Peace Corps into the Territories to spread calm. Barak hesitated. "We will be introducing international forces before we even know whether Arafat is ready and able to stop the violence and return to the negotiations table."

On November 1, Shimon Peres, accompanied by Peres' adviser Avi Gil and me, departed for Gaza. On the drive over, in an armored vehicle, Peres fumed: "Ehud does not leave me any room to maneuver, he has really strangled me." Avi Gil connected him by phone to bed-ridden Leah Rabin. "We are on our way to Gaza, to Arafat," Peres told her. "We'll see what happens."

In Gaza, Nabil Sha'ath, Mohammad Rashid and Nabil Abu Rudayna were waiting in Arafat's office. The reception was friendly, as usual.

"We are making all the possible mistakes. You have buried six people;

174

we have buried three soldiers. We are civilized people. There is no point to all this bloodshed," Peres began.

"You are bombing everywhere. Jericho, Ramallah, Nablus, Bethlehem, Karni, Rafah," Arafat replied.

"This can all end in a few hours," Peres responded coolly.

"Everything we agreed to in Sharm Al Sheikh does not exist," interrupted Arafat, "He [Barak] did not withdraw the tanks, he froze the peace process." "Nothing in the peace process has changed," Peres replied. "No one wants war. We are committed one hundred percent to what was agreed in Sharm."

"You are preventing the shipment of food, besieging the cities," barked Arafat. "Move your tanks away!"

"Within two hours of our return to Sharm, Barak gave an unequivocal order to the forces to stop all their operations," I intervened. "The announcement was made public in the media that day at 7 p.m. You on the other hand waited until after midnight to issue a vague announcement. Of course the violence escalated!"

"What happened to you Jilead [sic]?" Arafat asked, "You are speaking differently than usual."

"I cannot bear your manipulation of the facts," I answered him dryly. "You are trying to justify violence and wild incitement by your people."

"Let us think of something creative," suggested Peres. "Let's take a week without violence, in memory of Rabin."

We broke off for dinner, which was quite peaceful, full of jokes regarding a possible Israeli attack on Arafat's compound, in which we were all dining. Arafat hosted generously, as usual. At the end of the dinner, Peres tried to summarize. "We will issue a joint declaration regarding the cessation of violence to all our forces and units. Forty-eight hours later, assuming there's calm, the tanks will be withdrawn. Let's implement this," he turned to Arafat, "then you and Barak will approach President Clinton and ask him to create a commission to investigate the events."

"Withdraw your tanks, immediately," insisted Mohammad Rashid.

"Absolutely not," I responded.

"Withdraw your tanks and then we will do the rest," Rashid replied.

"I've come here on a mission of good will. Let's respect the Sharm agreement, and in a day or two after implementation we'll discuss all the issues relating to employment, economics, closures," Peres said.

"The most important thing is for you to remove the tanks. That is what we agreed in Sharm," Arafat answered.

Our hosts accompanied us to our cars. There was a feeling of a possible breakthrough.

"I am willing to put this to the test," decided Barak later that night, upon being briefed on the meeting. And so, according the timetable, we were to withdraw the tanks to rear positions and renew the intelligence cooperation. "If this succeeds," pondered the prime minister, "we have made an important step for peace. If we find out that Arafat has 'tricked' us – we should approach the Nobel peace prize committee and ask to replace the prize awarded to Arafat with an Oscar, for great acting," he said to Peres.

At 2 p.m., each leader was to make an identical, agreed upon statement to the media, calling for a ceasefire. "I don't intend to recite the history of Zionism," snapped Barak on the phone to Arafat, "so don't digress from the version we agreed on either, do not add and do not detract."

Using various excuses, Arafat's declaration to the media was being delayed.

"We're going from area to area, place to place, and stopping people from shooting. It takes time, patience," Abu Mazen asked the Americans to convey to us.

At around 3 p.m. that day, a car bomb exploded in the heart of Jerusalem, in an alley near the Mahaneh Yehuda market. Two people – Ayelet-Hashachar Levy and Hanan Levy – were killed and ten more were wounded. Ayelet-Hashachar was the daughter of the former minister Yitzhak Levy, who was among those briefed by the Cabinet secretary regarding the agreement with Arafat just twelve hours earlier. The Islamic Jihad claimed responsibility for the attack. As in the past, Palestinian extremists are the ones who set the tone for the direction of events.

"I have no assurance that this time we will be able to force Arafat into a ceasefire and return to normalcy," I said during a brief to reporters, "but there are indications that he is making an effort to get orders down to his people on the ground to stop the violence. It is possible, however, that this attack, at this time, with its specific circumstances in the heart of Jerusalem, have destroyed, for both sides, the slim chance of returning to sanity."

Chirac called to express his condolences and emphasized, "We have condemned the attack and demanded that Arafat return to the negotiations. It is very urgent to maintain the dialogue and to resume it now," concluded the French president. Barak listened patiently before responding. "Arafat wasn't speaking to some taxi driver, but to Shimon Peres! Peres called him personally from my office to check that the detailed steps were mutually acceptable. I myself heard that six hours after the withdrawal of tanks there would be a joint, reciprocal statement by the leaders. But there is something worse that not fulfilling a commitment to call publicly for the cessation of violence, and that is the reality itself. The shootings have been resumed in full force tonight. From Area 'A' they are shooting on us without end. The incitement continues. They are not combating terrorism. You, Mr President, would not allow shooting on Pont de Neuilly.

We know they are preparing car bombs in Gaza. I am biting my lip in the face of my people's anger. Arafat endangers the entire region with a new cycle of violence. This is the time for friends like you to go to him and say – we support your cause, but first stop the violence."

The possibility of an imminent Palestinian UDI triggered a flurry of activity at the Ministry of Foreign Affairs, the Ministry of Justice, the National Security Council, the IDF and the Prime Minister's Office. Work in different government offices, and other organizations regarding unilateral disengagement was accelerated. Concurrently, preparations continued for the prime minister's visit to the United States for the meeting of the Jewish Federations (GA) and for meetings in Washington. The principles of Israeli policy were summarized briefly:

- prevent Palestinians from attaining international achievements through violence;
- prevent internationalization of the conflict;
- prevent regional deterioration and allow for political dialogue.

Barak briefed Ben-Ami and me. "We have to clarify to the international community that there is a choice between moving forward on the basis of the Camp David ideas, that are basically similar in their interpretation of UNSCRs 242 and 338, and rewarding violence and unilateral Palestinian measures. In parallel, we have to work to stabilize the domestic political situation for at least two to three months."

On the way to the US, we received news that a Russian passenger plane had been hijacked en route to Israel. After a short consultation, the prime minister instructed that we return to Israel. It was an embarrassing situation. Under other internal political conditions this would have been unacceptable. It turned out that the hijacker was an eccentric, who bore no arms or means of sabotage. We finally arrived in Washington almost a full twenty-four hours behind schedule. Most of the planned meetings were canceled, except for the most important one, between Barak and Clinton. The president postponed his planned departure to Southeast Asia for this purpose.

The American public and media were immersed with the controversy surrounding "who was elected president last week." George W. Bush was a few hundred votes ahead of Al Gore during the re-count of some the twenty million Florida votes. The Gore camp was raising claims regarding the validity of the vote. It was clear that a decision would be reached, ultimately, in the Supreme Court. Barak's visit, held against this background, went almost unnoticed. But President Clinton, who was finishing eight successful years in office, was hoping to achieve something tangible in the Middle East.

The Barak–Clinton meeting took place a few days after Arafat's visit to Washington. "Arafat told me 'I must reach an agreement before the end of your term,'" related Clinton over dinner. Arafat's vision for Jerusalem included Palestinian sovereignty over the Arab neighborhoods, a special regime in the Old City, and making "Haram Al Sharif" Palestinian. He demanded ninety-eight percent of the territory under his sovereignty, but the president thought that an agreement regarding ninety-five percent could be reached, as long as territorial contiguity would be maintained, and there would be a safe passage between the Gaza Strip and the West Bank. On refugees, Clinton clarified to Arafat that Israel agreed to the establishment of a Palestinian state on one hand, and absorbing masses of refugees on the other, in effect creating a Palestinian or Arab majority within Israel proper. The president's impression was that Arafat's main problem involved the refugees in Lebanon. If that were to be solved, the whole refugee issue would be resolved, through an international fund that would finance the arrangement over the years.

On security, Clinton believed that an international force and a non-militarized Palestinian state would be sufficient. "I asked Arafat specifically – whether these parameters are in the framework of an agreement he is willing to sign. Arafat responded 'yes' – twice. Arafat wants an agreement," Clinton concluded, "but I don't know whether the compromises he can accommodate, cross your red lines, Ehud. The best way to examine this is to prepare a 'package' through your representative here, and with the help of Mubarak."

Barak was focused on the recent escalation of violence: "We will not accept negotiations and violence simultaneously. This is what Arafat wants," Barak told Clinton. "The daily average is thirty to forty shooting attacks on our people."

"I told Arafat that we could not start working until he made an effort to drastically reduce violence," assured Clinton. "He wants Amnon [Shahak] to work with his people to consolidate a stabilizing plan."

Barak was unimpressed. "Arafat leaves everything open-ended, so he won't be thrown from the negotiations table, and at the same time he continues to blackmail us. You have to confront him with the evidence we have about his role in perpetuating the violence – you can do this with words, while I can only do this with actions, some of which are irreversible."

"Arafat is indeed trying to keep all his options open," replied Clinton, "but unlike the past, he says he is determined to reach an agreement, and during my term. I am personally willing to do what is necessary, and so are the Egyptians and Jordanians. Send Amnon Shahak to him, to stop the shooting. Let's stop the violence and enter into secret negotiations. But if we do not succeed," Clinton thought aloud, "what then? Have you thought of a limited, much smaller agreement?"

Barak was firm. "It's clear that we will eventually make peace with the Palestinians but it's possible that it will not happen under their current corrupt leadership. We've worked with them over the past decade under the assumption that they will be responsible enough to bring forth an end of conflict. But they've rejected all our and your advances toward a fair solution based on mutual compromises. We have no intention of committing suicide."

Our exhausted team continued on to Chicago for the GA convention. Barak, who was already feeling sick on the flight from Israel, completely lost his voice, and despite the dozen cups of tea, and an odd purple scarf around his throat, he could barely speak above a whisper. Yossi Kucik, "Bouji" Herzog, Danny Yatom and I filled in for him in different forums of the Jewish leadership of North America. Barak would arrive during the last few minutes of each event, to shake hands, embrace, and to honor the audience. The timetable was intense.

In Israel, four Israelis were killed in shootings in the Territories. In retaliation, the IDF besieged Palestinian cities. We returned to Israel on November 14. On our way back, the prime minister spoke to Albright, furious. "This is ridiculous. We have four dead and Arafat claims it's not him? He is lying to all of us. He is forcing me to react."

In the morning, the coffin of Leah Rabin was placed near the Yitzhak Rabin memorial in Tel Aviv. A thousand people attended the heavily guarded funeral in Mount Herzl. Hilary Clinton, representing the president of the United States, delivered a moving eulogy. The American peace team, Dennis Ross, Aaron Miller and Ambassador Indyk represented the State Department. Arafat eulogized Leah from his office in Ramallah signing off with the words "Goodbye, sister."

Against the background of continued violence in the Territories, Barak intensified the domestic political efforts to form an emergency national unity government.

18

IT'S THE ONLY WAY

During the negotiations, and especially during the more intense periods of the political process, Ehud Barak, Shlomo Ben-Ami and I often met with experts, academics and senior officials from past administrations to examine and analyze concepts, models, positions and possible alternatives for the negotiations. In the second week of October, I convened an external brainstorming group to examine the positions and arrangements that were being discussed in the negotiations. The diversified group evolved into a political forum and contributed on an ongoing basis to our thinking and to shaping the overall policy. It accompanied us throughout the process as an external, independent and discreet forum with multidisciplinary experience. The lively discussions exposed the Israeli negotiations team to a range of new ideas, many of which were later implemented.

One of the issues discussed in the group was the socio-economic impact of the violent conflict. Some members of the team warned against stopping the transfer of funds to the PA. "Starving" the Palestinian population would leave them with nothing to lose. The effectiveness of economic sanctions was questioned altogether, some arguing that it might actually have an adverse effect of mobilizing the Palestinians against Israel, rather than creating pressure on the Palestinian leadership to move forward toward a resolution of the conflict. Arafat was not prepared to go the distance at this point, and the people in his inner circle, with the exception of Dahlan and Rajoub, were not strong enough to back him up on difficult decisions. The Palestinians, fighting for their independence, were ready to sustain enormous suffering, and their leadership was positioning itself as the voice of the people in its fight against the occupier, the settlements and the economic sanctions.

Another think-tank group, composed of lawyers and jurists, engineers and architects, economists and sociologists, was formed in order advise on the different aspects of Jerusalem – religion, nationality, urbanization, security and symbols. The work of the group and its relationship with the negotiators contributed to our attempts to resolve this most sensitive issue. The working assumption of the group was that alongside an Israeli Jerusalem, the internationally recognized capital of Israel, another municipality would be created – Al-Quds. One participant presented a three-phased program of normalization, growth and legitimacy. Normalization would be achieved by transforming Jerusalem into an "open city," after years of conflict had undermined its urban development and planning. The end of conflict would bring legitimacy to Jerusalem as the capital of Israel, and would start a new page in the relationship between the Muslim world and the Vatican.

One of the recommendations we received was to establish a multi-lateral sovereignty on Temple Mount – by Israel, Palestine, leading Arab countries and the permanent members of the UN Security Council. The redefined sovereignty charter recognized in international law would include specific arrangements in the area of security, freedom of access and management, granting Israeli sovereignty and Palestinian custodianship.

Based on the assumption that a divided Jerusalem was "a lesser evil" than an isolated Jerusalem, the team focused on the practical aspects of disengagement – legal, organizational, technical/physical, civic – believing that a well-planned, logical separation was the best basis for eventual coop-eration. This held true for the issue of security, which envisaged two separate police forces operating in Jerusalem and Al-Quds, each covering its area of sovereignty, but slowly building mutual trust and cooperation. A joint tourist police force would operate in the Old City. Our main fear was an eruption of uncontrollable violence due to an outburst of religious hatred by a quarter of a million worshipers at the Temple Mount during Ramadan or as a result of some crazy religious terrorist act of a Jewish extremist.

On November 19, 2000, Barak suggested that former President Weizman would meet with Arafat. "Let's maintain an optimism that will enable even further reduction in the level of violence," he told Arafat on the phone, emphasizing the importance of coordination meetings between senior-level Israeli and Palestinian commanders on the ground.

The following morning, a roadside charge exploded under a school bus in Gush Katif. Two adults were killed, eleven children were wounded, including three children from the Cohen family whose limbs were ampu-tated. The IDF attacked Gaza. Egyptian Ambassador Bassiouni was recalled to Cairo, and Jordan announced that at this time, it would not send an ambassador to Israel. On November 22, Barak met with Turkish Foreign Minister Jam. The Turks expressed a willingness to contribute to the efforts of both sides. To this end, Jam suggested that Ben-Ami and Nabil Sha'ath travel to Turkey for talks, or that the negotiations teams – in some form – convene for secret talks in Turkey. During the conversation we were informed of a terrorist attack in Hadera in which two people were killed and sixty-one were wounded. On the next morning, November 23, two soldiers were killed in Gaza; on November 24, another soldier and civilian were killed.

A group of prominent Labor politicians promoted the idea of a long-term Interim Agreement that would address a great number of the Palestinian demands, while leaving the issues of Palestinian refugees and Jerusalem to be concluded at a later stage. The initiative included the establishment of a demilitarized Palestinian state on sixty percent of the territory in Judea, Samaria and Gaza, settlement blocs on three to four percent of the area, with no land swaps. "Anything that would reduce the violence to a level with which we could live is worthy of being seriously considered," they said. Others suggested a Sadat-style initiative – a sweeping effort with a bit of theatrics – such as Barak going to Ramallah to speak in Parliament, or Arafat being invited to the Knesset in Jerusalem. All these proposals crumbled because of the inability to bring down the violence, the most basic precondition to resuming the negotiations.

Barak – with the mediation of Minister Ben Eliezer – was preparing the groundwork for expanding the coalition to include the Likud. The main challenge was to find a formula that would reconcile the guiding political principles of Barak's government – which strived to end the Israeli–Palestinian conflict through painful compromise – and those of the Likud, which supported Israel's continued possession of the Territories it occupied in 1967.

The following wording was finally concluded:

> The cabinet will reexamine the proposals raised in the course of the political negotiation in general, and in the Camp David summit in particular in light of the vital interest of Israel and the violent events that occurred over the past weeks. All coalition groups agree that a future resumption of political negotiations with the Palestinians/Arab nations on Permanent Status must be approved by the cabinet.

Even those closest to Barak were not sure they fully understood his political thinking. Was it really his intention to create a national emergency government, thereby losing the crucial support of the political left? Or was he just biding time in order to move toward signing an agreement as soon as the violence subsided. His domestic politics were unclear and appeared to be zigzagging, losing credibility with the Likud on the one hand and the Israeli peace camp on the other.

In a turbulent meeting of the Labor party faction in the Knesset, Barak had to withstand attacks by those who opposed an emergency government. The next day, November 28, Barak made a sudden, dramatic announcement, "I am ready for elections." The proposal to dissolve the Knesset was passed with a majority of seventy-nine to one, with twenty-seven abstaining.

The internal situation on the other side was hardly better. Hostility within the Palestinian leadership was at its peak. Old and ongoing rivalries surfaced in full intensity. Abu Mazen, who suddenly befriended Abu Ala, announced to Arafat that as long as Mohammad Rashid was in the picture, he would not join any Palestinian team or delegation. He accused Dahlan, a close friend of Rashid's, of having a hand in the escalating situation in Gaza, in order to gain credibility after having been accused of excessive flexibility in Camp David. In meeting with foreign diplomats, however, Abu Mazen and Abu Ala expressed an unconditional willingness to engage in secret negotiation with any authorized Israeli representative.

In the Fatah, there were growing divisions regarding activities against Israel. The more extremist elements were encouraged by Hezbollah's apparent success in driving Israel out of Southern Lebanon. They argued in favor of dragging Israel into extreme reactions that would ultimately serve the Palestinian cause. They also provoked incitement against the "traitors," the Old Guard, Abu Mazen and Abu Ala. Marwan Barghouti and his people, on the other hand, held a milder line, supporting violent but more popular actions limited to the Territories. As for the Islamic organizations, at the end of November they threatened that if Arafat tried to calm the revolt they would undermine his efforts with further, more intense attacks.

Seven weeks remained for the Clinton administration.

On the evening of November 30, I flew to Cairo for a meeting with Omar Suleiman, head of the Intelligence Services of Egypt and Mubarak's closest confidant. A few Israelis had contact with him, including the head of the Mossad, Ephraim Halevy, the former deputy head of the Shin Bet, Israel Hasson, and Yossi Ginossar. In preparing the meeting, I also learned the blessings for Ramadan by heart, and wrote them down in Hebrew, just in case.

I started the meeting with Suleiman with a report on the latest violent events, the number of wounded, the explosive charges, the sniper fire, the weapons and continuing incitement in the Palestinian media and mosques. Suleiman inquired about the political situation in Israel. "Barak's commitment to the peace process is unchanged," I replied, "but we need a declaratory commitment from Arafat to stop the violence, to cease the incitement, and to prevent terror attacks. Egypt could play a critical role in facilitating the negotiations because any agreement made, authorized by the president of Egypt, would be accepted among the Israeli public as a word set in stone."

"We must bring together the leaders to show the people, Palestinian and Israeli, that there is a future and hope," Suleiman said. "We have four to five weeks to change the atmosphere between the Israelis and the Palestinians. It is our intention to push the Palestinians to control the situation. We need a meeting between Barak and Arafat, to return all sides on the track to peace. We are willing to provide the place and the lodging, maybe in Sharm, Taba or Cairo." Before we went down for dinner on the banks of the Nile, we agreed that Suleiman would come to Israel two days later for a meeting with Barak.

Suleiman arrived at Barak's residence in Jerusalem with a message from President Mubarak that relations between our two countries would not be affected by any event. President Mubarak would spare no effort to achieve peace. Suleiman himself was working with the Palestinians in order to improve their control on the ground and urged Barak to continue maintaining patience and restraint. Mubarak made a special appeal to Barak to let humanitarian aid be sent to the Territories during Ramadan.

"I instructed the Commander of the Southern Command to ensure that shipments go through the checkpoints without problems," informed Barak. "If we are able to work together so that within two to three weeks there is calm on the ground, we can propose a summit with Arafat, Mubarak, King Abdullah and myself at President Clinton's – as long as our working groups will first be able to narrow the gaps on the core issues. It is clear to me that your positions are naturally closer to the Palestinians', but I trust that you can bring them to far more realistic positions."

Suleiman promised to do all that was possible with the Palestinians to calm the Territories.

"I have fifty more days in this position," Clinton told Yossi Beilin in Washington on December 1, "and I am willing to dedicate all of them except three to help settle the conflict."

Throughout the previous weeks, I had met secretly with Abu Ala at his home in Abu Dis. Spacious and comfortable, his house was tucked away in a labyrinth of steep, narrow alleys, surrounded by a fortress-like wall. Abu Ala was very resolute about Arafat's willingness to reach an agreement. He even said, "Jerusalem, including the Temple Mount, will not be a problem. On territory there will be a need for land swaps in ratios that will be agreed upon, but the main goal is to consolidate confidence-building measures, to completely stop the settlements, and to 'pay the bill' in terms of the Third Further Redeployment."

In the late evening hours of December 6, Amnon Shahak, Yossi Ginossar, Shlomo Ben-Ami and I met in the home of the prime minister in Jerusalem. Toward midnight Barak summarized, "We have an historic responsibility to exhaust the process until its very end, even if ultimately we are unsuccessful. So long as the terror attacks don't stop, we're walking a very thin line. We have to proceed on several parallel tracks, focusing on the reduction of violence, resuming security cooperation, preventing further attacks on the one hand, and advancing the negotiations based on the Camp David Understandings on the other."

Aware that his policy was being misinterpreted by the media and the public, we urged Barak to use one of his public appearances to give an inspirational speech to the people. Unfortunately, that never happened.

"President Mubarak wants Barak to succeed in the elections," Suleiman began during another meeting we had in Cairo on December 9. "He believes that only a Barak-led government can reach an agreement with the Palestinians. For this purpose, Egypt has prepared a proposal for a 'half final' Permanent Status agreement, which it intends to submit to the negotiations teams." The Egyptians envisaged some kind of Palestinian sovereignty over the Temple Mount in return for denying the Right of Return to Palestinian refugees. I emphasized that any formula proposed by Egypt regarding the Temple Mount must include recognition of the rights of the Jewish people in the State of Israel. Most importantly, the demand for the end of conflict and finality of claims had to be included in any proposal or formula.

"The Palestinians always deceive us," Suleiman said. "President Mubarak scheduled three weeks in his calendar to track what is happening on the ground. On Tuesday December 12, we will reconvene the heads of the security establishments, to be followed by two weeks of calm. We have to continue with the quiet track of three-person teams on both sides. The feeling of urgency is also clear to Abu Amar [Yasser Arafat]."

That evening, from the Knesset platform, Barak explained:

> Israel needs special new elections, so that we might have a new government with a mandate and renewed trust in he who heads it ... I hope that it will be a broad government ... this is the real referendum on the way of Israel to peace.

Arafat claimed that Barak's resignation would delay the peace process. The morning after the resignation, at the Sunday Cabinet meeting, Chief of Staff Mofaz assessed that the Palestinian leadership intended to reach an agreement with Israel before the end of Clinton's term.

The details of the Egyptian initiative were clarified. It involved transferring ninety percent of the territory within six months, including the Territories around larger Jerusalem such as Beit Hanina, Wadi Joz, Issawiya, Shoafat, Abu Dis and Al Eizariya. Concurrently, intensive negotiations on Permanent Status would take place. Three weeks after it was concluded, there would be a withdrawal from an additional five percent of the territory. If, by that time, the sides did not reach an agreement, an international conference would be convened for going forward. The Temple Mount and East Jerusalem would be deferred for an agreed period.

A domestic Israeli drama was unfolding. Benjamin Netanyahu returned to Israel and announced that he would challenge Barak. But he set a condition: that the early elections for prime minister should include early general

Knesset elections. After many upheavals and countless intrigues, it was determined that the elections would be restricted to electing the prime minister. The law, which restricted this election to Knesset members, was amended to benefit Netanyahu, but he stood by his word and did not announce his candidacy. Sharon, representing the Likud, would challenge Barak. Whatever Barak's inner feelings may have been on all this, he continued to convey self-confidence, which the public often interpreted as complacence.

Against the background of these developments, the smaller negotiations teams convened in Tel Aviv on the evening of December 10. On the Palestinian side there were Dahlan, Erekat and Abed Rabbo; on the Israeli side Shlomo Ben-Ami, Israel Hasson and me. "We are seeing each other at this very difficult period through a twisted prism," we said, "but we have not, for one minute, lost the determination to reach a comprehensive Permanent Status agreement. The political developments in Israel do not affect the peace process but days like today, which saw nine violent attacks, make it extremely difficult to engage the public's support."

"Arafat wants to continue the process we started at Camp David. He wants to sign a Framework Agreement on Permanent Status before President Clinton leaves the White House," Abed Rabbo said.

"This is our wish as well but a supportive environment and atmosphere are necessary for negotiations, that is, without violence or attacks," I replied.

"We are making an effort to isolate ourselves from the raging violence outside and examine the possibility of resuming the negotiations. God help us if anyone found out these negotiations were taking place," Ben-Ami added.

The discussion started with the issue of the Temple Mount. "We know what you need, and you know what we need," I began. "Let's start from the Egyptian proposals on this issue."

"This has to be part of Palestinian sovereignty in East Jerusalem and the Old City. Arafat has said many times that the Jewish Quarter and the Wailing Wall will be under your control," Abed Rabbo noted.

"Any solution in the Temple Mount has to reflect the Jewish faith, religion and tradition," I replied. "For us, the Temple Mount is a place for the dead, not for the living. We have to respect the symbols of each of the sides," Ben-Ami added. "We respect the Jewish relationship with the Mount of Olives, with the City of David, and with Mount Zion. We will give you everything you need, as long as it will be under Palestinian sovereignty," Erekat replied.

"There are so many solutions on the issue of sovereignty we can surely formulate something that will reconcile the Muslim and Jewish demands," Ben-Ami continued.

The next morning, after the teams agreed to meet again with the maps, Barak convened a meeting in his office, in a forum that would later be called the "peace cabinet" – which included Shlomo Ben-Ami, Yossi Beilin,

Amnon Shahak, Yossi Sarid, Danny Yatom and me. Shimon Peres joined from the second meeting on, and national security adviser Uzi Dayan also attended. "We must ensure that we have done everything possible to reach a reasonable agreement within a month, to a month and a half," Barak summarized the short meeting.

It is difficult to comprehend the number of plans, proposals, recommended plans of action, and just plain ideas that reached my desk from concerned citizens, academicians, veterans of the political system, executives and institutes, to name but a few. Proposals regarding the negotiations process, understandings regarding Arabs in general and Arafat specifically, historic lessons, maps, outlines for solutions, were all examined and addressed. This outpouring was heart-warming. Even those that criticized had a creative or innovative element that could serve as a catalyst for moving our work forward and consolidating a position.

The opening session of the fact-finding Mitchell commission took place on December 11, 2000. In his opening remarks, as the host, Barak was pointed and clear:

> Even before Camp David, the Palestinians outlined a violent scenario as an alternative to the failure of the summit. At the end of September they did turn to violence, in an effort to gain outside public support. In doing so, they violated their obligations to us in signed agreements, to solve every problem strictly through negotiation. In the last few months we have faced hundreds of shooting incidents toward the capital of Israel, including by the Palestinian security forces, with weapons that we gave them to maintain public order in the Palestinian Authority.
>
> The terrorist attacks were carried out by terrorists who were released from prison by Arafat himself. Who benefits from this situation? Whom does this violence serve? Clearly, not Israel. This is the essence of your work in the fact-finding commission.
>
> In Paris, Arafat avoided signing a ceasefire agreement. After the Sharm summit, he did not implement anything and did not fulfill his commitments. I sent Shimon Peres to him, together with Gilead Sher, who sits with us today. Of course, Arafat promised them that he would act to reduce violence. If words between leaders are nothing but molecules drifting in the air, and commitments are not even worth the paper they are written on, this is very frustrating. No country can accept shooting directed at its cities and an armed struggle as a means of achieving political goals.
>
> What has been presented in the world press as the excessive use of force is interpreted by the Israeli public as feebleness that

is unacceptable for any legitimate regime in the world. At the end, we will have an agreement with the Palestinians. And as you know a reasonable agreement can be achieved. We do not intend to rule over another people, but we intend to realize our right to be here, in the cradle of our civilization, and to defend ourselves.

Former Senator Mitchell, the chairman of the commission, detailed the mandate of the commission, and emphasized the transparency with which it intended to conduct its work. The committee would complete the report, which would be submitted to both sides as well as President Clinton.

In the evening I met with Erekat in Jerusalem. Erekat again told me that the Palestinians wanted a full framework agreement. Later that night, I called Arafat's Bureau Chief Nabil Abu Rudayna to protest the latest incident – shootings from Beit Jalla toward Jerusalem, injuring a citizen, shootings on Givat Ze'ev, an explosion in Harsina Hill in Hebron, firing on posts in the Gaza Strip and in Kfar Darom. It was a completely unacceptable situation, with a total of thirty-five shooting incidents before midnight.

The next evening, Hasson, Pini Meidan-Shani and I took off for meetings in Amman. I had a long private conversation with Foreign Minister Abdel Ilah al-Khatib. "We need a confidence-building measure," al-Khatib said. "In substance you have closed more than a few issues in Camp David. Jerusalem is a difficult issue, but the question of refugees is even more complicated." I warned against introducing initiatives and ideas without consulting with us first. "Every document has its own dynamic, and the minute it is put on the table, it can exacerbate a crisis rather than resolve it. We do not accept Arafat's behavior. After weeks of bloody violence on his part, he now waits for Israeli concessions. The parameters of a possible agreement between us and the Palestinians are clear and known to you, and we propose that they serve as the basis for moving forward." Late that night, we returned to Israel in the same light plane, buffeted by the pouring rain and stormy weather.

We all felt the urgent need for President Clinton's personal and direct involvement. "Don't you think it's a bit much for you to expect that the president dedicate his time to your discussions now?" Ambassador Indyk asked. "It's the only hope for a breakthrough." I answered. "Does Ehud share your opinion?" Indyk continued. "I don't know," I answered honestly, "I intend to speak to him shortly about it, and I hope he accepts my view."

This and other conversations prompted the Americans to accelerate their preparations for the negotiations round a week later in Washington, and to finalize the president's proposal, which would be presented to the sides at the end of December.

On December 14, Shlomo Ben-Ami, Israel Hasson and I arrived at Mohammad Rashid's magnificent house in Gaza for a meeting with Arafat.

The Palestinian side was represented by Rashid, Erekat, Dahlan, Abed Rabbo and Abu Rudayna.

Arafat was very late and we were just chatting, making small talk while waiting. My cellular phone rang. It was my father. My dear grandmother, Antoinette Sher-Simon, one of the bravest and most determined people I ever knew, had passed away after months of suffering. A member of an assimilated French family who became a fervent young Zionist, she fled from Paris in 1940 just hours before the Germans entered the French capital, escaping with her her only son, seven-year-old Yoel, my father. Her husband, my grandfather Avraham Sher, one of the defenders of Tel Hai in his youth and a member of the Hagana, was killed in December 1947 while escorting a convoy to besieged Jerusalem near the Castel, at the beginning of the War of Independence. All of us, three generations, loved her dearly and were very attached to her. I tried to support my father as much as I could from Gaza, in this unreal situation.

Ben-Ami urged Arafat to develop a timetable. "Your relationship with Barak is not good but no one before us and maybe no one after us will attempt to conclude an agreement with the same determination as we have. We are continuing with the process despite being attacked even by the left as having gone too far. We do not want to see the Palestinian people suffer but we can ignore neither the reality nor the serious threats of Hamas and Islamic Jihad. It is vital that we implement the decisions that were agreed in Sharm, and propose confidence-building measures. We are hostages of one another: no other way out, except through an agreement."

"Time is very short," responded Arafat, "we have to work seriously and quickly, because it will take the new administration a long time to study the issues. Today was a very bad day in Gaza."

Ben-Ami and Arafat went off for a private conversation, with the other participants left to talk among themselves. Arafat appeared encouraged from the discussion, apparently hearing things he wanted to on territory and the Temple Mount. His representatives would later quote what they claimed were parts of the conversation with Ben-Ami. The negotiation meetings continued on the afternoon of the following day, December 15, in Tel Aviv. The Palestinians vehemently protested the targeted killings. "Don't push us to extremes with the assassinations your government is carrying out," Dahlan evoked. "You expect us to stay silent when you murder us?!"

Within the military, there was almost a consensus that the Palestinians were deceitful and that they were preparing for armed conflict. The military's analysis, that a conflict was unavoidable, encouraged an aggressive approach, that we should subdue the Palestinians through pressure and even more force, thinking nothing of the negotiations. This kind of thinking in essence set the atmosphere and conditions for a self-fulfilling prophecy. On more than one occasion over the past months, in a severe deviation from the democratic procedures and governmental hierarchy, some senior military officials have made public remarks with definite political undertones. Assessments and analyses by the intelligence community found their way to the public before even being presented to the government and the prime minister. Through the guarantees given to the US and the Palestinians during the negotiations, the Cabinet counted on the IDF to assist in the attempts to attain calm. Testimonies from the ground, however, indicated that on several occasions, operations diverged from the political directives. Some of the prime minister's commitments, which were conveyed to the military by the prime minister's military secretary, seemed to simply evaporate along the way. Tanks were not withdrawn. Instead, their commanders made do by turning the barrels away; the fishing area in Gaza was not opened; an incredibly small amount of Palestinian workers were allowed to enter, in violation of a clear directive; closures were not removed. At some point former Chief of Staff Amnon Shahak gave up. This couldn't go on.

On the Israeli side, the public debate around the question of "negotiations under fire" would not die down. Many people engaged in a manipulative discussion, about whether Arafat could, or even wanted to control the situation on the ground. In doing so, they avoided the main question – what were the Israeli interests in continuing the dialogue? Israel was becoming a country under siege, in the main, a self-imposed siege. The negotiations were meant to salvage us from this situation once and for all.

The new characteristics of the conflict did not allow for an "Israeli victory." We might be led into a very dangerous situation, without an agreement. With international terrorism, Islamic anti-Zionist fundamentalism, fanned by blind religious fervor, and the pressure of extremist Arab countries in possession of mass destruction weapons, the foundations necessary for an agreement – trust and hope – had been worn thin on both sides. On the Palestinian side, extremist forces were pushing from the bottom-up, in an environment of hate and incitement supported by the top echelon. Marwan Barghouti had become a star in the media and Palestinian street, preaching for a popular and violent war against the occupation. The basic concept of "two states for two peoples" was being eroded on both sides.

Under these circumstances, the Camp David outline for a Permanent Status agreement was the best Israel could achieve, in hoping to end the conflict with the Palestinians.

The negotiations continued on December 16. "There are ten to fifteen decisions which the leaders only would have to take by themselves. Therefore, let's return to the substance," I suggested. "We need 10.5 percent of the land, for settlement blocs that will accommodate eighty percent of the settlers. You need your dignity. Which means, you need the borders of June 4, 1967, as a point of departure, with the necessary corrections, and a physical connection between the West Bank and the Gaza Strip. You need breathing space for the people in Gaza. We have to be guided by feasible solutions not by a perceived notion of 'justice.' Our perceptions of each other are conflicting, yet the issues are linked in a relationship that cannot be dissolved. We will have to uproot the inhabitants of sixty to eighty settlements, but these could immediately serve refugees returning to the area of the Palestinian Authority. This is the negotiations space between us, on the ballpark of territory."

Ben-Ami supported these thoughts. "It is humiliating to talk about percentages and parts of percentages when we are dealing with the homeland, and that's why Gilead's proposal to discuss the needs of each side is the right one. Each of us will have to confront our public. We will not infringe upon the safe passage, although it will be under our sovereignty. We will give you all that you need in terms of economic relations in our area. And it appears to me that we will not oppose an international force in the Jordan Valley."

The discussion focused on Jerusalem and Palestinian commitments not to excavate the area of the Temple Mount. "We agree to international supervision," Erekat noted. But he did not budge from his inflexible position regarding the Palestinian demand to use the term "Wailing Wall" instead of the "Western Wall" in the text. The Western Wall, in the Jewish tradition, is part of the wall that surrounded the Second Great Temple and is its only remnant. Its length is 480 meters. The "Wailing Wall" is the exposed part of the wall, a few dozen meters long, where worshipers pray and place notes in. Erekat also demanded Palestinian sovereignty over all the Arab neighborhoods in East Jerusalem, including three-quarters of the Old City.

As Erekat and I were concurrently carrying out talks with the Americans to plan continued negotiations in the US we emphasized the precondition accepted by both sides – that the region be calm, without violence or attacks, while we talked in Washington. We stood once again before a decisive stage in the process. The US was apparently about to present a comprehensive proposal for Permanent Status. If such a plan had been presented to the two sides at Camp David, or shortly thereafter in August/ September, things could have been substantially different.

19

DO YOU WANT TO
CONTINUE CRYING?

Beginning on Friday December 15, 2000, the political story in Israel focused on the possibility that Shimon Peres would present his candidacy for prime minister. Encouraged by public opinion polls that showed a tie between him and Sharon, and a clear win for Sharon over Barak, Peres decided to run for prime minister, for the sixth time in his life. However he would need the signatures of ten Knesset members to submit his candidacy. He was unable to get the necessary signatures from his own Labor party faction and had to turn to Yossi Sarid and ask for the support of the Meretz faction. Barak and his advisers tried to convince people around Sarid not to support Peres' candidacy. It was actually Yossi Beilin, a close confidant of Peres, who spoke against the candidacy, claiming that it would do harm to the peace camp. The deadline for submitting one's candidacy for prime minister was midnight, December 21.

The one person who was very agitated, stressed and concerned about this development was Shlomo Ben-Ami, the minister of foreign affairs. While he was at Bolling Air Force Base near Washington, his people back in Israel reported that Peres was demanding to replace him as minister of foreign affairs. Barak tried to calm Shlomo over the phone. "I have no intention of replacing you," he said. Another proposal, according to rumors, was to nominate Peres a supra-minister for peace. It was accepted by Barak, but rejected by Peres. Peres announced his intention to run but was prevented from actually doing so. Sarid's position, to withhold the ten signatures that Peres needed, prevailed in an internal Meretz vote.

The discussions at Bolling Air Force Base began on the evening of Tuesday, December 19. Bolling was a huge base, like a small city, on the outskirts of Washington. It was very cold outside and the forecast predicted snow that night. Minister Ben-Ami and I headed the Israeli team, accompanied by General Shlomo Yanai, IDF, and Colonel Daniel Reisner, IDF Legal Branch. Yasser Abed Rabbo, Saeb Erekat and Mohammed Dahlan led the Palestinian side.

The negotiators lowered expectations in advance. Upon our arrival I told reporters who waited at the airfield: "We have come here to promote the implementation of the Sharm agreement. This is a dialogue aiming to achieve an effective ceasefire, and to see if we can resume the political negotiations at some future stage." Erekat said similar things.

"This is it," Dennis Ross opened the round, dramatically. "This is the final shot, and there is no other. We will not have a summit if we are not completely confident that it will succeed this time around, and that we have a package on all the core issues."

I suggested that we set a rigid agenda. "We have to set the parameters for each of the issues, and to carry out in parallel a 'drafting' channel and a 'concept' channel," I said. "We have to ensure that there is no violence during this period, and to convey the feeling to people on both sides that we have moved forward from Camp David. The Americans," I emphasized, "are only aiding us, they cannot take our place as parties to an agreement." Abed Rabbo said that he had a mandate to reach a resolution on all the issues and to consolidate all the principles. The two sides declared their intention and consent to reach an agreement and to avoid failure.

The first issue was Jerusalem. We worked on a large aerial photo, in which we defined the Jewish neighborhoods, the Arab neighborhoods, contiguity in the "Holy Basin," the ground corridor toward the east, and a north–south passage. We also detailed all the Israeli and Jewish interests in the municipal area of Jerusalem.

Erekat presented the Palestinian map in which all the Israeli neighborhoods were linked by "strings" to western Jerusalem. An argument developed over the June 4, 1967 borders of Jordanian Al-Quds.

In meetings the next day, we geared up with a positive attitude, and tried to move forward, despite the differences. This was difficult, particularly after we received warnings from Israel and the Territories regarding terror attacks and military actions. It was clear to both sides that if we did not reach an agreement on Jerusalem, there would be no agreement at all. Ben-Ami and I pointed out that the Palestinians were backing down from their Camp David positions. "We should stop with the demagoguery," we told them, "and stop building ideologies on the basis of databases, like including the inhabitants of Jerusalem in the number of settlers, for a reduced calculation of settlement blocs and territory."

The Palestinians were resolute about an exchange involving Palestinian sovereignty over the Temple Mount, and in return for Palestinian recognition of eleven Jewish neighborhoods built in Jerusalem after the Six Day War.

"We have a symbolic claim on the Temple Mount. We have prevented ourselves from praying at – let alone excavating – the site, because of the sanctity of the location. The issue of the Temple Mount requires empathy by both sides. We are looking for a formula that recognizes that the Jews do not have to give up their linkage to the site. Then, either we divide sovereignty, or we just don't talk about it," Ben-Ami suggested. Dennis Ross proposed that the Americans present their own formula for "Haram Al-Sharif," that would be acceptable to both sides.

In internal discussions, some disagreement emerged between Shlomo Ben-Ami, who tended to be more flexible on our positions, and Hasson, Meidan-Shani and I, who worked in line with the principal guidelines of the prime minister. What could have been interpreted as differences in nuance at the beginning became differences in substance. From the beginning of the process in 2000, Ben-Ami's vital passion and determination to reach a Permanent Status agreement carried us through all the obstacles, energizing us, propelling us forward. No one cared what his motives were – Shimon Peres breathing down his neck, political considerations, or belief in this political credo. However, his running full steam ahead at this extremely crucial point of the negotiations became a real concern. Ben-Ami and I had two very honest and difficult private discussions on this issue during which I was put in the awkward position of explicitly asking the foreign minister to work within the guidelines set forth by the prime minister and the "peace cabinet."

Hasson chose not to challenge the erosion in our positions, isolating himself by sitting in an armchair on the sidelines, conspicuously indifferent, and refusing to attend meetings at the White House, even though he was on the guest list. Upon our return to Israel, he resigned from the negotiations team in protest, using very harsh words to describe Ben-Ami's behavior. According to the Palestinians, Hasson revealed to them his decision to resign in advance. We viewed this as a momentary weakness. We were able to later change his mind in a meeting at the prime minister's residence in Jerusalem.

This rift inside the Israeli delegation did not escape the attention of the Americans and Palestinians. "Not everything that Ben-Ami says is authorized by the prime minister," remarked Meidan-Shani to Rob Malley and Saeb Erekat over dinner in Washington.

The negotiations were tense and very difficult but both sides continued their earnest efforts to come up with creative solutions for the complex, sensitive issues, most notably the issue of Temple Mount and rehabilitating the refugees from Lebanon. Still, the fatigue, responsibility and frustrations were showing their effect on all of us. "Do you want to keep on crying?" Ben-Ami blurted out to Erekat at the heat of the discussion. "You want everything to be accepted based on your positions," I concurred to Abed Rabbo, "relying on the president's proposals when you feel like it, and tossing to the garbage what you don't like. An agreement means a package of compromises from *both* sides, not just from Israel!"

On the Temple Mount, Ben-Ami suggested far-reaching language that did not mention Israeli sovereignty at all. "The Palestinian state recognizes the sanctity of the place to the Jewish people, and the centrality of the site in the history, tradition and identity of the Jewish people. The Palestinians therefore commit not to conduct excavations on or beneath the site of 'Al Haram,' as not to harm Jewish holies. Moreover, in recognition of these values, the Jews can pray on the Mount in an area that will be agreed upon. This agreement, like the declaration which accompanies it, will be ratified in a summit of the Islamic nations." The Palestinians immediately rejected the formulation. "If you refuse to accept this – there's no deal. I say this with a broken heart," Ben-Ami reacted angrily. "You are causing us to act like historians, judges and people of faith. Your right doesn't bind me," Abed Rabbo replied bluntly. "I am really impressed that you are willing to agree not to excavate at the Temple Mount. Thank you, really, from the bottom of my heart," I offered cynically. Abed Rabbo got up, grabbed his coat, and had to be forcibly held back by his friends, Dahlan and Erekat, so as not to break up the meeting and leave for the airport.

Things were not looking much better on the territorial issue. The Palestinians continued to object to contiguity of Israeli settlement blocs. The most they offered was four percent of the territory in addition to land swaps, although they did not insist on a ratio of one to one.

In meetings with the American team, headed by Secretary of State Albright, we were not able to identify any Palestinian movement relative to their position at Camp David. On territory, we understood that the Palestinians would agree to a five percent annexation while for security purposes and settlement blocs, Israel would need an area totaling a minimum of eight percent. As for the division of sovereignty in the Old City, here too there was a need to return the Palestinians and the Americans to a formula with equal division of two Quarters for each side, under a special regime that would exist in the Old City. There would be recognition of Jewish and Israeli ties to the Temple Mount. The prime minister had to confirm with President Clinton again that unless there was a signed agreement, all understandings would be null and void.

In our first meeting with President Clinton at the White House on December 20, the president declared, "I am willing to do all I can, to reach an agreement but we first have to address the issue of the violence and to bridge the gaps between you. This effort can end no later than January 10."

"We cannot afford a failure. This will be a disaster. It is vital that both sides move away from their positions," Ben-Ami said.

Abed Rabbo expressed commitment, on behalf of Arafat, to reach an agreement in the coming weeks. "The atmosphere is promising, but the question of 'Haram Al-Sharif' is critical. Each side has a better understanding now of what are the real needs of the other side, and there is a chance to move forward. This is the moment – and it will not come again."

Clinton continued: "I tried to consolidate parameters within which the issues should be resolved. It's very important to discuss not only a solution, but to try and imagine how the day-to-day life will be. I suggest you continue your work within this set framework."

The president then went into the detail of his proposed framework: Territory – neither ninety percent nor one hundred percent of the territory, but some rate in between; Security – how would Palestinian sovereignty be respected while addressing Israeli security needs; Refugees – this could threaten the actual existence of the State of Israel; the international mechanism to compensate, resettle and rehabilitate refugees must be addressed; Jerusalem – find a functional formula for arrangements between the two capitals, the one including the Arab neighborhoods and the other the Israeli ones. At "Haram Al Sharif" there will be Palestinian sovereignty, while recognizing Jewish tradition. Clinton thought that actually describing the arrangements on the Temple Mount would create agreement between the sides. "The leaders you represent here are more willing today, than they were a few months ago, because each has seen the darkness that stands before him," the president said. "And you, their representatives, prove the serious intentions of those who sent you."

Yasser Abed Rabbo's brother passed away after a long battle with terminal illness. We came to his room to pay our respects. The Palestinians were sitting with him. This very gloomy and sad environment was so similar to the period of mourning we Jews traditionally practice. The next day, Abed Rabbo left Washington. Our next meeting with him was at the Erez checkpoint, three weeks later.

In the Territories, the newspaper *El-Hayat El-Jadida* published a caricature depicting Shlomo Ben-Ami with an ax in one hand, his other hand shaking a severed and bloodied extended hand – Palestine.

Friday December 22, after two additional days of grueling negotiations, was the eve of President Clinton's presentation of his ideas to the sides. Palestinians and Israelis alike were equally anxious. Would the first formal American plan reflect the minimalist positions of each side, or would the president overstep the area of agreement that would be acceptable to each of the sides, and raise ideas that would constitute an attempt to impose his position?

Erekat and Dahlan met with the Saudi ambassador for dinner, and returned later to meet with Ross. "What have you prepared for us?" they asked Ross, with audible concern. "Will we be able to swallow it?" Ross, who held a draft of the text that President Clinton would present to both sides the next day, read to them what they were going to hear the following morning. "This is difficult," was their reaction. "The question is not whether this is difficult," Ross replied. "I assume that this will also be the Israeli response. The question is whether it is possible for you, and will Arafat be able to live with it." In a conversation that lasted until after midnight, Ross asked the Palestinians if they preferred the president not to present his ideas, thereby making the entire draft irrelevant. "No," replied Erekat and Dahlan, "we ask that the president present the ideas. We'll deal with it."

The climax of this round of negotiations, and actually the high point of the entire American effort to bring the sides to a Permanent Status agreement, culminated in the presentation of President Clinton's ideas to us, on Saturday December 23, 2000.

The tension at the White House was palpable. The Israelis and Palestinians took pictures with one another, trying to ease the anxiety, aware that within a short moment the American plan for a peace agreement would be revealed. Clinton, dressed casually in jeans, entered the Cabinet room in which the members of the teams were seated, in suits and ties, and began his message at this dramatic moment by stressing that the ideas he would detail in the minutes to come were his best judgment. The ideas, he said, were not open to negotiation, but rather should provide a basis to reach agreement within two weeks. And the president proceeded:

Territory
Based on what I heard, I believe that the solution should be in the mid-90%s, between 94–96% of the West Bank territory of the Palestinian state.

The land annexed by Israel should be compensated by a land swap of 1–3% in addition to territorial arrangement such as a permanent safe passage.

The parties should also consider the swap of leased land to meet their respective needs. There are creative ways for doing this that should address Palestinian and Israeli needs and concerns.

The Parties should develop a map consistent with the following criteria:

- 80% of the settlers in blocs;
- contiguity;
- minimize annexed areas;
- minimize the number of Palestinians affected.

Security
The key to security lies in an international presence that can only be withdrawn by mutual consent. This presence will also monitor the implementation of the agreement between both sides.

My best judgment is that the Israeli withdrawal should be carried out over 36 months while international force is gradually introduced in the area. At the end of this period, a small Israeli presence would remain in fixed locations in the Jordan Valley under the authority of the international force for another 36 months. This period could be reduced in the event of favorable regional developments that diminish the threats to Israel.

On early-warning situations, Israel should maintain three facilities in the West Bank with a Palestinian liaison presence. The stations will be subject to review after 10 years with any changes in status to be mutually agreed.

Regarding emergency developments, I understand that you still have to develop a map of relevant areas and routes. But in defining what is an emergency, I propose the following definition:

> Imminent and demonstrable threat to Israel's national security of a military nature requires the activation of a national state of emergency.

Of course, the international forces will need to be notified of any such determination.

On airspace, I suggest that the state of Palestine will have sovereignty over its airspace but that the two sides should work out special arrangements for Israeli training and operational needs.

I understand that the Israeli position is that Palestine should be defined as a "demilitarized state" while the Palestinian side proposes "a state with limited arms." As a compromise, I suggest calling it a "non-militarized state."

This will be consistent with the fact that in addition to a strong Palestinian security force, Palestine will have an international force for border security and deterrence purposes.

Jerusalem and refugees
I have a sense that the remaining gaps have more to do with formulations than practical realities.

Jerusalem
The general principle is that Arab areas are Palestinian and Jewish ones are Israeli. This would apply to the Old City as well. I urge the two sides to work on maps to create maximum contiguity for both sides.

Regarding the Haram/Temple Mount, I believe that the gaps are not related to practical administration but to the symbolic issues of sovereignty and to finding a way to accord respect to the religious beliefs of both sides.

I know you have been discussing a number of formulations, and you can agree on any of these. I add to these two additional formulations guaranteeing Palestinian effective control over Haram while respecting the conviction of the Jewish people. Regarding either one of these two formulations will be international monitoring to provide mutual confidence.

1 Palestinian sovereignty over the Haram and Israeli sovereignty over *either* the Western Wall and the space sacred to Judaism of which it is a part *or* the Western Wall and the Holy of Holies of which it is a part.

There will be a firm commitment by both not to excavate beneath the Haram or behind the Wall.

2 Palestinian shared sovereignty over the Haram and Israeli sovereignty over the Western Wall and shared functional sovereignty over the issue of excavation under the Haram and behind the Wall as mutual consent would be requested before any excavation can take place.

Refugees
I sense that the differences are more relating to formulations and less to what will happen on a practical level.

I believe that Israel is prepared to acknowledge the moral and material suffering caused to the Palestinian people as a result of the 1948 war and the need to assist the international community in addressing the problem.

An international commission should be established to implement all the aspects that flow from your agreement: compensation, resettlement, rehabilitation, etc.

The US is prepared to lead an international effort to help the refugees.

The fundamental gap is on how to handle the concept of the Right of Return. I know the history of the issue and how hard it will be for the Palestinian leadership to appear to be abandoning this principle.

The Israeli side could simply not accept any reference to Right of Return that would imply a right to immigrate to Israel in defiance of Israel's sovereign policies on admission or that would threaten the Jewish character of the state.

Any solution must address both needs.

The solution will have to be consistent with the two-state approach that both sides have accepted as the way to end the Palestinian–Israeli conflict: the state of Palestine as the homeland of the Palestinian people and the State of Israel as the homeland of the Jewish people.

Under the two-state solution, the guiding principle should be that the Palestinian state will be the focal point for Palestinians who choose to return to the area without ruling out that Israel will accept some of these refugees.

I believe that we need to adopt a formulation on the Right of Return to Israel itself but that does not negate the aspiration of the Palestinian people to return to the area.

In light of the above, I propose two alternatives:

1 Both sides recognize the right of Palestinian refugees to return to Historic Palestine. Or:
2 Both sides recognize the right of the Palestinian refuges to return to their homeland.

The agreement will define the implementation of this general right in a way that is consistent with the two-state solution. It would list five possible final homes for the refugees:

1 The state of Palestine.
2 Areas in Israel being transferred to Palestine in the land swap.
3 Rehabilitation in a host country.
4 Resettlement in a third country.
5 Admission to Israel.

In listing these options, the agreement will make clear that the return to the West Bank, Gaza Strip and the areas acquired in the land swap would be a right to all Palestinian refugees.

While rehabilitation in host countries, resettlement in third countries and absorption into Israel will depend upon the policies of those countries.

Israel could indicate in the agreement that it intends to establish a policy so that some of the refugees would be absorbed into Israel consistent with Israel's sovereign decision.

I believe that priority should be given to the refugee population in Lebanon.

The Parties would agree that this implements Resolution 194.

I propose that the agreement clearly mark the end of the conflict and its implementation put an end to all its claims. This could be implemented through a UNSCR that notes that Resolutions 242 and 338 have been implemented through the release of Palestinian prisoners.

I believe that this is an outline of a fair and lasting agreement.

It gives the Palestinian people the ability to determine the future on their own land, a sovereign and viable state recognized by the international community, Al-Quds as its capital, sovereignty over the Haram, and new lives for the refugees.

It gives the people of Israel a genuine end to the conflict, real security, the preservation of sacred religious ties, the incorporation of 80% of the settlers into Israel, and the largest Jewish Jerusalem in history recognized by all as its capital.

This is the best I can do. Brief your leaders and tell me if they are prepared to come for discussions based on these ideas. If so, I would meet them next week separately. If not, I have taken this as far as I can.

These are my ideas. If they are not accepted, they are not just off the table, they also go with me when I leave the office.

The president read quickly, without stopping. After he finished, he left the room. Dennis Ross returned, re-read the ideas at note-taking speed, and responded to some questions for clarification.

Gidi Grinstein, our able and dedicated team secretary and coordinator, typed up every word as did the assistants of the Palestinian representatives. During the meeting, Gidi's computer battery went out, and he continued to take notes by hand. The text that was typed and written became the official version of those "unofficial ideas," and a basis for reference in all our internal discussions from here on.

Clinton had decided to adopt the "one text process": one proposal that conveys the judgment of a third side in terms of options that could be acceptable to the sides involved in the conflict. Such a document could be transferred to the sides for their comments. There are those who believe these procedures facilitate a positive response from the sides. This method, described in detail in the 1993 book *Beyond Machiavelli – Tools for Coping with Conflict* by Fisher, Kopelman and Schneider, was the one used by President Jimmy Carter and Secretary of State Vance during the 1978 Camp David summit with Prime Minister Begin and Egyptian President Sadat. The American negotiations team prepared twenty-three drafts of the agreement in ten days, and each draft was essentially a reaction to an issue that was raised by one of the sides. On the last day, Professor Fisher writes, President Carter decided that the developing document was the best that could be achieved. He turned to the sides to get their consent. In a few hours the Camp David Accords were signed.

Only now, five months after the Camp David summit in 2000, I thought to myself, were the unraveled ends woven back together. It is difficult to assess how Camp David would have ended if these proposals had been presented to the two sides at that time, with the two leaders present at this isolated location, with Clinton president for another five months. If only the Americans would have used those conditions to pressure the sides into closing the deal . . . This did not happen, and I could not easily dismiss the feeling of a missed opportunity.

Immediately following the presentation of the Clinton ideas the two sides began working feverishly. Ben-Ami and I thought that Israel should accept the ideas of the president as a basis for negotiations. Within this framework we would ask for some clarification and further elaboration of some unclear points, recall Israeli positions on issues in which they differed from the president's idea, and propose points that were not addressed.

For example, we expected that finality of claims would be included in the framework agreement itself. Also within the context of leasing arrangements, the area of the annexed blocs should be expanded. We believed that it was necessary to clarify that the safe passage would be under Israeli sovereignty and that the free access and worship in the places holy to the Jewish faith would be ensured. Israel also wanted to ensure the contiguity of its sovereignty in Jerusalem, the primacy of the special regime in the "Holy Basin," and Israeli interests in the Armenian Quarter, Mount of Olives, the tunnel system adjacent to the Western Wall, the structure just outside and adjacent to the Temple Mount above the Western Wall, which houses the police, the City of David, the Ofel, and Pool of Silwan.

Our first reaction was that the agreement should include further details regarding the mandate of the international force, taking into consideration Israel's needs. Arrangements regarding the airspace would be extended to include the electromagnetic spectrum.

On refugees, the agreement had to reinforce the principle of "lump sum" covering all financial needs.

Our initial recommendation was to respond in the affirmative but to clarify and detail some issues and add points that were not addressed.

An air force helicopter was waiting for us upon our return from Washington on the evening of December 24. We immediately flew to Shraga Camp, not far from Nahariya, to report to Barak and the other members of the "peace cabinet."

Shimon Peres thought that the Palestinians would question the president's proposals regarding the Temple Mount, the refugees and the Jordan Valley. He insisted on the importance of the time factor. "The Likud is accusing us of making so many concessions, they are actually doing us a favor by preparing the groundwork for concessions in the agreement." Yossi Sarid urged Barak to respond positively in principle, and use that answer as an asset in the election campaign. Yossi Beilin expected difficulties but said, "I am at peace with these parameters." He pressed Barak to meet with Arafat in the next two days. Dayan also believed it was necessary for Barak to meet with Arafat, even before giving an answer to the president on Wednesday.

Ehud Barak concluded. "Despite everything, we still have no assurance that Arafat will move to close the deal. I think it would be wrong to discuss the details in public at this point. We should stress that what's driving our strategy is the understanding that the alternative to an agreement is tragedy, we are therefore willing to discuss any far-reaching idea."

We all recommended that the prime minister meet with Arafat as soon as possible but the meeting never took place.

In Rabin Square in Tel Aviv, the bereaved parents of children who were killed in terrorist attacks and who supported the Barak government's peace efforts, raised a tent to gather signatures and express support. The public was apathetic, and the giant tent was left empty. I spoke to them every few days. Rami Elhanan, who lost his daughter, is an old friend from Jerusalem, and with Yitzhak Frenkental, whose son was assassinated, I had a strong personal bond. I came to visit them in their tent, and arranged for the entire group, including its Palestinian members, to meet with the prime minister in his office, in order to support and encourage him. I believe the meeting also gave strength to the parents.

On Wednesday, December 27, the extended Cabinet convened for a lengthy session on the ideas of President Clinton. The prime minister asked to hear the positions of the ministers and of outside experts. The discussion began in the morning, with an overall feeling that the country was at a crossroads. Barak emphasized that he did not intend to grant the Palestinians the Right of Return to Israel, neither formally nor practically. Weighing every word, he conveyed:

> I do not intend to sign a document that transfers sovereignty on the Temple Mount to the Palestinians. . . . This is one of the most important sessions this government has had since it was created, because it reflects unusual historic responsibility. There are, of course, risks. But we must remember that our responsibility is to exhaust the possibility of reaching an agreement that does not compromise Israel's vital security interests. The ideas of the president are not our ideal. On certain issues they go beyond what even we were willing accept, if we were to address each issue separately. But if the other side it willing to take this step, it would be wrong not to discuss the entire package. The government must face reality and lead a political process, as painful as it may be, instead of heading – eyes wide open – into wars after which we arrive at the same place, after having buried our dead.

Barak proposed that our response to President Clinton should be that the Israeli government viewed the ideas of the president as the basis for further negotiations toward a permanent peace agreement, provided the Palestinians viewed it as a basis as well.

In the afternoon, I convened an internal discussion of the working group on borders that worked in coordination with the "peace administration," and representatives of the Ministry of Foreign Affairs. Maps were laid out as we engaged in a serious and in-depth thinking process to the president's proposal regarding land swaps, taking into consideration all the interests – demographic, security, agricultural, habitation, and creating reasonable permanent borders.

A little storm began brewing in the interim. Head of the Shin Bet, Avi Dichter, and the Chief of Staff Mofaz, were afraid that their reservations and comments on the president's ideas would not receive the necessary attention in the Cabinet meeting. Dichter, level-headed and discrete as always, sent a short letter to the government members, outlining his main reservations. Mofaz was primarily concerned with the PA not fulfilling previous agreements and with ensuring Israeli control in order to prevent erosion in the demilitarization of the Palestinian state. The prime minister's response to the analysis of the chief of staff was terse: "Shaul, do you really think that the State of Israel can't exist without controlling the Palestinian people? It's the conclusion that comes out of your assessment."

On that afternoon I received a phone call from a senior journalist. He outlined a long document, in which the reservations of the IDF chief of staff were detailed, word for word. This was just a few hours before they were supposed to be presented to the Cabinet. I refused to comment. As Ariel Sharon would tell the IDF chief of staff and his senior officers, in a future Cabinet meeting: "The next time you want to tell me something, don't call the press, call me, directly."

Ambassador Indyk reported that "the Palestinians already responded to the White House. They expressed their gratitude for all the efforts that were made. But before responding to the ideas of the president, they wanted to receive answers on specific questions." The US adopted a very severe approach in response, telling the Palestinians: "We will not answer any question, until we know unequivocally that you accept the ideas and parameters the president has offered as a basis for continued negotiations." Indyk suggested that Israel continue its discussions in an effort to consolidate its answer, irrespective of the Palestinian position.

In a conversation with the national security adviser Sandy Berger at 2 a.m., Barak emphasized that he would not meet with Arafat unless the chairman replied with a "yes" or at the very least "yes, but," to the ideas of the president.

At Mubarak's request, Hasson, Yanai and I flew out to Sharm Al Sheikh and met with President Mubarak, Omar Suleiman and Foreign Minister Amre Moussa. I provided an overview of the Israeli response as it was conveyed after the Cabinet decision, and noted that we would require some clarifications on vital issues. Clarifications, I emphasized, not rebuttal of specific points.

I explained to Mubarak why the president's proposal was so difficult for Israel. Rabbis, mayors, politicians from every direction, and even people within the peace camp and the government itself, opposed the government position and attacked it vehemently, for their own reasons. "This is very difficult publicly, but we believe that the president's proposal is reasonable and balanced – for good and for bad – and Prime Minister Barak is determined to exhaust the possibility of reaching an agreement on this basis.

"Egypt's position is important despite your unsuccessful involvement, Mr President, in stopping Palestinian violence," I continued. "Today alone, there were three attacks in Israel, thirteen wounded in a bus terrorist bombing in Tel Aviv, one dead and two wounded in an explosion at the Sufah checkpoint in Gaza, and firing toward a bus near Hebron. We have been restraining ourselves in the face of an average of twenty shooting incidents a day. We are decided to continue on the path to peace against the backdrop of these difficult events."

I proceeded to outline the two main points of disagreement. "In 'Al Haram Al Sharif' we need a reasonable and creative solution that expresses the sensitivity toward the faiths of each side. We cannot sign a document that transfers sovereignty over our 'holy of holies' to the Palestinians. On the Right of Return, there is no way to implement it within the borders of Israel."

Mubarak, who listened carefully, asked to see the maps. Hasson laid out the aerial photos of the Old City, on one side of the table, and the enlarged photograph of the entire city, on the other side. He then went over the different areas, problems of contiguity, neighborhoods, zones of friction, problematic crossroads. "The Armenians are not Arabs," he noted. "We do not understand the Palestinian demand for sovereignty over the Armenian Quarter."

Mubarak was particularly interested in the difference between the Western Wall and the Wailing Wall, which we explained using the aerial photo. "We demand that our sovereignty be preserved over the Western Wall, the area above ground and underneath," I said. "This is the holiest place to the Jewish people, and it was so for over 600 years before the Al Aqsa Mosque was ever built. This is the site to which Jews have prayed throughout the Diaspora. According to our faith, the stone on the Temple Mount is the center of the world, the site of creation, the holy of holies, over which the Divine spirit presides for all eternity. For Muslims, it is only in third place in terms of significance, and they turn to Mecca when they pray. Nevertheless, we are interested in an arrangement that respects both religions. Our intention is not to change the reality of daily life, but to make arrangements for it."

Amre Moussa, who was very active in the discussion, asked for an explanation of the term "the space sacred to the Jews." We explained that this referred to the space under the area of the Haram, but its exact location was unknown.

On territory, Yanai explained that there were different calculations that yielded somewhat different results. In the end, the differences were minor, mounting to one-quarter to one-half of a percent, or fifteen to thirty square kilometers in total. The three of us showed the Egyptian president a map that presented eight percent annexation, but said we were willing to stick to the parameters set forth by President Clinton and ask to lease the remaining land necessary for Israel, of around two percent beyond the six percent, for an agreed period. We further described the border and showed the reasonable Palestinian contiguity on the map, emphasizing the expected difficulties with this outline – evacuating 50,000 or more people from ninety settlements.

The meeting lasted for three hours, at the end of which it appeared to us that Mubarak understood the details of the Israeli position, and recognized its fairness and reasonability. He asked to keep the map. We declined politely.

Moussa and Suleiman estimated that within twenty-four hours at the most, by Friday evening of December 29, Arafat would respond in the affirmative. Moussa believed that the Palestinians would accept the map that we presented, with a few adjustments.

Unbeknownst to us, Saeb Erekat was waiting on another floor during all that time. The original intention of the Egyptians, which was not conveyed to us in advance, was to get me together with Erekat for a kind of informal negotiation, under Egyptian auspices, regarding the president's ideas. I went to shake the hand of my old friend and exchange a few words but refused to conduct any substantive discussion. "We do not intend to negotiate until the Americans receive a positive Palestinian response to the president's ideas," I told Suleiman. "Do not force us into back-door negotiations, it's explicitly against my mandate."

After the Cabinet meeting and the follow-up staff-level meetings, the Prime Minister's Office prepared the full response document to the president's proposal. The main points included:

1 Thanking the president for his efforts and accepting his ideas as a basis for continued negotiations toward a Permanent Status agreement, provided that they remain, as they are, a basis for discussion acceptable to the Palestinians.
2 Certain elements of the president's ideas differ or run contrary to Israeli positions, as they were presented in the last stages of the negotiations:
   a Territory – Israeli needs to include eighty percent of the settlers in settlement blocs dictate greater needs than provided for by the president's ideas.
   b Jerusalem – Israel emphasized the importance of the special regime in the "Holy Basin," demanded a different expression for the relationship of the two sides to the Temple Mount, and expected that establishing a normal a life in the city would require a balance between different considerations the president presented, primarily issues of contiguity and demography.

   c Security – Israeli positions, as they were presented in the negotiations, differ from the president's ideas regarding the Palestinian
police force, the mandate for the international force, monitoring the
demilitarization of the Palestinian state, the airspace arrangement,
the timetable and the accompanying conditions.

   d Refugees – judging by the president's proposal it seems he may have
underestimated the extent of Israel's opposition to the Right of Return
of refugees into its border.

3 Elements in the president's ideas that require further clarification. The
following list does not question the internal logic of the president's ideas:

   a General – anchoring the concept of finality of claims, the status of
the agreement in relation to UNSCRs 242 and 338, the status of the
right to self-determination, and the status of issues discussed in the
past between the sides.

   b Territory and borders – the status of Palestinians in settlement blocs,
the status of the safe passage, the relationship between the territorial
arrangements and the division of territory, and the regime in the
holy places.

   c Jerusalem – in relation to the guiding principle "Arab – to Palestine,
Jewish – to Israel" (neighborhoods or individual homes), the meaning
of the term "the Western Wall" and the status of the holy sites to
Judaism.

   d Security – the status of the president's conclusion on security from
the Camp David summit regarding the role of the Palestinian
security force; the meaning of the non-militarization of Palestine, the
structure of the international force (preference for the United States
to take the lead), its tasks (supervising demilitarization and protecting
the areas of emergency deployment) and its relationship with the
Israeli force; control of the airspace and the electromagnetic spectrum.

   e Refugees – Israel's judgment with regard to refugees entering its
borders, addressing the Jewish refugees of the 1948 war, the issue of
a lump sum for the Israeli financial contribution.

4 It was noted that there is a long list of issues that were not addressed
in the president's ideas. Clarification of these issues is vital for completing
a framework agreement.

President Clinton assured us that the substance of the detailed response
document would remain secret.

The Palestinian response, which was reported to be positive, never really
came. It turned out that despite the understanding that Mubarak conveyed
in our meeting, the Palestinians successfully scared the Egyptians into
thinking that our "real positions" were quite different from the ones we
presented to him. Mubarak left Arafat alone and did not pressure him.

20

THE FUTURE OF THE REGION
IS IN YOUR HANDS

The world was on vacation for New Year's Eve, slowly returning to the work routine only four to five days later. In Israel, the "peace cabinet" convened on January 1, 2001. The prime minister assessed that Arafat would not be able to endorse an agreement that would not include the Right of Return. Therefore, the chairman was not going to make any step toward an agreement in the next ten days. "We have to focus on an immediate cessation of violence and we must continue preparing for unilateral disengagement," concluded Barak.

That evening, Dennis Ross reported that Arafat had responded in the affirmative to the ideas of the president, but had requested clarification on the issues of percentage of territory, the Western Wall and refugees. President Clinton, relayed Ross, demanded that Arafat arrive in Washington immediately. Only afterwards could the president say if he was satisfied with the answer. Clinton repeated his demand that Arafat stop the violence.

In a midnight phone conversation with Barak, President Clinton said, "Arafat is willing to conclude the negotiations during my term, and asked that negotiators on both sides move forward." Barak was skeptical. "Arafat is feeding the violence. It's being carried out directly by his security people. He's trying to extort maximum internationalization and concessions from us, and is dragging his feet. I cannot carry out any type of negotiations without a dramatic decrease in violence on the ground, cooperation on preventing terror attacks, and it is for Arafat to prove that he is actively combating terrorism. I am being asked to jump into an empty pool, with the hope that in mid-air Arafat will fill it with water! I am guided by Israel's basic interests, more than by a desire to win the election. Arafat now has to prove fiercely and harshly that he is able to put an end to violence immediately. Then, and only then, could I accept your invitation to participate in another round of talks."

"I will try to get a 'yes' from Arafat tomorrow," Clinton replied.

In the liberal *Haaretz* daily, writers and members of the "peace camp" – David Grossman, Meir Shalev, Nissim Calderon, Amos Oz, Zeev Sternhel and A. B. Yehoshua – published an advertisement stating their unequivocal opposition to the Right of Return. "Accepting this right would destroy the State of Israel," they said.

The danger of further deterioration in the Territories became a main concern. I urged Barak to restrain his election campaign advisers, whose aggressive messages over the media were causing enormous damage to the negotiations process and to his political standing alike. I feared the devastating results of a potential escalation similar to the events that preceded the 1967 Six Day War.

At the same time, the level of incitement, the verbal violence, and the riots within the country were reminiscent of those preceding the Rabin assassination. In a letter entitled "The Struggle Against Incitement and Political Violence," addressed to Minister of Internal Security Ben-Ami and to Attorney-General Rubinstein, I pleaded with them to take action:

> In the past few days the Israeli public has witnessed unprecedented and unbridled incitement. The blood of the prime minister and other civil servants has been forsaken. In several events, an incited and unrestrained crowd lashed out against bystanders, police, and journalists . . . these events constitute an ominous reminder of the darker days of our people and nation.
>
> I urge you to act immediately and decisively against these criminals, and to adopt all legal measures possible to investigate and bring them to justice . . . writing the necessary changes in the law, in order to provide law enforcement bodies with the authority and powers necessary for an uncompromising struggle against violence, racism and incitement.

On the early morning of January 3, Dennis Ross called to convey that Arafat agreed to the demand to resume cooperation on security. His impression was that Arafat "could live" with the parameters suggested by President Clinton.

Clinton's impression was that Arafat had accepted his ideas, although Arafat had what he called "opinions" about them. Clinton indeed thought Arafat was ready to resume negotiations. "I replied," Clinton told Barak on the phone, "that there would be no negotiations until there was a dramatic reduction in violent acts, and that he must act to stop shootings in all the areas, stop terrorists, and begin cooperation to prevent perpetration of terrorist attacks. I told him, 'I want you to start reporting to the head of the CIA, George Tenet, every day.' It appears to me that resuming the political process enables Arafat to address security issues. I think that a deal with him is possible, although difficult, in the coming two weeks. Now that both sides have accepted the parameters I presented, subject to their reservations, we have to move forward in closing the gaps. I suggest that you send someone here, so that I can hold separate discussions, en route to negotiations that will take place subject to fulfilling all the security demands."

Barak was interested in the specific responses Arafat had to the president's ideas. Did he raise fundamental issues like the Right of Return or the Temple Mount, outside the framework of the ideas?

"It is apparently clear to the Palestinians that they would have to concede the Right of Return," Clinton replied. "Why don't you send Shlomo or Gilli so that Arafat sees that something is happening in terms of dialogue."

"A clear and dramatic reduction in violence is an absolute precondition, to avoid being caught in his manipulations," Barak insisted.

At a meeting of the "peace cabinet" Shahak noted that "it is very doubtful that the Palestinians can prevent violence without some movement in the political arena. We should definitely send a representative to get updates on the Palestinian positions as they were delivered to Clinton." Peres also supported sending over an Israeli official equipped with our affirmative response to the president's ideas.

"Gilead will be in Washington tomorrow to meet with you and to hear details regarding your conversations with Arafat, as well as to discuss ways to continue combating violence," Barak informed the president. I left for the airport directly from the Prime Minister's Office, without even saying goodbye to my family.

Friday January 5, 2001. We entered the White House under tight security, "sniffer" dogs climbing into our cars, stern guards checking our IDs meticulously. A dozen or so reporters and photographers stood in the freezing cold outside. Inside, it felt like the last day of school before summer break, the staff having brought their children and other family members to see where they had worked during those years, and waiting for the chance for their photographs to be taken with the president.

I was escorted to the Oval Office for my meeting with the president. "The peace process and the future of the entire region are in your hands, Mr President," I opened, stressing the need for a vigorous US effort to press Arafat to reduce violence and incitement, resume cooperation on security and intelligence, and prevent terrorism. Clear standards had to be set to examine whether Palestinian efforts in this direction (including arresting wanted terrorists from the 120 most-wanted list we presented to the Palestinians, complete cessation of incitement by the PA or the PLO, and a measurable reduction in shooting incidents and explosives) would result in no further injuries. I suggested that a US–Israeli–Palestinian surveillance team be created to monitor events on the ground and to report directly to the president on a daily basis.

Contrary to reports at the time, both before and after the meeting, Permanent Status issues were not discussed at all during my conversation with the president. We did discuss possible policy alternatives given the time and location constraints, including replacing a framework agreement with a presidential declaration, on the basis of the president's ideas, subject to comments I submitted to the national security adviser Sandy Berger.

Clinton asked what troubled us the most about the substance of his ideas. Summarizing the detailed written document we submitted, I noted the central issues: the division of the Old City, contrary to the Israeli position that a special regime was needed for the entire area; the proposed arrangement on the Temple Mount; the proposed arrangement in the Jordan Valley, the wording relating to the refugees; the issue of airspace above Palestine; and the land swap.

We then discussed the possibility of a senior US official coming to the region to monitor the events on the ground, thus conveying the importance that the US was giving to the issue of security and cessation of violence as preconditions to a possible summit.

Reporters were waiting outside in the freezing cold. The White House Master of Ceremonies recommended that I address them without a coat to maintain a "respectable" appearance . . .

Dennis Ross tried to develop a timetable for moving forward. One of the ideas that was raised was to invite the "peace cabinet" to Washington to meet with Abu Mazen and Abu Ala. We also discussed the way in which to address the coordination of the parameters themselves, given the reservations from both sides. We did not reach any real agreement on these issues. One thing was clear, however, changes in the ideas of the president could only be carried out with agreement between the two sides themselves.

On January 6, before I returned to Israel, I met with Muhammad Rashid at the Willard Hotel. I began by stating that the future relationship between the Israeli and Palestinian people under any prospective government depended on Arafat's commitment to maintain calm and prevent terrorism. "Arafat's failure at this test sabotages any possibility of returning to negotiations on Permanent Status now and in the foreseeable future. The strategic goal of the State of Israel remains the end of conflict with the Palestinians through a framework agreement. But the political conditions in Israel, in addition to Arafat's delay in replying to the president, have made this goal practically unattainable."

My counterpart replied honestly. "Arafat is ready for an agreement and intends to complete it. He understands what the necessary concessions are and is committed to match them. He has practically conceded the Right of Return. All that he needs now is to find a way to save face before the Arab world and his own people. The issue of territory concerns him greatly. If he receives clarifications that the maps do not cut Palestine into little pieces, and that this map can be presented without shame in a Palestinian classroom, he will be satisfied."

Rashid then asked specific questions on Arafat's behalf:

– Do we intend to evacuate all the settlements in the Gaza Strip?

I replied that in a final agreement, which constituted the end of conflict, the answer was "yes."

– What is the status of the safe passage?

Formal unconditional Israeli sovereignty and effective Palestinian control was my response.

– Can the deployment period of Israeli forces in the Jordan Valley be shortened and can the "eyesore" created by the emergency deployment areas in Palestinian territory be prevented?

I replied that subject to the full accommodation of Israel's concept of security, we would be willing to discuss any issue that did not breach the parameters set by the president.

– Could we find a name for the Palestinian police that will not be humiliating?

In a final agreement we would be open to any proposals.

On the question of the location of land swaps, I replied that on the basis of comprehensive staff work we could present several alternatives, each with its internal logic, as long as the territorial issue was agreed.

Rashid made a point of emphasizing that Arafat was really willing and ready to move toward signing, and that the sense of a missed opportunity that was now being felt on the Palestinian side was even deeper than that of 1947.

Upon my return to Israel I briefed the "peace cabinet," which convened in the Prime Minister's Office, on Arafat's main reservations. These included the Western Wall and its definition, continued Israeli military presence on Palestinian territory after signing the agreement, and declaring the end of conflict – which Arafat believed was too soon, and should be concluded only upon signing the comprehensive agreement.

All those present, without exception, supported moving the process forward, focusing on the positive parts of the president's ideas. As Amnon Shahak put it: "This is a way of leaving something for the future, for either this government or the government that will replace it. It would be wrong and unwise to give up this opportunity." In sharp contrast to his "superficial" and "indifferent" image in the media and in some political circles, Shahak was always "the voice of reason" – collected, assertive and balanced in his assessments, discrete in his work, focused and goal oriented.

That night I spoke with Rob Malley and Dennis Ross. I understood from them that Arafat wanted to say "yes, but" from the beginning, but that from a conversation that was carried out later with Erekat, the Americans were convinced that the real answer was completely negative.

We rejected the proposal that Ross come to the region before the PA had a chance to prove itself in reducing violence. I told the Americans that the "peace cabinet" had decided to let President Clinton adopt any measure he saw fit, including toward reaching a framework agreement. I asked, on Barak's behalf, that George Tenet remain at least one more day in the region, until the violence-reducing mechanism was in place.

On the morning of January 8, I spoke to Tenet, who had not slept all night, busy with the security coordination meeting in Cairo that ended at 4.30 a.m. "I have to return back to the United States," Tenet told me, "but I am willing to fly back to the region in a few days, toward the weekend." I asked him to make sure he received daily reports from events on the ground and to pass them on to the president.

Most of the members of Barak's team who were involved in the peace process believed, now as in the past, that Barak must meet with Arafat without delay. Yossi Ginossar was the most adamant. "We will continue to march in place, unless a meeting like this takes place. There is no way to break this vicious cycle without meeting Arafat."

It was unclear whether Arafat gave clear instructions to prevent terrorism. The IDF's Central Command communicated an *increase* in violence. The only chance to bring about calm within a few days involved some type of political contact. Our intelligence heads were still of the opinion that Arafat would ultimately be ready to "close the deal" within the framework of Clinton's proposals. But the prime minister's assessment was that an agreement would not materialize before the elections.

On January 7, Clinton spoke at a meeting of the Israel Policy Forum, at the Waldorf Astoria in New York. His speech included clarifications to the ideas he had detailed on December 23. To the Israelis, it appeared that Clinton had made some revisions that were more inclined toward accepting the Israeli reservations. The speech was warm and supportive, and the president never hid the sympathy and great appreciation he had for Ehud Barak.

> No dilemma I have ever faced approximates in difficulty or comes close to the choice that Prime Minister Barak had to make when he took office . . . but he has demonstrated as much bravery in the office of prime minister as he ever did on the field of battle . . .

Clinton, however, did not hesitate to criticize continued construction in the settlements "in the heart of what the Israelis already know will one day be part of a Palestinian state." He also spoke about the refugee problem. Although his wording was within the framework of understandings that were reached, for those not in tune with the nuances, his statements could have been interpreted as an agreement in principle – at least partially – to the Right of Return of refugees to Israel.

In a phone conversation with Barak, after the speech, Clinton was interested to know what the prime minister thought of his address. Barak responded that he had to read the speech thoroughly but that it appeared balanced except for the president's remarks on the Right of Return, which may have led some people to believe the president supported it. Barak gave Clinton an update on the ongoing violence: "It is now midnight," Barak said, "today alone we had twenty shootings, including a three year-old boy who was wounded by three bullets. We received the plan that Tenet prepared. We will need him back here again, toward the end of the week."

Clinton suggested sending Dennis Ross the next morning, with proposals for channels of negotiations. Barak didn't think that Ross alone had the power to bring about movement, suggesting that Clinton himself should come to the region, but the president refused, saying: "This will hurt me, and maybe you as well. We cannot afford to be fooled by Arafat."

After a useful meeting at Erez checkpoint, the security track was yielding some glimmer of hope. Amnon Shahak and Saeb Erekat led this track together. They were joined by Avi Dichter, and generals Shlomo Yanai, Giora Eiland, Yitzhak Eitan and Doron Almog on the Israeli side, and Rajoub, Dahlan, Amin Al-Hindi, Ismael Majayda and Tawfiq Tirawi on the Palestinian side.

The "peace cabinet" convened again, in advance of a meeting with Arafat that was at long last planned for that evening. Shahak hoped that this time the meeting would be substantive. Barak, as in previous meetings, emphasized that if he knew that Arafat was planning on reaching an agreement, he would make a far-reaching effort. But he felt that no real effort to reduce violence was taking place on the Palestinian side and that no attempt was being made to allow the Israeli government to move forward with the process.

Yossi Beilin continued to urge Barak to meet with Arafat. "Hope is our work tool."

Yossi Sarid added, "We have to start 'going wild' and shift gears, because it appears to the public that we are dragging our feet." Sarid also saw no harm in a Barak and Arafat meeting.

But Barak was not convinced that he personally needed to meet with Arafat under the current situation. "It is worth considering, maybe Amnon should meet with him," Barak said, knowing well that Shahak was already set to meet Arafat that evening, but fearing a leak. "We have ten days left, and we have to move the process forward responsibly by allowing President Clinton to advance the process."

Marathon-like preparations for the negotiations began under the assumption that they would take place if and when the level of violence came down. The Palestinians appointed Abu Ala, Yasser Abed Rabbo and Saeb Erekat for the negotiations. The message was conveyed by Yossi Ginossar at midnight on January 10. The number of attacks that day fell to thirteen and Shahak suggested that the "peace cabinet" preconditioned the continuation of the three-on-three negotiations on complete cessation of the attacks. I urged the prime minister again to consider meeting with Arafat right away. "Consider the composition of the Palestinian team that he appointed for these marathon negotiations. There is no choice but to expect that we will quickly reach a dead end," I assessed. "Meanwhile, the foundations of the president's proposal are dissipating. We see evidence of this in Clinton's last speech."

Barak replied that were the elections not so close, it is possible that we should have accepted the proposal to negotiate. But under the current circumstances, he was not sure that this was right. He proposed that on the Israeli side the negotiators included Shimon Peres, Shlomo Ben-Ami and me. In parallel, Amnon Shahak would continue his meetings with Arafat.

Yossi Sarid lamented the loss of momentum. "We are creating a difficult impression, proceeding up to a month before the election, and then stopping."

The following day, January 11, Ambassador Indyk relayed that Arafat made a commitment to the president that he himself would participate in the negotiations. I told Indyk that as a result of Abed Rabbo's statement in the media that "Barak is a war criminal who must be put on trial," no Israeli minister would meet with Abed Rabbo – no matter what position Arafat appoints him to in the negotiations – unless he publicly recants this perverse and baseless charge. "There is a limit to what we are willing to take, even during a bloody confrontation," I said.

The likely prospect that the prime minister would be replaced in the upcoming elections had seemingly not sunk into the Palestinian consciousness at that stage. "Sharon will not be elected," Erekat declared confidently, "and if he is elected, I will invite you to a feast right before I resign." However, Sharon was to be elected, and Erekat did not resign.

During this period, Jean Frydman, one of Barak's closest friends, worked to prepare the foundation for resolving two of the fundamental problems in the Middle East: Palestinian refugees and water. A self-made wealthy businessman, Frydman was among Barak's earlier supporters, encouraging him to run for head of the Labor Party and for prime minister. Frydman's directness and discreteness put him in a position of a close and influential confidant and adviser to Barak.

Frydman and Jacques Segala, a well-known public relations person from France, came up with a new Israeli initiative:

- Conditional on an ongoing ceasefire, Israel would recognize a demilitarized Palestinian state and would end occupation.
- The borders of the state would be temporary, until negotiations on permanent borders between the two states could be concluded.

- The temporary borders would be based on Israel's security needs, minimum annexation of areas inhabited by Palestinians, evacuation of some settlements – preferably those in the Gaza Strip and others in isolated locations.
- Relations from time of recognition onwards would be those of two states and subject to international law.
- The Right of Return for Palestinian refugees would be implemented in the Palestinian state only. Joint projects for the Palestinian state, Israel, Jordan and Egypt would be developed in the areas of economic relations, water, energy and infrastructure.

I supported this initiative in principle. It appeared reasonable, well designed, preserved the main assets for future negotiations, and unilaterally ended the occupation in most of the Territories. There was no doubt that such a plan would also help Barak politically in the election campaign. Barak, however, was not enthusiastic. From his perspective, the initiative contradicted the approach of the end of conflict and gave rise, prematurely, to a very difficult dilemma for the settlers – where would the line be?

At midnight on January 11, 2001, the negotiations on the Palestinian side of Erez checkpoint began. We refused to begin the meeting until we "cleared the table," as Shahak put it. "We are not here to represent a war criminal." I had told the Palestinians in advance that there would be no meeting until Yasser Abed Rabbo promptly took back the allegations he tarnished the prime minister with.

"If there is a need to apologize, we are prepared to do so. Things are also being said on your side and we have not made an issue out of it. I take back the things that were said," Abu Ala replied.

"No way! I will not agree to this!" Abed Rabbo jumped up.

Abu Ala asked for a short break. After a "back and forth" that lasted for about an hour, the Palestinians returned to the negotiations table with an official apology for what Yasser Abed Rabbo had said. The negotiations resumed.

Erekat began to detail what Arafat presented to Clinton. "On Jerusalem, Arafat requested that there be a detailed map which relates to all the neighborhoods in the city. We cannot accept the term Western Wall, instead we can only accept the term 'Wailing Wall,' which defines something smaller. Sovereignty over 'Haram Al Sharif' has to be transferred to the Palestinians – above, below and to the sides – geographically and topographically.

"As for security," continued Erekat, "Arafat told the president that the minute an American-led international force would come in, he would be kicked out of the Arab League. We would not be willing to accept emergency areas of IDF deployment in our territory, any IDF presence beyond the long thirty-six-month withdrawal, and Israeli air force training in our airspace. Regarding demilitarization we would be willing to accept the term 'state with limited arms.'"

On territory, Arafat rejected the proposal of long-term leasing of lands. He insisted that all land swaps be equal in quality and quantity to the annexed territory, without damaging the aquifers or the contiguity, and while preserving the principle that Palestinian towns or inhabitants would not be annexed to Israel.

On refugees, Arafat insisted that the Right of Return be mentioned explicitly, although there would be discussion, taking into consideration Israel's concerns about the future identity.

Shlomo Ben-Ami said: "Finally, on end of conflict. This will happen only upon signing a peace accord, subject to international guarantees regarding implementation of the agreement and the immediate release of all prisoners from Israeli prisons.

"Both sides have reservations about the president's proposals. You must submit the clarifications you have requested to the Americans, not to us." He continued: "All your reservations are beyond the scope of the president's parameters, which means that you are not interested in concluding this process under President Clinton. It's a shame. We have gone a long way. We renewed the negotiations after Arafat explicitly declared that he wanted to reach an agreement. Here you prove the opposite and try to negotiate the parameters themselves. We have to go back to the prime minister to reconsider our position."

I looked over my notes from the meetings with the American peace team and the president. I told Erekat, "I am very sorry, but there is absolutely no resemblance between the report I received from the Americans and your presentation, Saeb."

"We have a serious problem. You come to us with demands, which in term of content and timing are a few steps behind the ideas the president presented regarding a possible arrangement," Ben-Ami added.

We realized that only Clinton could get the Palestinians back to the parameters he had proposed. Unless he did, we would have endless, fruitless negotiations.

That evening Shahak, Peres, Ben-Ami and I met with Arafat himself at his headquarters in Gaza together with Saeb Erekat, Mohammad Rashid, Abu Ala, Yasser Abed Rabbo and Mohammed Dahlan. We sat around tables, pretty distant from each other. On the two sofas in the middle, Shimon Peres and Yasser Arafat sat side-by-side.

"In 1996, we lost the elections because of violence," Peres began. "We have to maintain a decrease in violence as a main goal, and at the same time try to narrow the gaps between us. We would like to see a friendly and respectable Palestinian state. This has not changed, despite all the problems. We will achieve this and live like other nations."

"We have to do something before Clinton leaves. We have six to seven days and this is a heavy task. We will not stop to negotiate on January 20, but at least we can allow Clinton to say to his successor and to the world – 'this is my plan,'" Arafat replied.

"We were surprised to find out that some of your reservations go beyond the president's parameters," intervened Ben-Ami. "Under these conditions, it is beyond human capacity to achieve something in the time remaining. We did not come here to create an arrangement to get through the election period. If we can reach an agreement by January 25, and not by January 20, won't we continue?"

"Begin and Sadat opened everything, and reached an agreement anyway," Arafat answered.

"Yes, but we have many more areas of disagreement – Jerusalem, refugees, security," Ben-Ami added.

Peres suggested preparing an inventory of the agreed issues, and leaving the remaining issues for later discussion, when both sides felt they were prepared to continue. "You have to impose strict discipline on your people in the next three weeks," he told Arafat.

Arafat was non-committal. "We have to achieve what we can. We have to work hard for that."

Barak was convinced that Arafat did not want to, and could not make progress toward an agreement, primarily because of the Right of Return. He instructed us to limit the meetings with Arafat to contact through Yossi Ginossar, and only on the area of security.

On January 16, as the election campaign broadcast propaganda started, we met in Jerusalem with Abu Ala and Erekat (who arrived late, after being detained for over half an hour by a soldier at the Az-Za'ayyem checkpoint at the outskirts of Jerusalem). The meeting took place against the backdrop of rioting settlers in the Mawassi area in the Gaza Strip, and the destruction and razing of structures, facilities, orchards and Palestinian fields, as retribution for terrorist attacks.

"There are complaints, strikes and demonstrations in front of Arafat's office," Abu Ala described. "You are humiliating the Palestinian leadership at checkpoints."

"This is precisely why we are here," I replied. "We have to relay all the problems and the friction to the joint security committee that is meeting tonight. There is no time to waste in exchanging accusations. It should be clear to you how the process you described began – the murder of an Israeli at the door to his home. Let's see how we move forward on the basis of the president's ideas."

"We refuse to move forward according to the president. We want to see maps: what is territory, what is Jerusalem," Abu Ala replied angrily.

"So what is the basis for this discussion, if you do not want to talk about the president's ideas? You have no maps to show us. You rejected the president's ideas with your reservations. You present nothing constructive. At the same time you are undoing all the ends from which we can weave some common understandings. Under these conditions, we can negotiate amongst ourselves; we do not need to meet with you," I replied.

However, we laid out a map of the Territories, with eighty percent of the Israeli population in 9.6 percent of the land, in blocs marked for Israeli annexation. We also presented an aerial photograph of Jerusalem. Major-General Yanai described the data on the basis of which the calculations were made – 187,000 Israeli settlers in the West Bank and another 7,000 in Gaza.

"If we presented you with what we really needed, it would go beyond the scope of the president's parameters. But you have gone beyond those parameters, which has made the discussion impossible," Shlomo Ben-Ami said, having joined the meeting.

During a meeting of the "peace cabinet" immediately after, a pessimistic Barak stated: "There will be no real political breakthrough. Reason cannot tolerate negotiations under violence and the time constraints. The public does not accept it, and there is no power to decide on the other side. We have to consolidate our positions in a clear document to Clinton and Bush, and tell the public that we need separation into two states in an agreement, respectfully. However, having tried more than any other government before us to reach an agreement, we have to take the initiative and pursue this objective unilaterally. We have conducted negotiations under the shadow of violence in order to exhaust all possibilities of reaching an agreement under Clinton."

Surprisingly, this statement did not go down very well.

"What I have just heard from Ehud Barak about a public declaration regarding the failure of the negotiations will result in increased violence, not in its reduction. I, as an Israeli citizen, am embarrassed by what happened yesterday in Gaza, but this cannot weaken our resolve," said Amnon Shahak.

Peres was even more pointed. "What you are suggesting could be a real catastrophe. This is the biggest mistake that can be made. The Palestinians will think that we have stopped to negotiate and Arafat will do everything in his power to make hell on earth. Arafat understands the alternative and is ready to conclude guidelines toward a resolution. If we are left without him, the situation will be completely chaotic, with violent gang warfare."

Barak raised his voice, addressing his words to Peres. "You yourself have said that the Israeli government has gone too far toward the Palestinian positions. Don't try to hold the stick on both ends. The risks we have taken upon ourselves politically are a result of our willingness to make this move. We cannot blame ourselves. But, given the circumstances, the government of Israel must make a realistic evaluation of the situation. The Palestinians do not understand the meaning of the crossroads we face, of a regime change."

Sarid also attacked the idea of unilateral disengagement, and urged us to keep all the channels of dialogue open. "If we cut contact with the Palestinians, it will be fatal, and there is no chance in the world that we will win the elections. We have to continue negotiations in all channels and at the highest levels, in order to prepare the hearts and minds on our side."

"Clinton has given up and has allowed Arafat to sidetrack the parameters. Nevertheless, ceasing contact will be perceived by the rest of the world as our fault," Ben-Ami added.

Yossi Beilin tried to focus on the practical. "There is a real dilemma – to carry out negotiations under fire or to give up hope. We have to conduct negotiations on two tracks, one official which conveys hope, and another secret, substantive."

Barak accepted Beilin's position. "Despite the risk and the low probability that we will reach substantive agreements, we have an interest in continuing dialogue."

If there was anyone who spent most of his adult life dealing with the fundamental questions regarding the existence of Israel as a state and as a society, it was Yossi Beilin. There were few people who could compete with Yossi in terms of the depth of his analysis and the scope of his knowledge on all issues relating to Permanent Status peace with the Palestinians. Deeply empathetic to the plight of the Palestinian people, Beilin was willing to go against the current, no matter what the cost, in order to bring about an end to their suffering.

On the afternoon of January 18, 2001, negotiations in working groups continued at the David Intercontinental in Tel Aviv. Present were Abu Ala, Erekat, Abed Rabbo and Samih El Abed on the Palestinian side and Ben-Ami, Yanai, Hasson, Meidan-Shani, Grinstein and myself on our side.

We presented a map of our security, settlement and strategic needs, and an enlarged map of Jerusalem. It was my impression that the Palestinians had no real interest whatsoever in negotiating within the parameters laid out by the president. They rejected any attempt to convince them to present maps of their own both on the issue of territory and on Jerusalem. I did not hesitate to convey my dismay. "You tell the world that you are serious, but in this room you sit holding hands and grade us on our efforts, instead of tightening your belts and working cooperatively with us. We don't intend to present any more maps, until you present us with your maps on territory, land swaps, and Jerusalem."

Throughout this period it was apparent that the Palestinians were not making any real effort to ensure that the agreements on security issues were relayed to those responsible on the ground. The commonly held view was that the violent incidents would continue up until the elections and beyond.

On the evening of January 20, the "peace cabinet" met at the prime minister's house in Kohav Yair. The main issue was, and remained, the cessation of violence. The American administration was changing hands while we were two and a half weeks before an election.

Sensing possible progress on the question of refugees, Peres introduced the idea of conducting intensive negotiations until six days before the elections, to be resumed after the elections. Among the plethora of places suggested for holding such talks were Europe, Eilat, Taba, Sharm Al Sheikh, Cairo, Turkey, Cyprus, as well as an American aircraft carrier which would be anchored somewhere in the Mediterranean. Ultimately, with the prime minister's agreement, we decided on Taba. Barak set one condition whereby the security meetings would be held at the same time as the political talks. The prime minister asked that Ben-Ami, Shahak, Sarid and I make our way down south. He proposed that he and Peres brief Beilin who would lead the commission on refugees.

Before we went down to Taba, Barak met with Ben-Ami and me in his office. "I don't know if we'll get anywhere and if anything is even possible," I told the prime minister, "but the parameters suggested by the president, subject to our reservations, are the blueprint for a permanent solution."

Barak asked us both to seek out possible channels at Taba, which would enable us to make progress, and as usual he cautioned from recording any Israeli positions that deviated from the parameters suggested by the president.

In various discreet and closed forums, Clinton spoke out angrily against Arafat. At the moment of handing over power to George W. Bush, the outgoing president called the chairman of the PA "a liar who destroyed the whole process and cheated us." It has been reported that Dennis Ross used similar words when briefing the incoming secretary of state, Colin Powell: "Don't believe a word that Arafat says. He's a con man."

21

WE'LL BE COUNTING THE
CORPSES ON BOTH SIDES

On January 21, the sides met again around a long narrow table at the Taba Hilton. It was the very same hotel where, in September 1995, a month and a half before Yitzhak Rabin's assassination, the Interim Agreement "Oslo B" had been signed. Abu Ala, Saeb Erekat, Hassan Asfour, Nabil Sha'ath, Yasser Abed Rabbo and Mohammed Dahlan represented the Palestinian side. The Israeli team included Shlomo Ben-Ami, Amnon Shahak, Yossi Beilin, Israel Hasson, Pini Meidan-Shani, Gidi Grinstein and me.

It was with some trepidation and hesitation that the Israeli representatives came to Taba. Some of us believed that the government should indeed prepare the infrastructure for future post-election negotiations so that they would be guided by long-term factors. We all knew that even under a best-case scenario, in which agreements were reached on most issues, the prime minister would not sign. Moreover, his representatives in the Israeli delegation would not approve any document before the elections. Others, including Hasson and Meidan-Shani, opposed this last minute effort at the "end of term" calling into question the validity of the government actions. Still others, like Amnon Shahak, realized that there was no realistic chance of reaching an agreement at Taba, but felt that there was no reason not to pursue dialogue right up to the elections. This was also my view.

Those of us who were intensively involved in the entire negotiations process, regarded Taba as little more than a theoretical ploy, designed to pass a political reality based on Clinton's ideas on to the incoming Republican administration.

Attorney-General Elyakim Rubinstein found a middle ground in trying to address the issue of negotiations during an election campaign. On December 25, 2000, he sent a "personal letter" to the prime minister. The letter was leaked from the attorney-general's office to the press before Barak himself had a chance to look at it. It laid out the difficulties involved in the issue but did not make any specific recommendation as to how to proceed. The long letter, written in very poetic style, could be summarized in one simple sentence: there was no legal or constitutional impediment to responsibly carrying out political negotiations, even under the current political conditions. It appeared, however, that in the actual act of writing the letter and then leaking it to the press, the office of the attorney-general, in a sharp abuse of its mandate, was expressing an ideological position and a political opinion.

On January 25, in response to a petition brought by various right-wing activists, the Israeli High Court of Justice ruled that the prime minister was entitled to continue with the negotiations.

At the start of the opening session at Taba, both sides declared their serious intentions, despite the ticking political clock.

Shlomo Ben-Ami said, "It is not impossible to achieve something here. President Clinton had left us his ideas, which are a reasonable basis for discussion despite the reservations on both sides." "The Clinton ideas are not a basis," retorted Abu Ala. "They are at least a convenient tool to work with, aren't they?" Ben-Ami shot back.

We decided to split into two working groups. One group, headed by Sha'ath and Beilin, would focus on refugees, while the second group would discuss all the other issues. The two groups would coordinate with the drafting team, headed by Erekat and myself.

The first issue to come up was the territorial question. Ben-Ami asked the Palestinians to produce a map of their own as an alternative to our maps. The Palestinians sidestepped the request. Abu Ala raised a fundamental objection to the idea of long-term lease.

Dahlan turned to the question that concerned him most. "The most important issue for the future relations between the two states is how we deal with terrorism. Don't try to control us. Let us do it ourselves. We have to completely separate between Israelis and Palestinians in the Territories in order to prevent friction. You shouldn't need more than a year for the withdrawal of Israeli forces and the evacuation of settlements. You will not have control of our airspace; it would violate our sovereignty. How you name our security force is not important, we can decide on it later on, but we want a real state, capable of defending itself with its own army, which will however not be capable of threatening Israel."

At 1 a.m. I phoned the prime minister to discuss our first day. I believed that both on the territorial and security questions there was a good chance of a solution that would be acceptable to Israel and to the Palestinians. We assessed that such understandings would need to be accompanied with a few "side letters," namely on the issue of refugees. Such side letters are often used to secure commitments on sensitive or "loaded" issues that the parties do not want to be made public.

During our meeting on territory the next day, we laid out a map of the Ariel territorial bloc, and next to it, another map showing that ninety-two percent of the territory would come under Palestinian control.

Abu Ala was angry. "We are not prepared to consider partial or outdated maps, nor maps that show Palestinian villages in areas that you propose to annex. The percentages of land remaining under Israeli control are too high." Erekat came to his aid: "We're wasting our time."

"In the map in front of you, only seventy-three percent of the settlers have been included and not eighty percent. We will have to find a solution for the remaining seven percent. The practical implications of this map are that for it to be implemented, we would have to vacate ninety settlements," I responded.

I proposed to draft a framework agreement based on the Clinton proposals, a long-term lease by Israel of Palestinian territory for the purposes of meeting Israel's strategic defense requirements, and the end-of-conflict principle. "With regard to Jerusalem," I emphasized, "there is no way to end the dispute unless we agree on a special regime relating to the 'Holy Basin' and the Old City." I said that even if there was no major breakthrough, we should at least seek to set down a clear summary of all the issues. "Such a summary could at the very least provide a basis for a substantive joint declaration at the end of these talks."

Erekat stated that he was prepared to start drafting an agreement, provided that the discussion on territories was held on the basis of a ninety-five percent map.

In private, Shahak wondered aloud, "Perhaps it would be a good idea to draw up maps which adopt a new theoretical approach – one, for example, which rejects the idea of Ariel as indispensable? Perhaps instead, we could think of building an alternative town between Latrun and Jerusalem. After all, those settlement blocs are the result of a combination of the settlements themselves and our own strategic needs."

We agreed among ourselves that since there was a fair chance that nothing would be achieved in this round, and that we would thus be amenable to any viable alternative, provided that any such alternative would not be made public as a formal position.

The criticism from home on the very act of holding the talks at Taba started right at the beginning and gathered momentum by the second day. Even Minister Haim Ramon, known to be a staunch advocate of an overall agreement, which involved painful compromises, attacked Barak harshly and called for the immediate freeze of these "immoral" talks until after the elections.

In an interview with Yediot Ahronot I was asked to comment on what Ramon had said. "There can be nothing more moral, democratic or even Zionist," I responded, "than to conduct negotiations at all times. The ultimate decision will be made by the people in a referendum – in other words, by each one of us. Haim, as a party to both the vision and the process, knows better than anyone else the value of peace, if it spares even just one drop of blood." I stressed the importance of continuity, which in itself can help prevent a complete degeneration into violence and to engender some hope in both peoples. Responding to Ramon's comparing the negotiation to a "corpse," I said "If we stop now, we'll be counting corpses on both sides."

At a discussion with Dahlan and Erekat that evening, Yanai went over the security issues that were still outstanding, including the deployment of Israeli forces in an emergency, in the event of a substantial threat from the East. "We're talking about specific small areas," he stressed. "Regarding the early-warning stations, there appears to be agreement on three sites. We have also agreed to the idea put forward by Clinton, regarding a Palestinian liaison officer placed at each warning station alongside the Israeli operators."

The head of AGAT then turned to the demilitarization of Palestinian forces. "We appear to be at odds on this issue. You have to understand that we cannot accept the presence of armed forces west of the Jordan River. We also need to ensure that all crossing points on your external border are under supervision, to make sure that no military equipment can come into the Palestinian state. We are suggesting cooperation between the sides and conducting joint supervision. At Camp David," Yanai recalled, "the president offered his help in bringing this about. We accepted the idea. We recognize your sovereignty over the airspace of Palestine, when it is created. We cannot, however, relinquish use of this airspace for the operational needs of the Israeli Air Force. It takes a fighter jet no longer than two to three minutes to fly from Amman to Israel's populated centers. We cannot possibly take such a risk.

"An easier subject involves the coordinated effort to combat terrorism, and a little less straightforward issue involves joint activity along the border. It was in this regard that President Clinton proposed that Israel, the Palestinians, a third party and possibly Jordan, operate as a joint force. Both sides rejected this idea. We do not know the Palestinian reaction to another force."

Dahlan, asking Saeb Erekat to translate from Arabic to English so that nothing would be lost from the meaning in Arabic, gave a measured but very angry response: "We are at the end of the game now, not the beginning. We are six months after Camp David. Don't cover up trying to rob us of our rights, under the guise of security arrangements. It won't work. These matters are intimately connected with the question of sovereignty, and our national and individual pride." He refused to even discuss the individual points Yanai raised, except for the issue of the combat against terrorism. "Yes," he said, "we have to set up a joint mechanism to fight terrorism. We are the best partners you have for that."

During a break in the meeting I said: "Both sides are making the same mistake. We are looking at the emerging agreement in a specific order, examining the compromises and concessions on each subject separately, and torturing ourselves. Instead, we should look at the dividends of a peace agreement, at the 'day after.' By the same token it was wrong to examine the security issue separately from all other subjects."

Meanwhile, it had become apparent that in the other rooms there had been dramatic erosion in the formulated Israeli positions. Barak had phoned me and asked that I convey to Shlomo Ben-Ami and Amnon Shahak that we could not go below eight percent annexation for Israel, including as part of any leasing arrangements or any other long-term arrangements. Even in this size area it would be very difficult to accommodate eighty percent of the settlers. Knowing, as we did, the usual Egyptian habit of bugging our conversations, we were very careful not to exchange sensitive information inside the hotel. In order to talk we would go out on to the narrow balcony at the end of the corridor, shutting the door firmly behind us and saying what we had to say, hoping that we were the only ones listening.

In the morning session of January 23, the Israeli and Palestinian claims on territory were raised again. This time the Palestinians brought the geographer Samih El-Abed, bearing a handful of maps. "Yesterday we saw one map which we did not like, and we have a number of comments. We were surprised by the annexation of Latrun, we have a problem with Gush Etzion, and there is absolutely no chance that we can agree to the annexation of Ma'ale Adumim, Givat Ze'ev and Har Homa to Israel," Abu Ala began. Samih El-Abed laid out the Palestinian map, which presented as small clusters or balloons at the ends of strings the Israeli settlements that would, according to the Palestinians, constitute the blocs of Ariel, Latrun and Gush Etzion. The Palestinians included certain Jewish neighborhoods of Jerusalem, such as Ramot and Neve Yaakov, in what they defined as "settlements." "In total," they said, "we are offering 4.5 percent of the area."

While the map reflected a manipulation of the demographic and geographic realities, it constituted a substantial improvement on what had been presented to us six months ago at Camp David. It was based on the idea of settlement blocs, rather than isolated settlements.

Our initial response pointed out that the map did not include areas that we had indicated were vital, including Ma'ale Adumim and Givat Ze'ev. The Palestinian calculations included Jerusalem, which Israel held was not to be included in calculations of territorial percentages nor population counts. The map did not address our stated strategic interests beyond settlements, which required an annexation of 650 square kilometers altogether. Furthermore practical implication of the presented map meant vacating some 130 Israeli settlements, constituting between 100,000 and 120,000 inhabitants. Our position, which was accepted in principle by the

American administration at Camp David, was to include some eighty percent of the settlers in a contiguous strip of territory. The map proposed annexation, which would include only 60,000 settlers representing only around thirty-five percent of the settler population. "In summary," I concluded, "the map you produced does not meet the criteria set by President Clinton or the test of reality. Do you have a better map?"

"The president's parameters are not a basis for discussion, and they are certainly not the Bible. Do not try to address your strategic interests in our territory. We might be prepared to consider a leasing arrangement once we have become a state," concluded Abu Ala.

Beilin and Sha'ath reported progress on refugees while using the papers and materials from Camp David. Later the Palestinians would deny this, saying that Sha'ath completely refused to rely on papers that were consolidated in Sweden or even in Camp David.

On January 23, 2001, two Israelis, Moti Dayan and Etgar Zeituni, owners of a restaurant in Tel Aviv, were kidnapped in Tulkarem and murdered in cold blood. Barak instructed the government ministers in Taba to return to Jerusalem for consultations. "I expect a strong public outcry at the funerals tomorrow," Barak said to the new secretary of state, Colin Powell, in a phone conversation that night. "We expect the Palestinians to resume security cooperation with us with renewed zeal and greater determination." He said that if – as seemed likely – we were unable to reach agreement, we would have to agree on some joint declaration or partial agreement.

The initiative to bring about a meeting between Barak and Arafat, possibly in Europe, was being consolidated. There were a number of possibilities, foremost of which was the World Economic Forum in Davos. Other options were Sweden or another European country. UN Secretary-General Kofi Annan, Prime Minister Göran Persson, representatives of the EU, and, of course, the Americans and other leaders were all involved.

On the evening of Wednesday January 24, a secret meeting was arranged by the Egyptians for Abu Ala and Dahlan, Israel Hasson, Pini Meidan-Shani and me. The meeting took place south of Taba, at a site chosen by the Egyptian security service. The aim of the meeting was for each side to present the "bottom line," as a possible short cut to an agreement.

The meeting was very dramatic. "We are at the moment of truth," we said to our counterparts. "The historic achievements that we can attain could evaporate in just a few days and with them the concept of a Palestinian state. We will arrange a plane for you. Fly to Abu Amar in Gaza and convince him to close a deal."

"Our boss does not want an agreement," was their response.

We were left to discuss a summit meeting at the end of the week, to explore less desirable alternatives, short of an agreement and possibly a

DOP. Such an outcome would at least allow us to make it through the elections in Israel and prepare the foundation for continued negotiations, if and when the next Israeli government was ready to do so.

In developing the joint declaration, it seemed once again essential that there be a meeting between Barak and Arafat to decide on the wording of the declaration and to make the necessary decisions regarding issues that were left specifically for the leaders to decide. We discussed the location, framework and possible substance for a meeting of the political leaders, as well as the final declaration that would be delivered by Abu Ala and Ben-Ami on Sunday, marking the end of the Taba talks. According to the plan, the meeting between the two leaders would be followed by a ceremony in which they would sign the joint declaration, and would deliver a speech that would be coordinated in advance. We would then have the elections. If Barak were re-elected, which appeared increasingly unlikely, we would resume the talks two weeks after the elections, aiming to complete them by April 30.

At the Princess Hotel in Eilat, the two delegations adjourned for a Sabbath dinner. The members of both teams sat round a festive table, all with skullcaps on their heads for the reciting of the "Kiddush." I imagine I was not the only one there who thought that it would be a long time before Israelis and Palestinians would again sit down together again for a joint meal.

Ben-Ami and Beilin thought it would be a good idea to gather an inventory of the understandings that had been reached at Taba in a summarizing document – Agreed Minutes – which was not legally binding. I was very much against the idea. We had by now a consolidated draft on many issues, which had been drafted painstakingly during hundreds of hours of negotiations. Every word had been weighed carefully. The potential implications of every provision, arrangement and wording had been examined. I saw no need or benefit in drafting a rushed and flawed document that had the potential to further erode our positions and cause significant political damage. I was relieved to learn that Erekat agreed that a short draft of the closing statement was the preferred route to take.

The closing statement was prepared by the Israeli team, headed by Ben-Ami, on the basis of the draft that Erekat and I had prepared, and had passed on for approval to the Palestinians. In the statement the talks were described as having been "serious, in-depth and practical." It was also said that they were "unprecedented in their positive atmosphere . . . but taking into consideration the circumstances and time constraints, it was impossible to reach an agreement on all the issues, despite the substantive progress that had been made on all the issues discussed. The parties declare that they have never been so close to reaching an agreement."

But instead of sticking to the agreed text, both Ben-Ami and Abu Ala preferred to speak freely and respond to the press questions. From January

28 onwards, all our efforts were focused on decently concluding this chapter in the political life of the outgoing government. It was decided that the meeting between Barak and Arafat would take place at Davos, as part of the annual World Economic Forum. Should the results of that meeting prove positive, the leaders would then move to Sweden for further discussions. In the midst of the intensive preparations for the prime minister's trip abroad, Barak, his military secretary Eizencot and I abruptly stopped and turned to the television set for a report on Arafat's speech in Davos. Shimon Peres, who had just given a speech, was in the audience.

Arafat spoke in Arabic. In his speech he said:

> The current government of Israel is waging a fascist war against our people. Israel is fighting a savage and barbaric war against the Palestinians, especially against our children. Israel conquers, destroys and exterminates the Palestinians with depleted uranium.

Arafat repeated this allegation a number of times in English. He proceeded to accuse Israel of:

> starving the Palestinian people and preventing them from obtaining medical treatment. [Israel] even prohibits us from receiving assistance from our brothers in other countries . . . Peace? Whoever wants peace does not order targeted killings, doesn't destroy and devastate like the government of Israel and its army.

Arafat blamed chief of staff General Mofaz as being personally responsible for the war.

All of us present at the Prime Minister's Office knew instantly that nothing could be done to rescue the remnants of the peace process. The peace efforts were about to plunge into an abyss from which they could not be resurrected. Arafat had gone too far. He had behaved exactly as he had on previous occasions, when the eyes of his own people and of the world had turned to him. He did the same in that shameful scene in Cairo in May 1994, during which he refused to sign the maps of the agreement. And now he had done it again, rudely, willfully and premeditatedly.

"What Israel has done has been in reaction to the violence of the Intifada," offered Peres in a conciliatory rather than a reprimanding tone, turning to extend a hand to "my friend and dear partner, Arafat." Attacked by the press, Peres would later explain "it was not the time and the place for a confrontation."

The Israeli newspapers covering the event were divided as to whether Arafat prepared for this in advance and was just eagerly awaiting an appropriate opportunity, or whether his remarks were off-the-cuff. Some believe that Abu Ala originally prepared a positive and focused speech aiming to create a bridge toward the envisaged agreement. But Erekat, according to this version of the story "drove Arafat crazy" with proposed changes and tiring amendments to the draft. When it finally came time for Arafat to speak, he did not have a final draft and improvised his stories and lies on the spot. I have no doubt in my heart that Arafat had consolidated these thoughts in his own mind for a while, but had not shared his intentions with Erekat and Sha'ath, who were with him.

In any case, within minutes, and ignoring anything else Arafat might have said ("Peace is my strategic choice"), Barak instructed that his trip be canceled. As much as he had wanted to shape a different reality and bring upon a permanent peace agreement, this time it was over, dead, finished. In the evening we announced that the prime minister had decided there was no point in further contact with the Palestinians until after the elections, and that we were suspending the dialogue.

A file containing a comprehensive report reviewing the peace process and the status of the issues under negotiation, to be conveyed in person from outgoing Prime Minister Barak to the incoming Prime Minister Sharon, was deposited in a safe in the Prime Minister's Office.

22

AND THOU SHALL MAKE
PEACE IN THE LAND

On March 7, 2001, approximately twenty months after Barak's government was formed, the twenty-ninth government of Israel, headed by Ariel
Sharon, was sworn in. At the Knesset, the prime minister turned to his
successor:

> Mr Prime Minister elect,
> ... The challenge facing your government is in security and
> the peace process, reducing the level of violence and resuming
> peace negotiations. The outgoing government [leaves you] a desk
> free of commitments, which will enable you to promote security
> and peace in your own way.
> ... The policy I pursued did not create the difficult reality of
> the conflict, but exposed its true face. It appears that the Palestinian
> leadership, unfortunately, is not yet ready for an historic recon-
> ciliation with the State of Israel and for the necessary compromises
> ...
> Political wisdom requires that we do not waste time, but instead
> use it with a sense of urgency, to minimize the dangers, to
> strengthen the security of Israel and ensure its future by working
> toward an end of conflict with its neighbors and toward peace
> agreements.

How is it that such intensive efforts toward peace did not bear fruit?

Under the circumstances described in this book there was a reasonable
chance of promoting permanent peace and ending the Israeli–Palestinian
conflict. It did not work out, but we believe we were not to blame.
Murderous Palestinian terrorism, encouraged by Arafat, as well as poisonous and cruel incitement, set the negotiations table ablaze, leaving it in
smoking ruins.

Israel must not yield to terrorism, shootings, suicide bombers and car
bombs. It is from us, from within, drawing on our strength, that the realization must come that continued control over another people is completely

231

unnecessary. It continues to present a strategic burden on Israel. There is no avoiding compromise. We have to concede territory in order to preserve the Jewish character and security of the State of Israel. Any other solution would mean conceding either the Jewish or democratic identity of Israel, or even conceding our inseparable place in the free world, of which we were always proud of being part.

The territories we occupy remain our principal levers for achieving a real peace. Returning to the gradual path of interim measures could replace these levers with short-term achievements, after which we will be left with no assets to bargain with during Permanent Status negotiations. Ehud Barak understood this well; and we, the members of the negotiating team, shared this understanding.

I believe that, at the end of the day, the result will be determined by the deepest interest of all those involved in the conflict. I therefore have no doubt that, even though the road may be longer, we – Israelis and Palestinians – will return to the path of peace.

We were determined, compassionate, persistent and serious in our attempt to return Israel to a state of sanity and self-reliance, within logical and defensible borders. Through the bloody violence that has swept the region since the failed Camp David summit, and through whatever violent reality we are condemned to still endure, the agenda will not change. The core issues that were defined will remain as they are, and so will the solutions.

In the prayer book of the "Kol Haneshama" community in Jerusalem, there is a prayer for the well-being of the State, with a phrase that reads: "Establish peace in the land, and everlasting joy for its inhabitants." I came across this sentence by chance, while preparing for my son's Bar Mitzvah. I was informed that the prayer was composed by Chief Rabbi Yitzhak Herzog, in consultation with Nobel Prize laureate, the renowned writer S. Y. Agnon, close to the founding of the State of Israel. Then, too, there was no peace, but the phrase carries with it the hope that the situation will change. I end this book with that hope.

APPENDIX

Israeli draft of the Framework Agreement on Permanent Status
Internal Working draft of the Negotiation Team
Introduction and Sections 1–2: Negotiated (updated Sept. 1, 2000); Sections 3, 4, and
Annex 4: As read to, and discussed with the Palestinians (up to Sept. 1, 2000); Remainder:
Internal – based on the internal draft and on talks with the Palestinian negotiators
FOR INTERNAL USE ONLY

Framework Agreement on Permanent Status

Preamble

The Government of the State of Israel (hereinafter "Israel") and the Palestine Liberation Organization (hereinafter "PLO") acting as the sole legitimate representative of the Palestinian people (hereinafter "the Parties"):

Reaffirming	their determination to put an end to decades of confrontation and conflict and to live in peaceful coexistence, mutual dignity and security [I: based on] [P: while recognising their mutual legitimate national and political rights to achieve] a just, lasting, and comprehensive peace settlement and historic reconciliation through the agreed political process;
Reaffirming	their obligation to conduct themselves in conformity with the norms of international law [P: and the Charter of the United Nations];
Recognising	each other's right to a peaceful and secure existence of their respective territory and peoples, within secure and recognised boundaries free from threats or acts of force;
Confirming	that the FAPS is concluded within the framework of the Middle East peace process initiated in Madrid in October 1991, the Declaration of Principles concluded on September 13, 1993, and the subsequent agreements including the Sharm El-Sheikh Memorandum concluded on September 4, 1999;
[P: Reaffirming	that the Palestinian people have the right to self determination under international law];
Reiterating	their commitment to United Nations Security Council Resolutions 242 and 338 and confirming their understanding that the FAPS is based on, [I: provides

- 1 -

- Nothing is Agreed Until Everything is Agreed -

TBC – To Be Completed

Israeli draft of the Framework Agreement on Permanent Status
Internal Working draft of the Negotiation Team
Introduction and Sections 1–2: negotiated (updated Sept. 1, 2000); Sections 3, 4, and
Annex 4: As read to, and discussed with the Palestinians (up to Sept. 1, 2000); Remainder:
Internal – based on the internal draft and on talks with the Palestinian negotiators
FOR INTERNAL USE ONLY

---

the basis for,] [P: and will lead to] the implementation of these resolutions and for the settlement of the Israeli-Palestinian conflict;

Viewing   the FAPS as a historic milestone in the creation of peace in the entire Middle East;

Therefore the Parties hereby agree on the following

Article 1 – Purpose of the Framework Agreement on Permanent Status

1. [I: The Framework Agreement on Permanent Status (hereinafter "FAPS") marks the end of the conflict between the Parties.] [P: The End of Conflict between the Parties will occur with the full implementation of the Comprehensive Agreement on Permanent Status].

2. The FAPS establishes firmly the basic principles that will determine the [P: core] content of the Comprehensive Agreement on Permanent Status (hereinafter "CAPS") that will be concluded so as to complete the process towards peace and final and effective reconciliation.

3. [I: The FAPS identifies] [P: The FAPS and the CAPS identify] all the claims of the Parties emanating from the conflict and arising from events occurring prior to its signature. No further claims may be raised by either Party. Save as agreed, the settlement of these claims will be achieved by the conclusion of the CAPS. Any further issues claims arising from the past relations of the Palestinian People and Israel will be raised only in as much as they are recognized within the FAPS [P: and / or the CAPS].

4. [I: The Parties shall conclude arrangements to ensure that claims, emanating from the conflict and arising from events occurring prior to the signature of the FAPS, shall not be raised by individuals of either Party against the other Party.]

5. The FAPS sets forth the principles, mechanisms and schedules for resolving each of the issues [I: outstanding] [P: reserved for Permanent Status negotiations] between the Parties and contains the

- 2 -

- Nothing is Agreed Until Everything is Agreed -

TBC – To Be Completed

235

modalities of the negotiations towards the CAPS and the transition to Permanent Status.

6. The CAPS will embody the detailed arrangements relating to the matters agreed upon in the FAPS and will provide for the modalities of their resolution. The CAPS shall be concluded [P: no later than September 13, 2000] [I: A determined effort will be made to conclude the CAPS in a timely manner and not later than January 1, 2001].

7. The FAPS and the CAPS shall be read together as constituting the Permanent Status Agreement (hereinafter "PSA"), creating a permanent condition of peace and reconciliation between the Parties. The CAPS will be consistent with and subordinate to the FAPS.

8. Hence, the FAPS marks the end of the Interim Period and the beginning of the transition to Permanent Status and to the establishment of the Palestinian State. All existing agreements, arrangements and procedures between the Parties, including the Interim Agreement and other related agreements, shall remain in force pending the entry into force of the CAPS, or until substituted by other relevant agreements or understandings, as appropriate, except as agreed in the FAPS.

Article 2 - The Relations between the State of Palestine and the State of Israel[1]

---

[1] Articles to be incorporated in other parts of the text:

1. [I: Disputes relating to the interpretation or application of the agreements between Israel and Palestine shall be referred to the agreed coordination, cooperation, or resolution mechanisms as provided for in this FAPS.]

2. [The legislative bodies of Israel and Palestine shall consult together directly and develop programs for cooperation and coordination.]

3. [Israel and Palestine shall develop a comprehensive cooperation program along their agreed international borders.]

4. [Israel and Palestine shall take all necessary and effective measures in their power to enhance cross-border enforcement of law and order and to prevent cross-border criminal activities.]

5. [Israel and Palestine shall both respect the rule of law and work together in cooperation between their two respective legal systems, to vigorously

- 3 -

- Nothing is Agreed Until Everything is Agreed -

TBC – To Be Completed

9. The right of the Palestinian people, by virtue of [I: its] [P: their] right to Self-Determination, to establish [I: its] [P: their] independent State shall be exercised by the Palestinian Party [I: by DMY] [P: on a date specified thereby] within the international borders agreed in [Article III of the FAPS] [This Agreement].[2]

10. [I: The Palestinian Party agrees that upon the coming into existence of Palestine, all the functions at present performed by the entities constituting the Palestinian Party will pass to Palestine. Palestine shall replace the Palestinian Council and the Palestinian Authority, which shall hereupon stand dissolved. All the undertakings and obligations by the PLO and Palestinian Authority will be succeeded by Palestine.]

11. The State of The State of Israel shall recognize the State of Palestine [within its agreed international borders as defined in [Article III of the FAPS] [This Agreement] (hereinafter "Palestine") upon its establishment. The State of Palestine shall immediately recognize the State of Israel. [P: Hence, Israel and Palestine shall establish full diplomatic relations with each other.]

12. Without derogating from the Parties' obligation to perform the agreements between them, relations between Israel and Palestine shall be based upon the provisions of the Charter of the United Nations, the principles set out in the Declaration on Principles of International Law concerning Friendly Relations and Co-operation among States, and other principles of international law governing relations among states in times of peace.

---

enhance the respect and enforcement of the law. To that effect, they will establish appropriate mechanisms of mutual legal assistance and cooperation.]

6. [Israel and Palestine shall encourage cooperation among their civil societies, and local authorities and shall devote special attention to the development of joint programs in the areas of culture and education with the aim of promoting reconciliation between their peoples.]

7. [Israel and Palestine shall respect the freedom of worship in holy sites.] [May be incorporated within a special article].

[2] The two alternatives are left until the whole text is agreed, after which point reference shall be made to "this Agreement".

- 4 -

- Nothing is Agreed Until Everything is Agreed -

TBC – To Be Completed

13. Relations between Israel and Palestine shall be founded on peaceful coexistence. Without prejudice to their status as separate entities, the two States shall endeavor to ensure the freedom of movement of persons, vehicles, goods, and services between their territories, in accordance with the arrangements and procedures set forth in the CAPS.

14. Without prejudice to the freedom of expression and other human rights as commonly practiced in democratic states, Israel and Palestine shall create the appropriate atmosphere for a lasting peace and reconciliation by promulgating laws to put an end to incitement for terror and violence, by vigorously enforcing them through the appropriate programs in their respective educational systems.

15. With a view to the advancement of the relations between the two States and peoples in all spheres of common concern, Palestine and Israel shall conclude arrangements and cooperate in areas of common interest including, but not limited to, those mentioned in this Agreement.

16. [I: Israel and Palestine shall not enter into any military, economic, or political union or confederation with third parties whose objectives are directed against the interests of the other Party without consultation with and agreement of the other Party.]

17. [I: Neither party shall be a party to an agreement or alliance with third parties, which has political, military, economic, or social intentions or objectives directed against the other parties or which is inconsistent with their agreements.]

18. The Parties are committed not to intervene in each other's internal affairs, or to take any action that may undermine the security or economic and social integrity of the other Party. Neither Party shall provide, or attempt or offer to provide diplomatic representation in any way, shape or form to citizens of the other Party without the consent of the other Party. [Accordingly, except as specifically agreed, no individual may hold dual Israeli-Palestinian citizenship.]

19. Israel and Palestine shall work together with the regional and international community to enhance regional security and political

- 5 -

- Nothing is Agreed Until Everything is Agreed -

TBC – To Be Completed

Israeli draft of the Framework Agreement on Permanent Status
Internal Working draft of the Negotiation Team
Introduction and Sections 1–2: Negotiated (updated Sept. 1, 2000); Sections 3, 4, and
Annex 4: As read to, and discussed with the Palestinians (up to Sept. 1, 2000); Remainder:
Internal – based on the internal draft and on talks with the Palestinian negotiators
FOR INTERNAL USE ONLY

stability free of hostile alliances and coalitions, and promote economic growth and prosperity.

20. [I: In view of the beginning of the new era of peace, the PLO undertakes, upon the declaration of Palestine, to cease its former existence, to change its title, charter, and stated objectives to reflect the requirements of the new era of peace and the coming into being of Palestine.]

21. The mechanisms required for all the above will be established in the CAPS.

Article 3 – Borders, Settlements and Territorial Arrangements

22. This Article and Map no. 1 attached hereto provide the permanent borders and the related territorial arrangements between Israel and Palestine.[3]

23. A number of matters, or specific areas as shown in Map no. 1, will be covered by temporary or permanent Special Arrangements. These Special Arrangements will include, according to circumstances, divisions of jurisdiction and responsibilities between Israel and Palestine and long-term special regime arrangements or lease agreements. The agreed categories of areas or matters to be the subject of Special Arrangements are set out in this Agreement. Their details shall be agreed upon in the CAPS or in subsequent protocols thereto.

24. Special Arrangements through or within Israeli and Palestinian territories respectively shall include:

   a. Routes for Joint Usage through Israeli and Palestinian territories for the local movement of Palestinian and Israeli persons, vehicles, or goods respectively;

   b. Areas populated by Israeli and Palestinian citizens within the territory of the other party.

25. Special Arrangements through, over, or within Israeli territories shall include:

---

[3] An agreed map should be attached to this text.

- 6 -

- Nothing is Agreed Until Everything is Agreed -

TBC – To Be Completed

   a.   The Safe Passage between the West Bank and the Gaza Strip aiming to provide for efficient and unimpeded movement of Palestinian persons, vehicles, and goods, under Israeli sovereignty;

   b.   Civil flights arrangements between the West Bank and the Gaza Strip;

   c.   Palestinian economic needs.

26. Special Arrangements through, over, or within Palestinian territories shall include:

   a.   Passageways to provide for the movement of Israeli citizens and security forces;

   b.   Usage and control of the airspace and electromagnetic sphere;

   c.   Israeli strategic defense and security needs within specified locations, zones or areas as detailed hereinafter.

27. The Parties shall view the delimitation of their permanent international borders and the creation of the agreed permanent Special Arrangements as the implementation of UNSCRs 242 and 338 and shall recognize them as final, permanent, irrevocable, and inviolable. The Parties may maintain territorial claims solely with regard to those areas specified in Map no. 1 as territories whose permanent sovereign status or permanent arrangements are reserved in the FAPS for future negotiations.

Article 4 – Jerusalem, Hebron and Holy Sites

28. The Parties recognize the universal historic, religious, spiritual, and cultural significance of Jerusalem and its holiness enshrined in Judaism, Christianity and Islam.

29. The Haram Al-Sharif / Har Ha'bait / Temple Mount (hereinafter "Temple Mount") and the Holy Sepulchre will be under the Custodianship of Palestine and Israeli sovereignty. The religious authorities of Palestine will carry the administrative and religious responsibilities in Temple Mount, except for the specified Jewish Site:

- 7 -

- Nothing is Agreed Until Everything is Agreed -

TBC – To Be Completed

Israeli draft of the Framework Agreement on Permanent Status
Internal Working draft of the Negotiation Team
Introduction and Sections 1–2: Negotiated (updated Sept. 1, 2000); Sections 3, 4, and
Annex 4: As read to, and discussed with the Palestinians (up to Sept. 1, 2000); Remainder:
Internal – based on the internal draft and on talks with the Palestinian negotiators
FOR INTERNAL USE ONLY

a. The existing law enforcement arrangements on Temple Mount shall remain in force;

b. An agreed site shall be specified on Temple Mount for Jewish worship. This Site shall be under the responsibility of Israeli religious authorities;

c. The historic character of Temple Mount and its archaeological artifacts shall be preserved;

d. There will be only symbolic use of flags and emblems on Temple Mount.

30. The Holy Basin of Jerusalem - the Old City and the adjacent religious and historic sites including the Mount of Olives, Mount Zion, City of David - shall be the subject of an agreed Special Regime. Israel and Palestine shall work together to respect the unique universal status of this area and to maintain its historic, cultural, religious, and architectural characteristics. The national institutions of both Parties shall not be located herein and shall be situated at the same distance from Temple Mount.

31. [The Zone of Jerusalem (ZOJ) shall consist of the territories within the municipal boundaries of Jerusalem and the adjacent Palestinian and Israeli populated areas such as Abu-Dis, Eyzariya, ar-Ram, Az-Zaim and Ma'ale Edumim, Givat Ze'ev, Anata, Michmas, and Givon.[It has been pointed out that should a map of the zone of Jerusalem be attached, this article would become redundent.]

32. The ZOJ shall consist of territories under recognized Israeli sovereignty, territories under recognized Palestinian sovereignty and certain areas of East Jerusalem, whose permanent sovereign status has been determined by the Parties prior to the signing of this Agreement. Other areas of East Jerusalem whose permanent sovereign status has not been determined, shall be negotiated for an agreed period.

33. For this duration, present arrangements shall be revised to provide Palestinian neighborhoods in East Jerusalem with functional responsibilities in agreed municipal spheres including, inter alia, agreed partial powers and responsibilities in planning and zoning, public order and law enforcement, provision of certain municipal services, and dispute settlement.]

- 8 -

- Nothing is Agreed Until Everything is Agreed -

TBC – To Be Completed

Israeli draft of the Framework Agreement on Permanent Status
Internal Working draft of the Negotiation Team
Introduction and Sections 1–2: Negotiated (updated Sept. 1, 2000); Sections 3, 4, and
Annex 4: As read to, and discussed with the Palestinians (up to Sept. 1, 2000); Remainder:
Internal – based on the internal draft and on talks with the Palestinian negotiators
FOR INTERNAL USE ONLY

34. The ZOJ shall contain the respectively recognized capitals of Israel and Palestine: the Israeli municipality of Yerushalaim, which, within its recognized Israeli sovereign territories, shall serve as the united undivided capital of Israel and the seat of the Palestinian Embassy to Israel. The Palestinian municipality of El-Quds, which, within its recognized Palestinian sovereign territories, shall serve as the capital of Palestine and the seat of the Israeli Embassy to Palestine.

35. The ZOJ shall be managed as a functional, environmental, and economic whole, whose unity shall be preserved. Its urban needs and other issues of common concern shall be managed through agreed institutions and mechanisms to be provided for in the CAPS.

36. Israel and Palestine will aim to guarantee the free and unimpeded movement of persons, vehicles and goods in the ZOJ subject to the agreed arrangements and procedures.

37. Israel and Palestine shall reach an agreement on special security arrangements for the ZOJ including entrance and exit control in light of the City's status and particularly security arrangement necessary for the protection of religious sites. The parties will co-operate to the fullest extent in the formulation and implementation of such arrangements.

38. Hebron -

Article 4A – Holy Sites in Jerusalem and Hebron

39. The Parties are committed to the freedom of worship in and access to holy sites, subject to the requirements of public order. All possible measures will be taken to protect such sites and preserve their dignity.

40. The Haram Al-Sharif / Har Ha'bait / Temple Mount and the Haram Al-Ibrahimi / Mearat Hamachpela / Tomb of the Patriarchs are subject to divine providence, and holy to Jews and Moslems alike. The right for access to and worship in them will be guaranteed by the two States[4].

---

[4]   Rachel Tomb and Yossef Tomb should be addressed in Article 3.

- 9 -

- Nothing is Agreed Until Everything is Agreed -

TBC – To Be Completed

242

Israeli draft of the Framework Agreement on Permanent Status
Internal Working draft of the Negotiation Team
Introduction and Sections 1–2: Negotiated (updated Sept. 1, 2000); Sections 3, 4, and
Annex 4: As read to, and discussed with the Palestinians (up to Sept. 1, 2000); Remainder:
Internal – based on the internal draft and on talks with the Palestinian negotiators
FOR INTERNAL USE ONLY

41. There shall be freedom of worship in the Holy Sites. No form of racial or religious discrimination shall be permitted with respect to the rights of visit and access to any of the Holy Places, except in so far as the performance of certain religious rites and ceremonies may require the exclusion from them of the adherence of other faiths during the performance of such religious rites and ceremonies.

42. There shall be freedom of access to the Holy Sites in Jerusalem for all persons without discrimination subject to the laws of Israel or Palestine respectively and to the agreed arrangements and procedures.

43. Israel and Palestine shall agree upon special arrangements for persons entering their territories for sole purpose of visiting the Holy Sites. These persons shall be subject to the operation of the laws of Israel and Palestine respectively as modified by the terms of this Article.

44. Israel and Palestine shall have the right to exclude entirely or limit the period of visit of any person claiming to visit the Holy Sites if they believe that the visit of any such person may be prejudicial to their security. Any person thus excluded may require the respective State to state its reasons to the ...

45. It shall be no excuse or justification in law for a person found in Israel without having satisfied the formal entry requirements to claim that he was visiting or intending to visit the Holy Sites;

46. Israel and Palestine undertake to respect the **autonomous privileges** in religious affairs enjoyed by the various religious sects including in the Holy Sites, which have been under their custody and jurisdiction by law and custom, freedom of association, jurisdiction in religious affairs, freedom of dress and freedom of communication with their parent organizations outside Israel or Palestine.

47. The organization of and the conduct of services in the Holy Sites shall be regulated exclusively by the personnel of the community or communities exercising rights in and over the Holy Site.

48. The Holy Sites shall remain in the custody and subject to the jurisdiction of the communities who by law and custom have exercised rights in and over them. The rights and interests of all communities in the Holy Sites shall be as they were on the eve of the

- 10 -

- Nothing is Agreed Until Everything is Agreed -

TBC – To Be Completed

signing of, subject only to such agreed or otherwise unlawful changes made since have taken place.

49. Security - TBC;

50. Commissioner and Council - TBC;

51. Dispute resolution - TBC;

52. This Article relates to the Holy Places specified in the schedule to this Agreement.

Article 5 - Security Related Matters

General

53. The Parties recognize that the establishment of a stable and mutually beneficial relationship between them will require mutual understanding and cooperation in security and security-related matters, and take upon themselves to base their security relations on mutual trust, advancement of joint interests and cooperation.

54. Israel and Palestine shall each take all measures necessary in order to prevent acts of belligerency, hostility and violence directed against the other Party, and against individuals falling under its authority and their property.

55. Both Parties further recognize that effectively combating terrorism, in all its aspects, will be a crucial element in their joint endeavor to attain stable and peaceful relations.

Security Arrangements

56. The Demilitarized Palestinian State shall maintain a non-military Palestinian Police and Security Force (PPSF), comprised of ground and maritime elements, for the purposes of ensuring internal security, law enforcement and public order, and the fight against terrorism.

57. The size, armament, deployment, activities, structure, facilities, infrastructure, training, capabilities, and equipment of the PPSF shall be solely as appropriate and required for the fulfillment of its responsibilities for internal security, law enforcement and public order

- Nothing is Agreed Until Everything is Agreed -

TBC – To Be Completed

Israeli draft of the Framework Agreement on Permanent Status
Internal Working draft of the Negotiation Team
Introduction and Sections 1–2: Negotiated (updated Sept. 1, 2000); Sections 3, 4, and
Annex 4: As read to, and discussed with the Palestinians (up to Sept. 1, 2000); Remainder:
Internal – based on the internal draft and on talks with the Palestinian negotiators
FOR INTERNAL USE ONLY

and shall be as detailed in Annex ___. No other armed forces shall be established or operated by Palestine. Accordingly, Palestine shall ensure the dismantling of all other armed elements within its territory.

58. Palestine shall not allow the entry into, deployment, stationing or operation in or passage through its land, air, or sea of any military or security forces, personnel, armament, equipment, or material of any third Party, unless otherwise agreed by both States.

59. The Palestinian Party shall not maintain any military forces, capacities or infrastructure in any location, nor shall it become a party to any alliance, agreement or co-operative activity that is of a military, para-military, or security character.

60. Special arrangements relating to the importation, development or production of security and military equipment or potential dual use items (civilian/military) in Palestine shall be agreed upon in the CAPS.

61. Israel, for the purpose of protecting its vital interests, shall maintain a land force presence and early warning facilities in specified zones, locations and areas designated for that purpose, as delineated in Map no. 1. Special arrangements concerning the on-going free, secure and unimpeded movement of Israeli security personnel and equipment to and from the zones, locations or areas; the jurisdiction and division of responsibilities therein; and the status of the Israeli security personnel are detailed in Annex ___.

62. In case of an imminent threat of an armed attack, Israel may, by notice to Palestine, temporarily reinforce its military forces in the zones, locations or areas, for the duration of that threat.

63. Israel and Palestine recognize Palestinian sovereignty over its airspace. Both Parties further acknowledge that, for security and safety reasons, the Israeli and Palestinian airspace is practically indivisible. In light of the above, and in recognition of the vital importance of the airspace to Israel's security interests, the Parties have agreed that the airspace shall remain under unified Israeli control and administration, in accordance with the arrangements detailed in Annex ___.

- 12 -

- Nothing is Agreed Until Everything is Agreed -

TBC – To Be Completed

Israeli draft of the Framework Agreement on Permanent Status
Internal Working draft of the Negotiation Team
Introduction and Sections 1–2: Negotiated (updated Sept. 1, 2000); Sections 3, 4, and
Annex 4: As read to, and discussed with the Palestinians (up to Sept. 1, 2000); Remainder:
Internal – based on the internal draft and on talks with the Palestinian negotiators
FOR INTERNAL USE ONLY

---

64. Israel and Palestine recognize Palestinian sovereignty over its electromagnetic spectrum. Both Parties further acknowledge the fact that, due to geographical and topographical realities, it is practically impossible to administer this electromagnetic spectrum in separation from Israel's electromagnetic spectrum. In light of the above, and in recognition of the vital importance of the electromagnetic spectrum to Israel's security interests, the Parties have agreed that the electromagnetic spectrum shall remain under unified Israeli control and management, in accordance with the arrangements detailed in Annex ___.

65. Israel and Palestine shall establish a Border Security Regime along their borders, with the aim of regulating cross-border movement and enforcing the rule of law.

66. With the goal of minimizing friction, Israel and Palestine will implement agreed planning and zoning limitations in specified areas.

67. The Parties agree to establish procedures and arrangements for ensuring the security of the Israeli Settlements in Palestine, and for free, secure and unimpeded access thereto.

68. Israel and Palestine shall employ agreed mechanisms and arrangements for monitoring and verification of the provisions of this Article, in particular the demilitarization of Palestine. Detailed provisions in this regard are set out in Annex ____.

69. Israel and Palestine shall establish a joint Security Co-operation Committee (SCC). In addition to its other functions, the SCC shall serve as the forum for the resolution of all security-related disputes. The structure, composition, mandate and mode of operations of the SCC and its related mechanisms shall be as detailed in the CAPS.

70. The provisions of this Article, and other security related provisions of this Agreement, shall be further detailed in the CAPS.

- 13 -

- Nothing is Agreed Until Everything is Agreed -

TBC – To Be Completed

Article 6 – Refugees

71. The Parties are cognizant of the suffering caused to individuals and communities on both sides during and following the 1948 War. Israel further recognizes the urgent need for a humane, just, and realistic settlement to the plight of Palestinian Refugees within the context of terminating the Israeli-Palestinian conflict.

72. A resolution of the Palestinian refugee problem in all its aspects will be achieved through an international effort with the participation of, as appropriate, the Arab States, the European Union, the United States, and the rest of the international community. Israel, in accordance with this Article, will take part in this effort.

73. The termination of Palestinian refugee problem shall incorporate possible return to the State of Palestine, integration within the Host Countries, and immigration to other third countries.

74. In light of the new era of peace, the Palestinian Party recognizes that the Right of Return of Palestinian refugees shall apply solely to the State of Palestine. Israel recognizes the right of Palestinian refugees to return to the State of Palestine.

75. Israel shall, as a matter of its sovereign discretion, facilitate a phased entry of [XX] Palestinian Refugees to its territories on humanitarian grounds. These refugees shall be reunited with their families in their present place of residence in Israel, accept Israeli citizenship and waive their legal status as refugees.

76. An International Commission (Commission) shall be established. Canada, the European Union, the Host Countries (Jordan, Syria, Lebanon, and Egypt), Japan, Norway, the State of Palestine, [the PLO], the Russian Federation, the United Nations, the United States and Israel shall be invited to participate therein. Special attention will be given to the special role of the Hashemite Kingdom of Jordan with respect to the Palestinian Refugees within its borders.

77. An International Fund (Fund) shall be established and supervised by the Commission and the World Bank. The Fund shall be managed as an international financial institution ensuring transparency,

- 14 -

- Nothing is Agreed Until Everything is Agreed -

TBC – To Be Completed

Israeli draft of the Framework Agreement on Permanent Status
Internal Working draft of the Negotiation Team
Introduction and Sections 1–2: Negotiated (updated Sept. 1, 2000); Sections 3, 4, and
Annex 4: As read to, and discussed with the Palestinians (up to Sept. 1, 2000); Remainder:
Internal – based on the internal draft and on talks with the Palestinian negotiators
FOR INTERNAL USE ONLY

accountability, and due process. It will collect, manage and disburse the resources pertaining to the rehabilitation of and compensation to Palestinian refugees.

78. The objective of the Commission and the Fund is to provide for a comprehensive and conclusive settlement of the Palestinian Refugee Problem in all its aspects.

79. The Fund shall establish and manage a Registration Committee in order to compile a definitive and complete register of property claims of the refugees due to the 1948 War. The modalities, criteria, timeline, and procedures of the registration of claims, their verification and *pro-rata* evaluation shall be drawn up as appropriate by agreement upon the establishment of the Fund and within its framework.

80. The Parties affirm that the register of the claims verified by the Registration Committee shall constitute the definitive statement of all Palestinian refugee's property claims.

81. Every Palestinian refugee-household that became a refugee in 1948 or its direct descendents may, within an agreed period, submit one sole claim due to the 1948 War to the Registration Committee for the purpose of compensation for its property. No further individual claims may be filed beyond the agreed date.

82. The Parties agree that a just settlement of the Israeli-Arab conflict should settle the claims by Jewish individuals and communities that left Arab countries or parts of Mandatory Palestine due to the 1948 War and its aftermath. An international mechanism affiliated with the above Commission and Fund will be established to deal with such claims.

83. The rehabilitation of refugees in their current places of residence or their relocation to their new places of residence shall be carried out on the basis of comprehensive Programs for Development and Rehabilitation (PDRs). The PDRs will be concluded between the Commission, the Fund and the relevant country with the aim of enabling the refugee to rebuild his life and the life of his family.

84. The PDR shall provide for gradual elimination of the formal and practical aspects of the refugee problem including the phased

- Nothing is Agreed Until Everything is Agreed -

TBC – To Be Completed

Israeli draft of the Framework Agreement on Permanent Status
Internal Working draft of the Negotiation Team
Introduction and Sections 1–2: Negotiated (updated Sept. 1, 2000); Sections 3, 4, and
Annex 4: As read to, and discussed with the Palestinians (up to Sept. 1, 2000); Remainder:
Internal – based on the internal draft and on talks with the Palestinian negotiators
FOR INTERNAL USE ONLY

withdrawal of UNRWA within ten years and the transfer of its responsibilities to the Host Country, the provision of full personal-legal status to all refugees that wish to live in such Host Country and the settlement of its national refugee-related claim.

85. The Parties shall call upon the international community to support the permanent settlement of the Palestinian refugee problem by defining a Lump Sum [of XX] and to develop immigration options for those refugees wishing to immigrate to third countries. The Lump Sum shall provide for all the financial requirements for the comprehensive and final settlement of the Palestinian refugee problem including those of rehabilitation and all individual or collective claims.

86. Eligibility of a claimant for property compensation shall be proportionate, limited by and subject to, the resources accumulated by the Fund as well as by allocations to rehabilitation programs. Transfer of compensation to a claimant shall be conditioned by such claimant's waiver of further proprietary claims.

87. The Parties call upon the international community convene a conference for that purpose.

88. In the context of and within such international pledge, Israel will address the issue of a financial annual contribution of XX for XX years.

89. The mandate of the Fund and the Commission shall be concluded between the Parties in the CAPS based on this Article.

90. The Commission, the Fund and the Sate of Palestine shall design and implement a PDR for the permanent resolution of the Palestinian refugee problem in the State of Palestine within ten years of the conclusion of the CAPS. The State of Palestine shall view the implementation of this program as a final settlement of its national claim in this respect.

91. UNRWA records shall be the main basis for the implementation of this Article. Records from other relevant sources shall be subject to the Commission's scrutiny and approval.

- 16 -

- Nothing is Agreed Until Everything is Agreed -

TBC – To Be Completed

92. The wishes and claims of the Palestinian refugees shall be taken into account to the extent and manner agreed between the Parties in the FAPS and the CAPS.

93. The timeline for the implementation of this article is provided for in Annex XXX.

94. Israel shall have no further commitment or obligation emanating from the Refugee issue beyond those specified in this Agreement.

95. The implementation of this Article and the completion of the Commission's work as described in paragraph (X) shall resolve the Palestinian refugees problem in a permanent way thus amounting to the implementation of all relevant international resolutions.

96. The Parties encourage the Refugee Multilateral Working Group to continue its work on the basis of its agreed terms-of-reference specifically focusing on those individuals who personally became refugees during the 1948 War.

Article 7 – Economic Relations

97. Israel and Palestine shall work together to create an environment conducive to economic growth, prosperity and stability to their mutual benefit.

98. Israel and Palestine shall establish a Free Trade Area (hereinafter "PIFTA"), which shall govern their trade relations. Thereafter, each party will independently determine and regulate its own tax policy.

99. The PIFTA Agreement will address, inter alia, the border economic regime (including the establishment of customs stations and their operation on a cost reimbursement basis), as well as the issues of rules of origin, transit arrangements, intellectual property rights, transparency, cooperation on customs matters, double taxation and protection of investments. The Agreement may provide for the harmonization of standards and indirect taxation on specific agreed items.

100. The PIFTA shall come into being following the establishment of an effective economic border. Until such time, all existing economic agreements, arrangements and procedures as set out in the Interim

- 17 -

- Nothing is Agreed Until Everything is Agreed -

TBC – To Be Completed

Israeli draft of the Framework Agreement on Permanent Status
Internal Working draft of the Negotiation Team
Introduction and Sections 1–2: Negotiated (updated Sept. 1, 2000); Sections 3, 4, and
Annex 4: As read to, and discussed with the Palestinians (up to Sept. 1, 2000); Remainder:
Internal – based on the internal draft and on talks with the Palestinian negotiators
FOR INTERNAL USE ONLY

Agreement and subsequent agreements shall remain in effect, except as otherwise agreed. The existing tax clearance system will be terminated upon the establishment of a fully regulated effective economic border.

101. Each State shall grant workers of the other access to its labor market, without discrimination in comparison to third parties. Each State shall have the sole discretion to determine the policy and number of individuals of the other side eligible to work in its territory.

102. The two States, through their Joint Economic Committee, shall conclude additional agreements and arrangements on economic-related issues such as agriculture and fishing, industry and trade issues, insurance, tourism, telecommunications, and transportation.

Article 8 – Water and Wastewater

103. The Parties acknowledge the importance of water in meeting their vital needs. Accordingly, and with a view to continued cooperation, in the spirit of goodwill, they have agreed on the following principles for the comprehensive and final settlement of all the water and wastewater issues between them.

104. The Parties further acknowledge their mutual need for additional quantities of water, while recognizing that their existing natural resources are insufficient to meet these needs. In this context, both Parties accord special importance to the development of new water resources, with emphasis on the desalination of sea-water and brackish water and the reuse of treated wastewater.

105. Israel recognizes the water rights of Palestine and Palestine recognizes the water rights of Israel, as provided for in this Article.

106. Both Parties recognize their respective sovereign rights over the water resources within their territory that are not shared between them. They further recognize the necessity to agree on the [*equitable and reasonable*] allocations from their shared water resources.

- 18 -

- Nothing is Agreed Until Everything is Agreed -

TBC – To Be Completed

Israeli draft of the Framework Agreement on Permanent Status
Internal Working draft of the Negotiation Team
Introduction and Sections 1–2: Negotiated (updated Sept. 1, 2000); Sections 3, 4, and
Annex 4: As read to, and discussed with the Palestinians (up to Sept. 1, 2000); Remainder:
Internal – based on the internal draft and on talks with the Palestinian negotiators
FOR INTERNAL USE ONLY

107. In light of the above, the agreed and final allocations to each Party from the various water resources, taking into consideration their domestic, agricultural and industry needs, are set out in Annex_____.

108. Both Parties attach great importance to protecting and preserving their water resources. In this context, they recognize that effective treatment of wastewater will contribute significantly to the protection of their water resources and may serve as an important source for additional water.

109. The Parties will jointly approach the international community for the purpose of securing the funds necessary for the implementation of all agreed water and wastewater projects, for their mutual benefit, to be detailed in the CAPS. In this context, they jointly call upon the United States to sponsor the establishment of an International Water Fund for this purpose.

110. In addition, the Parties undertake to adopt all necessary measures:

   a. To effectively collect, treat and reuse or dispose of wastewater originating in their territory, including the construction, operation and maintenance of all required installations.

   b. To preserve the quality of the shared water sources, and prevent any harm thereto;

   c. To prevent continuation originating from point and non-point sources, including *inter alia*, solid waste, industry, agriculture and other land uses and activities;

   d. To preserve the quantity and ensure the quality of the current surface flows into Israel, for the protection of the environment.

111. It is further agreed that failure by a Party to fulfill any of its undertakings under paragraph 8 above, or use by a Party of water resources in excess of the agreed allocations in accordance with paragraph 5 above, will result in its bearing full responsibility for all resulting costs and damages incurred by the other Party.

112. The provisions of paragraphs 6 through 9 above will be further detailed in the CAPS.

- 19 -

- Nothing is Agreed Until Everything is Agreed -

TBC – To Be Completed

113. In addition, the CAPS shall address additional water and wastewater related issues, including inter alia:

   a. Establishment, structure, composition, mandate and mode of operation of a Joint coordination and cooperation mechanism;

   b. Joint monitoring and supervision mechanisms;

   c. Ownership of water and wastewater related infrastructure;

   d. Water and wastewater infrastructure crossing the territory of the other Party;

   e. Bilateral and multilateral cooperation;

   f. Dispute resolution;

   g. Financial aspects and arrangements relating to water and wastewater;

114. Pending the entry into force of the CAPS, all existing agreements, arrangements and procedures relating to water and wastewater shall remain in force, except as otherwise specifically agreed between the Parties.

Article 9 – Other Bilateral Issues

115. The two States shall conclude in the CAPS detailed arrangements and understandings in the different spheres of their future bilateral relations, including with regard to the issues provided for hereunder.

Civil Affairs

116. The Parties recognize that cooperation in civil affairs will constitute a cornerstone of the future relationship between the two States in light of their close physical proximity and the need to create an environment which is supportive of security, stability, good neighborly relations, growth and prosperity.

117. Relations between the two States shall be based upon, as appropriate, on exchange of information, consultation, coordination, and cooperation on the basis of accepted international standards.

- 20 -

- Nothing is Agreed Until Everything is Agreed -

TBC – To Be Completed

Israeli draft of the Framework Agreement on Permanent Status
Internal Working draft of the Negotiation Team
Introduction and Sections 1–2: Negotiated (updated Sept. 1, 2000); Sections 3, 4, and
Annex 4: As read to, and discussed with the Palestinians (up to Sept. 1, 2000); Remainder:
Internal – based on the internal draft and on talks with the Palestinian negotiators
FOR INTERNAL USE ONLY

118. The Parties shall formulate specific agreements, arrangements or procedures in the different areas of civil affairs including: agriculture; archaeology; cooperative planning; cooperation programs; education and culture; electricity; environmental protection; fuel and gas; health; holy sites; industrial estates; postal services; telecommunication; Tourism; and Transportation.

Legal Affairs and Law Enforcement

119. Israel and Palestine shall both respect the rule of law and work together in cooperation between their respective legal systems, to vigorously enhance the respect for and enforcement of the law. To that effect, they will establish appropriate mechanisms of mutual legal assistance, coordination, and cooperation.

120. Israel and Palestine shall create the appropriate atmosphere for peace by promulgating laws to put an end to incitement for terror and violence, by enforcing them and by the appropriate programs to that effect in their education systems.

121. Each Party undertakes to take all necessary and effective measures in its power to prevent cross-border criminal activities. They further undertake to ensure that any perpetrators of such acts are brought to justice.

122. The Parties shall formulate specific agreements, arrangements or procedures in the different areas of their legal relations including, *inter alia*, the following:

    a.   Co-operation in combating criminal activities;

    b.   Criminal jurisdiction;

    c.   Civil jurisdiction;

    d.   Legal assistance in criminal matters;

    e.   Legal assistance in civil matters;

    f.   Intellectual property;

    g.   Rights, liabilities and obligations;

    h.   Private claims against Israel and the PE;

- 21 -

- Nothing is Agreed Until Everything is Agreed -

TBC – To Be Completed

i.   Jewish and Israeli property;

j.   Legal education.

Border Regime

123. Recognizing the need for mutual stability and security, the two States will adopt a fully regulated border regime for the passage of people, vehicles and goods between them.

124. For this purpose, the two States will establish border crossings between them - the number, location, mode-of-operation and related procedures including all related security arrangements, and economic and civil aspects shall be detailed in the CAPS.

Safe Passage

125. The Parties agree to establish a Permanent Safe passage Route, between the West Bank and the Gaza Strip, aiming to provide for efficient and unimpeded movement of Palestinian persons, vehicles and goods, under Israel sovereignty.

126. Pending the establishment of the agreed Safe Passage Route, the existing safe passage arrangements will remain in force.

127. Detailed arrangements relating to the Permanent Safe Passage will be agreed in the CAPS.

Article 10 – Coordination and Cooperation Mechanisms and Dispute Resolution

Coordination and Cooperation Mechanisms

128. Israel and Palestine will establish coordination and cooperation mechanisms in the various fields, as detailed in this Agreement and in the CAPS, and as otherwise agreed between them.

129. Israel and Palestine will further establish a Senior Executive Committee (SEC), comprised of high-level officials from both sides. The SEC shall be responsible for supervising and guiding the activities of all the joint coordination and cooperation mechanisms. In addition, the SEC shall serve as the senior forum for the formulation

- 22 -

- Nothing is Agreed Until Everything is Agreed -

TBC – To Be Completed

Israeli draft of the Framework Agreement on Permanent Status
Internal Working draft of the Negotiation Team
Introduction and Sections 1–2: Negotiated (updated Sept. 1, 2000); Sections 3, 4, and
Annex 4: As read to, and discussed with the Palestinians (up to Sept. 1, 2000); Remainder:
Internal – based on the internal draft and on talks with the Palestinian negotiators
FOR INTERNAL USE ONLY

of joint policy decisions, and shall serve as the highest forum for the resolution of disputes relating to the interpretation or implementation of the FAPS or the CAPS.

Dispute Resolution

130. Any difference relating to the application or interpretation of this Agreement or the CAPS shall be referred to the appropriate coordination and cooperation mechanism.

131. Any such difference, which is not settled through the appropriate coordination and cooperation mechanism, shall be referred to the SEC for mutual resolution.

132. Disputes, which are not be settled by negotiation, may be resolved by a mechanism of conciliation to be agreed upon by the Parties.

133. The Parties may agree to submit to arbitration disputes relating to the application or interpretation of this Agreement or of the CAPS, which are not settled through negotiation or conciliation.

Article 16 – Timetable for Withdrawal of Israeli Forces

134. Israel will withdraw its forces from Palestinian territory, as defined in Article 3 and Map no. 1, in accordance with the timeline attached as Annex ____ to this agreement.

135. Recognizing their mutual interest in maintaining stability, Palestine will take all steps in its power to ensure that the Israeli process of withdrawal will not be interfered with or hindered, in any way.

136. Palestine will take sovereign control of each specific area or location from which Israeli forces have withdrawn, in accordance with the provisions of this Agreement.

137. Pending the completion of the withdrawal of Israeli forces from each specific area or location, the existing agreements, arrangements and procedures currently applicable therein will remain in force.

138. The provisions of this Article are without prejudice to the provisions of Article 5 (Security) to this Agreement in relation to security zones, designated areas, military locations and passageways.

- 23 -

- Nothing is Agreed Until Everything is Agreed -

TBC – To Be Completed

Article 17 - General Provisions

139. The Parties shall bring the FAPS to the approval of their respective legislative bodies within ___ weeks of its initialing. Immediately thereafter, Israel will present the FAPS for public approval through a referendum, to be completed within ___ weeks. The FAPS will be signed no later than ____ weeks from the date of the completion of the approval process by the Parties. The FAPS shall enter into force upon signature.

140. Upon its entry into force, the FAPS will be submitted to the United Nations, calling for both General Assembly and Security Council confirmation that the FAPS constitutes the sole agreed basis and mechanism for the fulfillment and implementation of all relevant United Nations Resolutions.

141. This Treaty does not affect and shall not be interpreted as affecting, in any way, the rights and obligations of the Parties or the rights and obligations of the two States under the Charter of the United Nations.

142. The Parties undertake to fulfil in good faith their obligations under this Agreement, without regard to action or inaction of any other party and independently of any instrument inconsistent with this Agreement. For the purposes of this paragraph, each Party represents to the other that in its opinion and interpretation there is no inconsistency between its existing obligations and this Agreement.

143. The Parties and the two States shall further take all necessary measures for the application in their relations of the provisions of the multilateral conventions to which they are or shall be a party, including the submission of appropriate notification to the Secretary General of the United Nations and other depositories of such conventions.

144. Both Parties will also take all the necessary steps to abolish all pejorative references to the other Party, in multilateral conventions to which they are parties, to the extent that such references exist.

145. The Parties undertake not to enter into any obligation in conflict with this Treaty. Subject to Article 103 of the United Nations Charter, in the event of a conflict between the obligations of the two States under

- Nothing is Agreed Until Everything is Agreed -

TBC – To Be Completed

Israeli draft of the Framework Agreement on Permanent Status
Internal Working draft of the Negotiation Team
Introduction and Sections 1–2: Negotiated (updated Sept. 1, 2000); Sections 3, 4, and
Annex 4: As read to, and discussed with the Palestinians (up to Sept. 1, 2000); Remainder:
Internal – based on the internal draft and on talks with the Palestinian negotiators
FOR INTERNAL USE ONLY

the FAPS or the CAPS and any of their other obligations, the obligations under the FAPS or the CAPS will be binding and implemented.

146. The Preamble to this Agreement, and all Annexes, and Appendices attached hereto, shall constitute an integral part hereof.

Made and signed in XXX, this XX day of XX, 2000

- Nothing is Agreed Until Everything is Agreed -

TBC – To Be Completed

Annex 1

Protocol on the Negotiations of the CAPS

1. The Parties to the CAPS shall be the Government of Israel (GOI), on the one side, and the Palestine Liberation Organization (PLO) and the State of Palestine for the Palestinian side, on the other.

2. The Palestinian Authority shall nominate the Palestinian delegations for the negotiations on all issues pertaining to the future bilateral relations between Israel and Palestine, excluding those issues and elements specifically reserved for the PLO.

3. Negotiations on the CAPS shall commence immediately pursuant to the initialing of the FAPS. All such negotiations prior to the approval and subsequent signature of the FAPS shall be *ad referendum*. The negtiations on the CAPS shall address all the issues referred for CAPS in this Agreement.

Third and Final Redeployment of Israeli Military Forces

4. The Third Further Redeployment (FRD3) shall be carried out in consultation with the Palestinian Party with the aim of enhancing Palestinian territorial contiguity towards coming into existence of the Palestinian State. The FRD3 shall not include settlements, military locations and military installations and territories whose status shall be addressed in the Map no. 1.

5. The Third Further Redeployment (FRD3) will be carried out in three stages as follows:

    a. Not later then DMY, Israel shall transfer to the PPG XX% from Area C to Area B and XX% from Area B to Area A including territories previously requested by the Palestinian Side in the areas adjacent to the present municipal boundaries of Jerusalem;

    b. Not later then DMY, Israel shall transfer to the PPG XX% from Area C to Area B and XX% from Area B to Area A ....

- 26 -

- Nothing is Agreed Until Everything is Agreed -

TBC – To Be Completed

Israeli draft of the Framework Agreement on Permanent Status
Internal Working draft of the Negotiation Team
Introduction and Sections 1–2: Negotiated (updated Sept. 1, 2000); Sections 3, 4, and
Annex 4: As read to, and discussed with the Palestinians (up to Sept. 1, 2000); Remainder:
Internal – based on the internal draft and on talks with the Palestinian negotiators
FOR INTERNAL USE ONLY

---

c. Not later then DMY, Israel shall transfer to Palestine XX% from Area C or Area B to Area A. The Third phase of the FRD3 shall constitute the first phase of the implementation of Map no. 1 and the CAPS.

- Nothing is Agreed Until Everything is Agreed -

TBC – To Be Completed

Israeli draft of the Framework Agreement on Permanent Status
Internal Working draft of the Negotiation Team
Introduction and Sections 1–2: Negotiated (updated Sept. 1, 2000); Sections 3, 4, and
Annex 4: As read to, and discussed with the Palestinians (up to Sept. 1, 2000); Remainder:
Internal – based on the internal draft and on talks with the Palestinian negotiators
FOR INTERNAL USE ONLY

Annex

The Palestinian Police and Security Force

1. Palestine shall be demilitarized, as detailed in the Agreement and this Annex.

2. The PPSF shall be a non-military force, comprised of ground and maritime elements, responsible for maintaining internal security, law enforcement and public order within the territory of Palestine.

3. The PPSF shall not engage in any cooperation of a military nature with any entity.

4. All aspects related to the PPSF shall be guided by accepted Western European practice regarding police and internal security forces. In this context, the size of the PPSF will be agreed upon between the Parties in the CAPS, based on accepted international practice for population to police ratios.

5. The Palestinian Party has informed Israel that in light of the non-military nature of the PPSF, there shall be no mandatory recruitment into it, and it shall be based on voluntary enlistment only.

6. The CAPS shall address all aspects of the armaments and security equipment of the PPSF. Without derogating from the above, the PPSF shall not be equipped with any of the items listed in Schedule ____.

7. The number of the PPSF's armaments and items of security equipment shall be commensurate with its size and responsibilities.

8. The PPSF shall not establish or maintain any infrastructure of a military nature, such as antitank ditches and fortifications.

9. The development or production of armaments and security equipment within the territory of Palestine, as well as their import or introduction, shall be fully compatible with the provisions of this Agreement.

10. The Parties may agree on specific amendments and adaptations to the above, as required.

- 28 -

- Nothing is Agreed Until Everything is Agreed -

TBC – To Be Completed

Israeli draft of the Framework Agreement on Permanent Status
Internal Working draft of the Negotiation Team
Introduction and Sections 1–2: Negotiated (updated Sept. 1, 2000); Sections 3, 4, and
Annex 4: As read to, and discussed with the Palestinians (up to Sept. 1, 2000); Remainder:
Internal – based on the internal draft and on talks with the Palestinian negotiators
FOR INTERNAL USE ONLY

Schedule

1. Tanks and other military armored vehicles.

2. Military aircraft and helicopters, and unmanned aerial vehicles.

3. Artillery, mortars and other high trajectory weapons.

4. Any missiles, rockets and rocket launchers.

5. Air defense weapon systems.

6. Anti-tank weapon systems.

7. Electronic warfare and military oriented intelligence capabilities.

8. Military naval vessels.

9. Land and naval mines.

10. Underwater weapon systems.

11. Any other military equipment, systems, materials and capabilities, or potential dual-use equipment, systems, materials and capabilities designed, adapted or used primarily for military use.

- 29 -

- Nothing is Agreed Until Everything is Agreed -

TBC – To Be Completed

Israeli draft of the Framework Agreement on Permanent Status
Internal Working draft of the Negotiation Team
Introduction and Sections 1–2: Negotiated (updated Sept. 1, 2000); Sections 3, 4, and
Annex 4: As read to, and discussed with the Palestinians (up to Sept. 1, 2000); Remainder:
Internal – based on the internal draft and on talks with the Palestinian negotiators
FOR INTERNAL USE ONLY

Annex 4

Protocol on Israeli Land Force Presence and Early Warning Facilities

General

1. Israel will maintain a land force presence and early warning facilities in Palestine, comprised of Security Zones in the Jordan Valley and along the Egyptian border, Designated Areas for times of emergency, Military Locations for early warning, and Passageways, all as specified in the attached map ____.

Security Zone

2. In the Security Zones, Israel will be entitled to maintain a continuous, self-sufficient military presence for a period of ___ years. Israeli personnel will be entitled to free and unrestricted access to the Security Zones, through the Passageways.

3. While Palestine will have civilian powers and responsibilities in the Security Zones, Israel will maintain overriding security powers and responsibilities therein. Palestine undertakes to ensure that Palestinian activities will not prevent, hinder or otherwise prejudice the effective use of the Security Zones by Israel.

4. Upon expiration of the ___ year period, the Security Zones shall be redefined as Designated Areas, unless otherwise agreed between the Parties.

Designated Areas

5. In the Designated Areas, Israel may maintain pre-positioning sites, under its responsibility, containing a continuous, self-sufficient military presence. Israel will be entitled to free and unrestricted access to these Designated Areas and installations, through the Passageways.

6. In case of an imminent threat of armed attack, Israel may, by notice to Palestine, temporarily deploy forces to the Designated Areas, for the

- 30 -

- Nothing is Agreed Until Everything is Agreed -

TBC – To Be Completed

duration of the threat. During these temporary situations, Israel will have all security powers and responsibilities within the Designated Areas.

7. Palestine undertakes to ensure that Palestinian activities will not prevent, hinder or otherwise prejudice the effective use of the Designated Areas by Israel.

Military Locations

8. In the Military Locations, Israel will be entitled to maintain a continuous, self-sufficient military presence. Israel will be entitled to free and unrestricted access to these Military Locations, through the designated access routes, as specified on the attached map ___.

9. Israel will maintain all powers and responsibilities in the Military Locations. Israel undertakes that the activities of the Military Locations will not adversely effect the daily life of Palestinians. Palestine undertakes to ensure that Palestinian activities will not prejudice the effective use of the Military Locations by Israel.

10. Israeli pre-positioning sites in the Designated Areas will be treated as Military Locations.

Passageways

11. The Passageways will serve for the free and unrestricted Israeli movement to and from the Security Zone and the Designated Areas. In case of an imminent threat of armed attack, Israel will be entitled to priority, free and unimpeded use of the Passageways by Israeli forces and personnel.

12. Palestine undertakes to ensure that Palestinian activities will not prevent, hinder or otherwise prejudice the effective use of the Passageways by Israel.

Other Provisions

13. All Israeli personnel within the Security Zone, the Designated Areas, the Military Locations, or on the access routes or passageways, will be under sole Israeli jurisdiction and responsibility.

- 31 -

- Nothing is Agreed Until Everything is Agreed -

TBC – To Be Completed

14. The Parties will agree, in the CAPS, on monitoring and verification procedures to ensure the implementation of the provisions of this Annex.

- 32 -

- Nothing is Agreed Until Everything is Agreed -

TBC – To Be Completed

Annex

Airspace and Electromagnetic Spectrum

Airspace

1. Recognizing Palestinian sovereignty over the airspace above Palestine, both Parties further acknowledge that the airspace between the Mediterranean Sea and the Jordan River is indivisible, for practical purposes.

2. Accordingly, the Parties agree to the following:

   a. Palestine agrees that the ultimate control and administration of the unified airspace shall rest with Israel.

   b. Israel recognizes the necessity to facilitate the smooth, safe and routine flow of civil aviation traffic to and from Palestine. Such traffic will be managed by the Palestinian Civil Aviation Authorities, in co-ordination with the Israeli authorities, and in accordance with the provisions of this Agreement.

   c. The Israel air-force will have the right of usage of Palestinian airspace up to the Jordan River, subject to the understanding that flights over densely populated areas shall be under the same limitations as those applicable in Israel.

3. Detailed arrangements relating to civil aviation, including air routes for internal Palestinian flights, shall be agreed in the CAPS.

Electromagnetic Spectrum

- 33 -

- Nothing is Agreed Until Everything is Agreed -

TBC – To Be Completed

Israeli draft of the Framework Agreement on Permanent Status
Internal Working draft of the Negotiation Team
Introduction and Sections 1–2: Negotiated (updated Sept. 1, 2000); Sections 3, 4, and
Annex 4: As read to, and discussed with the Palestinians (up to Sept. 1, 2000); Remainder:
Internal – based on the internal draft and on talks with the Palestinian negotiators
FOR INTERNAL USE ONLY

Side letter / Declaration by the Palestinian Side

1. On January 1, 2001, the independent sovereign State of Palestine shall be established based on and realizing the legitimate right of the entire Palestinian people for self-determination.

2. The Government of Palestine shall be the sole representative of the Palestinian State in its international affairs ... to sue and be sued in the name of Palestine and Palestinians to conclude contracts etc.

3. Upon the establishment of Palestine, the [Palestinian Authority] [Palestinian Provisional Government] shall cease to exist and Palestine shall assume all its remaining undertakings and obligations, as well as all those concluded for its benefit by the PLO.

4. The Palestinian Side undertakes that its legislation, and executive and judicial decisions shall be consistent with this Agreement;

5. This FAPS is a historic compromise ... an irrevocable renunciation of any claims for that are under the sovereignty of the other side ...;

6. The PLO shall modify its title, charter, structure, objectives and modes of operation ... shall not represent Palestine in all of its international affairs.

Transitional Arrangements

1. Settlements, the majority of the inhabitants of which will express their wish for relocation to Israeli Territories, shall be transferred to Palestine in the context of the Israeli contribution to the settlement of the Palestinian refugee problem.

Safe Passage

- 34 -

- Nothing is Agreed Until Everything is Agreed -

TBC – To Be Completed

BIBLIOGRAPHY

Copeland, Dale, *The Origins of Major Wars* (Cornell University Press, 2000).

Enderlin, Charles, *Paix ou Guerres* (Stock, 1997).

Fisher, R., Kopelman, E. and Schneider, A. K., *Beyond Machiavelli – Tools for Coping with Conflict* (Penguin Books, 1996).

Gowers, Andrew and Walker, Tony, *Behind the Myth: Yasser Arafat and the Palestinian Revolution* (Corgi, 1990).

Independent Task Force – Council on Foreign Relations, *Strengthening Palestinian Public Institutions* (Council on Foreign Relations Press, 1999).

Lewis, Bernard, *A Middle East Mosaic: Fragments of Life, Letters and History* (Random House, 2000).

Rubenstein, Danny, *The Mystery of Arafat* (Steerforth Press, 1995).

Said, Edward, *The Question of Palestine* (Vintage Books, 1980).

Sayigh, Yezid, "Arafat and the Anatomy of Revolt," *Survival*, Vol. 43, Autumn 2001, The International Institute of Strategic Studies.

Schelling, Thomas C., *The Strategy of Conflict* (Oxford University Press, 1960).

Schemla, Elisabeth, *Ton Rêve est mon Chauchemar* (Flammarion, 2001).

Shell, G. Richard, *Bargaining for Advantage* (Penguin Books, 1999).

Woolf, Bob, *Friendly Persuasion: How to Negotiate and Win* (Berkely Books, 1990).

Archives and internet websites

CNN

Haaretz

Israel Government Press Office

Israel Ministry of Foreign Affairs

Maariv

New York Times

Yediot Aharonot

YNet

INDEX

Page references in *italics* indicate illustrations. Subentries are in chronological order.